Teach Yourself VISUALLY™

Word 2019

by Guy Hart-Davis

Visual
A Wiley Brand

Teach Yourself VISUALLY Word 2019

Published by
John Wiley & Sons, Inc.
9200 Keystone Crossing, Suite 800
Indianapolis, IN 46240
www.wiley.com

Library of Congress Control Number: 2020937948

ISBN: 978-1-119-72448-3

Manufactured in the United States of America

V10019273_062220

Trademark Acknowledgments

Contact Us

For general information on our other products and services please contact our Customer Care Department within the U.S. at 877-762-2974, outside the U.S. at 317-572-3993 or fax 317-572-4002.

For technical support please visit https://hub.wiley.com/community/support.

Sales | Contact Wiley at (877) 762-2974 or fax (317) 572-4002.

CHAPTER 1

Getting Started with Word

In this chapter, you meet the Word working environment, including the Word Start screen and Backstage view, and you learn the essentials of navigating the interface with the keyboard and mouse and entering text using the keyboard. You also learn about using Word on tablets, phones, OneDrive, and Teams.

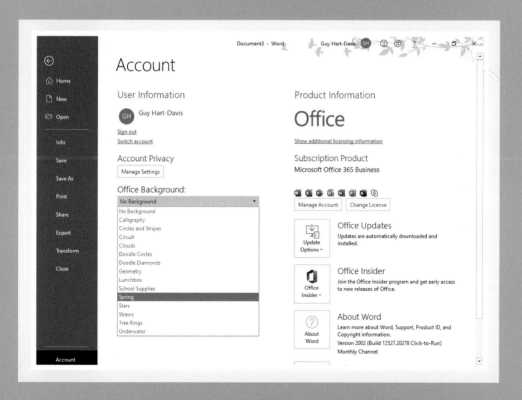

Chapter 12   Printing, Sharing, and Mail Merge

Table of Contents

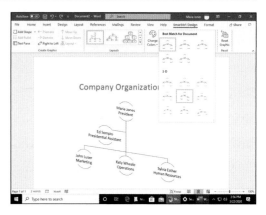

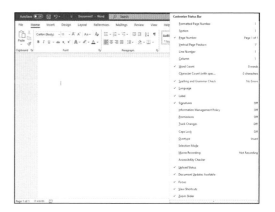

Chapter 9 | Working with Tables and Charts

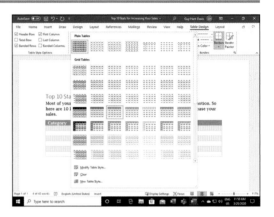

Table of Contents

Chapter 8	Reviewing and Finalizing Documents

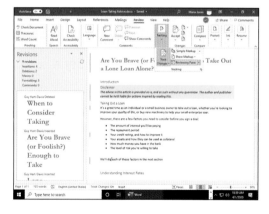

Chapter 6   Formatting Paragraphs

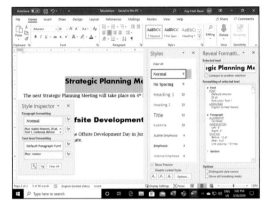

Chapter 7   Formatting Pages

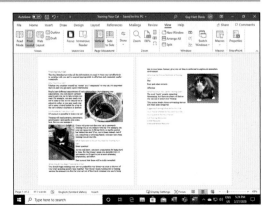

Table of Contents

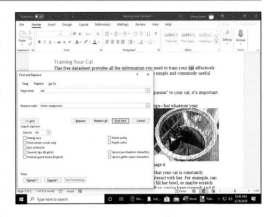

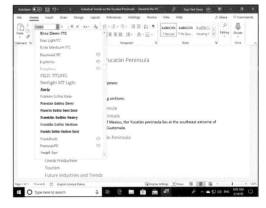

Chapter 2 Creating and Saving Documents

Chapter 3 Entering Text in Documents

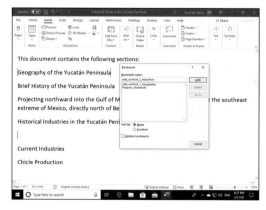

Table of Contents

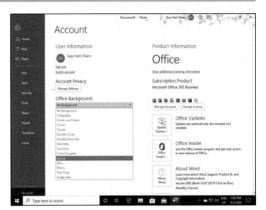

How to Use This Book

Who This Book Is For

This book is for the reader who has never used this particular technology or software application. It is also for readers who want to expand their knowledge.

The Conventions in This Book

❶ Steps

This book uses a step-by-step format to guide you easily through each task. **Numbered steps** are actions you must do; **bulleted steps** clarify a point, step, or optional feature; and **indented steps** give you the result.

❷ Notes

Notes give additional information—special conditions that may occur during an operation, a situation that you want to avoid, or a cross reference to a related area of the book.

❸ Icons and Buttons

Icons and buttons show you exactly what you need to click to perform a step.

❹ Tips

Tips offer additional information, including warnings and shortcuts.

❺ Bold

Bold type shows command names, options, and text or numbers you must type.

❻ Italics

Italic type introduces and defines a new term.

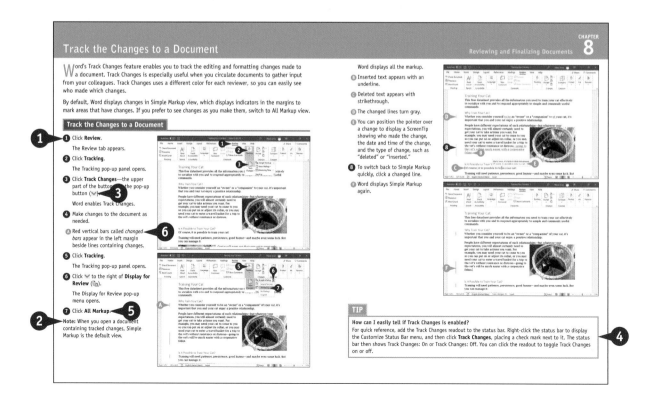

About the Author

Guy Hart-Davis is the author of more than 150 computer books, including *Teach Yourself VISUALLY iPhone 11, 11 Pro, and 11 Pro Max; Teach Yourself VISUALLY MacBook Pro and MacBook Air, 5th Edition;* and *Teach Yourself VISUALLY Android Phones and Tablets, 2nd Edition.*

Author's Acknowledgments

My thanks go to the many people who turned my manuscript into the highly graphical book you are holding. In particular, I thank Devon Lewis for asking me to write the book; Lynn Northrup for keeping me on track; Liz Welch for skillfully editing the text; Doug Holland for reviewing the book for technical accuracy and contributing helpful suggestions; Evelyn Wellborn for proofreading the book minutely; and SPi Global for laying out the book.

Open Word and Use the Start Screen

Microsoft Word is the world's most widely used word processing app. As of this writing, the current version of Word is Word 2019, which runs on Windows 10 and on macOS. This book focuses on Word 2019 for Windows. Microsoft also provides versions of Word for Apple iOS devices, which are the iPhone and iPod touch; for iPadOS, the iPad's operating system; and for Android, Google's operating system for smartphones and tablets.

To use Word, you first launch it. This section shows you how to pin Word to the Start menu or to the taskbar, and how to launch it from those locations.

Open Word and Use the Start Screen

Pin Word to the Start Menu or to the Taskbar

1 Click **Start** (⊞).

The Start menu opens.

2 Locate the Word icon (W) and entry. For example, scroll down.

Note: You can click **Word** (W) to launch Word.

3 Right-click **Word** (W).

The context menu opens.

A To pin Word to the taskbar, click or highlight **More**, and then click **Pin to taskbar**.

4 Click **Pin to Start**.

Windows pins Word to the Start menu.

Launch Word from the Start Menu

1 Click **Start** (⊞).

The Start menu opens.

2 Click **Word** (W).

Word opens.

Note: You can get Word either by buying an Office 2019 perpetual license or by paying for a Microsoft 365 subscription. Microsoft is gradually moving to the subscription model, and this is generally a better choice because the software receives ongoing updates as long as you subscribe, whereas the perpetual license receives only bug fixes and some updates.

Launch Word from the Taskbar

1 Click **Word** (w) on the taskbar.

Word opens.

Meet the Home Screen and Close Word

When Word opens, it displays the Home screen.

B If you have signed in to Microsoft 365, your ID appears here.

C The New area presents templates you can click to start a new document.

D You can click **Search** and type a search term to search for a document or template.

E The Recent list shows recent documents. You can click a document to open it.

F You can click **New** to create other types of new documents.

G You can click **Open** to open other existing documents.

1 Click **Close** (✕).

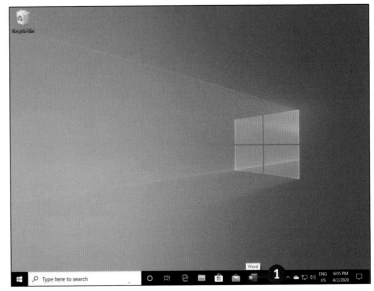

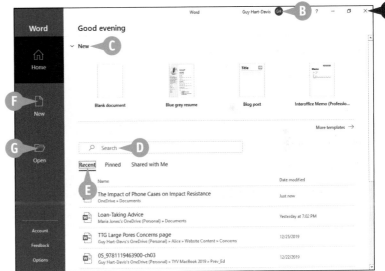

TIP

What do the Pinned tab and the Shared with Me tab contain?

The Pinned tab contains a list of documents you have "pinned" to keep them available. This gives you an easy way to open documents you use often.

The Shared with Me tab contains a list of documents that others have shared with you via Microsoft's OneDrive online service or through other means.

Understanding Office and the Cloud

Word and the other Microsoft Office apps, such as the Excel spreadsheet app and the PowerPoint presentation app, offer full integration with Microsoft's OneDrive online service, SharePoint servers, and Teams collaboration app. This integration enables you to work no matter where you are and which type of device you have available. For example, you can sign in to OneDrive on your laptop or iPad and get to work in Word; or you can sign in to Teams and open a Word document for editing directly in the app.

Sign In to the Cloud

Signing in to Office.com or your Microsoft 365 subscription connects your Office programs to the world beyond your computer. Office Online offers free access to the online, limited-edition versions of Word and other Office programs that you can use on any computer. Purchasing a Microsoft 365 subscription gives you access to full versions of the Office desktop programs and the

online versions of the products. Signing in gives you access to online pictures and clip art stored at Office.com and enables Word to synchronize files between your computer, OneDrive, and SharePoint.

OneDrive Storage Space

Subscriptions to Microsoft 365 include space on Microsoft's OneDrive cloud storage service. The amount varies depending on the plan; for example, the Microsoft 365 Personal plan gives one person 1 terabyte—1 TB, 1000 GB—of storage space, and the Microsoft 365 Family plan gives up to six family members 1 TB each. Word and the other apps save all documents by default to OneDrive so that you can access your documents from anywhere.

Using Office Online Apps

You can open and edit Word, Excel, OneNote, and PowerPoint documents from OneDrive using Office online apps, which are scaled-down editions of Office programs that you can use to easily review documents and make minor changes.

Take Your Personal Settings with You Everywhere

Word keeps track of personal settings like your recently used files and favorite templates and makes them available from any computer. When you open a document, Word gives you an easy way to return to the last location you were editing. This makes it easy for you to get back to work when you move from one computer or device to another.

Your Documents Are Always Up to Date

Word saves your documents by default in the OneDrive folder on your computer, from which you can access them quickly. Windows then synchronizes this folder with OneDrive in the background.

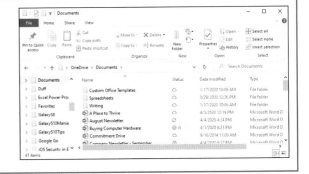

Share Your Documents from Anywhere

You can share your documents both from within Word and from OneDrive. If the document is stored on OneDrive, you can send the recipient a link so that they can work with the original document. If the document is stored on your PC, you can send the document itself; you can also send the document from OneDrive to give the recipient a separate copy to work with.

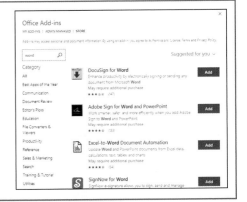

Take Advantage of the Office Store

The Office Store contains add-in applications that work with Word and the other Office apps. For example, the dictionary you use to look up words in Word does not automatically install when you install the program. But when you need an add-on for Word, you can download it from the Office Store.

Explore the Word Window

Like most of the other Office apps, Word's interface uses the Ribbon, a control strip across the top of the window, and a Quick Access Toolbar that appears either in the window's title bar or below the Ribbon. The Ribbon contains most commands available in Word, and the Quick Access Toolbar contains frequently used commands.

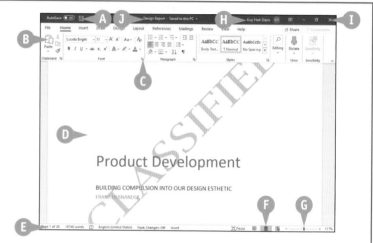

Ⓐ Quick Access Toolbar

Contains buttons that perform common actions.

Ⓑ Ribbon

Contains buttons organized in tabs, groups, and commands.

Ⓒ Dialog Box Launcher

Appears in the lower-right corner of many groups on the Ribbon. Clicking this button (🔽) opens a dialog box or task pane that provides more options.

Ⓓ Document Area

The area where you type and edit content. The insertion point, a blinking vertical bar, shows where text will appear when you type.

Ⓔ Status Bar

Displays document information and the location of the insertion point.

Ⓕ View Shortcuts

Contains buttons to switch among Word's different views of a document.

Ⓖ Zoom Controls

Changes the magnification of a document.

Ⓗ Microsoft 365 Indicator

If your name appears, you are signed in to your Microsoft 365 subscription. You can click ▾ to display a menu that enables you to manage your Microsoft account settings. If you are not signed in, this area shows a Sign In link.

Ⓘ App Window Controls

These buttons enable you to control the appearance of the app window. You can minimize the Ribbon, and you can minimize, maximize, restore, or close the app window.

Ⓙ Title Bar

Shows the document and app titles.

Sign In to Your Account

You can use Office.com or your Microsoft 365 subscription to work from anywhere. Once you sign in, you can use the free Office online apps, such as the Word app. Word remembers some of your personal settings such as your Recent Documents list so that you always have access to them. Desktop product users typically sign in using a Microsoft 365 subscription.

When you work offline, Word creates, saves, and opens your files from the local OneDrive folder. When you reconnect, Word uploads your changes to the cloud automatically.

Sign In to Your Account

1 Open Word.

The Word Home screen appears.

2 Click the **Sign in** link.

Note: If you are viewing a document, you can click the **Sign in** link in the upper-right corner of the screen.

The Sign In window appears.

3 Type the Microsoft account email address associated with your Microsoft 365 subscription.

4 Click **Next**.

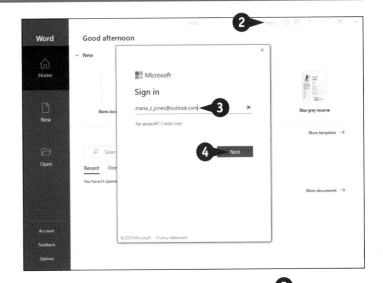

Note: If the Enter Password window appears, type your password, and click **Sign In**.

A Your name in this area indicates that you have signed in to Microsoft 365.

5 If you need to sign out, click your name, and then click **Sign out** in the pop-up panel that opens.

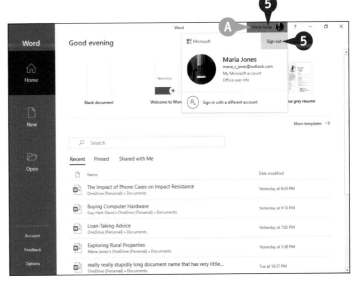

Work with Backstage View

You can click **File** at the left end of the Ribbon to display Backstage view. Backstage is the place to go when you need to manage documents or change program behavior. In Backstage view, you find a list of actions that you can use to open, save, print, remove sensitive information, and distribute documents as well as set Word program behavior options. You can also use Backstage to manage the places on your PC's hard drive, on your network, or in your OneDrive space that you use to store documents.

Work with Backstage View

1 Click **File**.

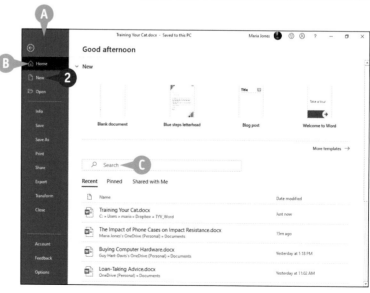

Backstage view appears.

A The left pane acts as a menu for navigation and commands for manipulating Word and the active document.

B This pane lets you quickly create new documents and open recent documents, frequently used documents you have "pinned," and documents shared with you.

C The Search box enables you to search by keywords for documents.

2 Click **New**.

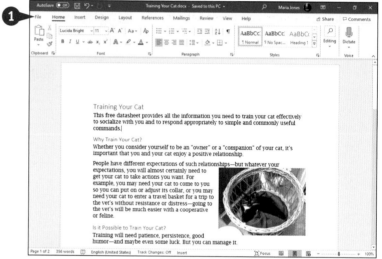

The New pane appears.

D You can double-click a template in the New area to quickly create a document based on that template.

E You can click **Search for online templates** and type search terms to search for online templates.

F You can click a Suggested Search to display templates in that category, such as Resumes and Cover Letters.

3 Click **Info**.

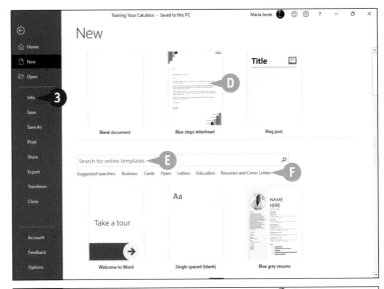

The Info pane appears.

G You can view information about the document and its properties, such as its size and last modified date.

H You can take actions, such as inspecting the document or managing it.

4 Click **Back** (⊖).

Word closes Backstage view and redisplays the open document.

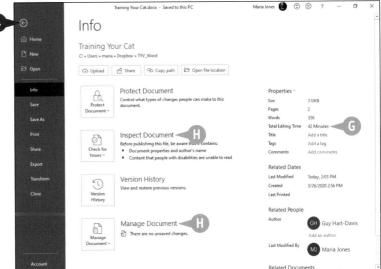

What does the Options link in Backstage do?

Clicking **Options** in the left pane in Backstage opens the Word Options dialog box. This dialog box contains scores of options for configuring Word to look and behave the way you prefer. You will explore the Word Options dialog box at various points throughout this book.

Change the Color Scheme and Background

The Office apps include several themes that you can apply from the Account screen in Backstage view or from the Word Options dialog box. The Colorful theme gives each app a different main color—navy blue for Word, forest green for Excel, and so on. The Dark Gray theme, the Black theme, and the White theme apply the name's shade to each app.

You can also apply an Office background, such as Clouds or Tree Rings, to an app. The background graphics appear on the right side of the title bar.

Change the Color Scheme and Background

Note: The color scheme and background apply to all the Office apps, so if you change the color scheme and background in Word, the changes appear in Excel, PowerPoint, and the other apps as well.

1 Click **File**.

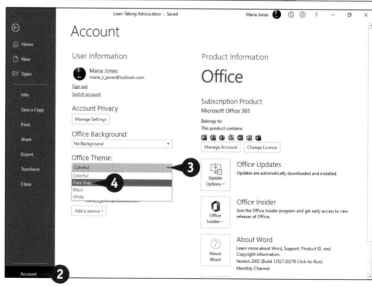

Backstage view opens.

2 Click **Account**.

The Account pane appears.

3 Click **Office Theme** (⌄).

The Office Theme drop-down list opens.

4 Click the Office theme you want.

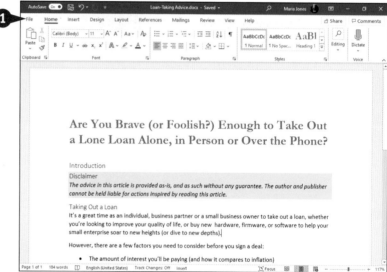

Word takes on the colors of the theme you chose.

Note: Some theme changes are more subtle than others.

5 Click **Office Background** (✺).

6 Move the pointer (🗘) over a choice in the menu to highlight that choice.

Ⓐ A background pattern appears at the top of the window. The pattern remains as you work on documents.

7 Click the pattern you want to use, or click **No Background**.

8 Click **Back** (🔙) to return to your document.

The Office theme and background you selected appear.

Ⓑ The background appears in the title bar.

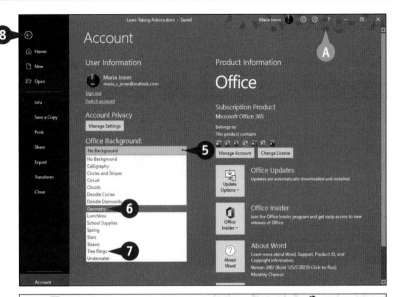

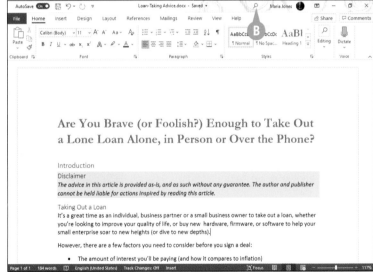

Locate Commands on the Ribbon

Word's Ribbon contains a huge number of commands, and it can be difficult to remember where to find a command you do not use frequently. To help you locate Ribbon commands, Word provides the Search feature.

You can still use the Ribbon directly, as described in the next section, "Give Commands Using the Keyboard and Mouse." The Search feature is most useful when you are not sure where on the Ribbon to find the command you need.

Locate Commands on the Ribbon

1 Open a document.

Note: See Chapter 2 for details on opening documents.

2 Click **Search** (🔍).

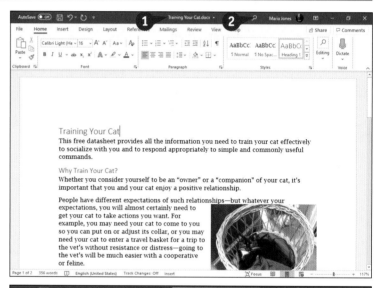

The Search pop-up panel opens.

A The Recently Used Actions list shows some recent actions you have taken.

B The Suggested Actions list suggests options that may be useful.

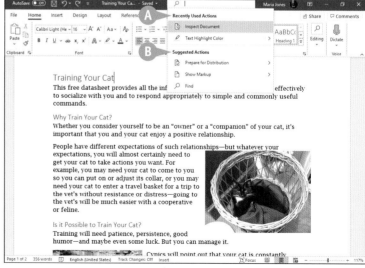

3 Type a brief description or a keyword describing what you want to do.

C The Actions list shows matches for what you typed.

4 Click a command to perform its action.

D If the command includes an arrow (>), you can either click the command itself to perform its default action, or click > to display a list of all its actions, and then click the action you want to perform.

Note: If you click a command that has no default action, Word displays the list of all the command's actions. You can then click the action you want to perform.

E The program performs the action you clicked. In this example, Word places a border around the first paragraph.

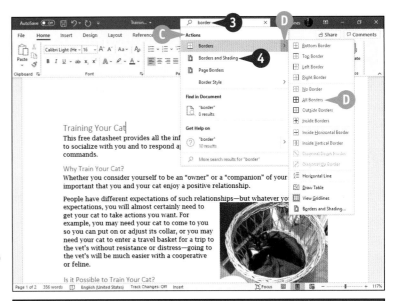

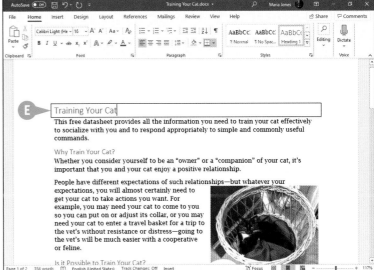

Will I need to type a description of the action I want to take if it is the same action I have previously taken?
No. The Search box remembers your previous searches and displays them on the menu that appears when you perform step **2**.

Can I delete my previous searches?
No. The Search feature retains your searches in the Recently Used section of the menu that appears when you click in the search box.

Give Commands Using the Keyboard and Mouse

You can keep your hands on your keyboard and select commands from the Ribbon or the Quick Access Toolbar, or you can use the mouse.

The Ribbon contains buttons organized in tabs, groups, and commands. Tabs appear across the top of the Ribbon and contain groups of related commands. Groups organize related commands; the group name appears below the group. Commands appear within each group. By default, the Quick Access Toolbar appears above the Ribbon and contains the AutoSave switch and the Save, Undo, and Redo commands. To customize the Ribbon or the Quick Access Toolbar, see Chapter 11.

Give Commands Using the Keyboard and Mouse

Give Commands with the Keyboard

1 If appropriate for the command you intend to use, place the insertion point in the right word or paragraph.

2 Press **Alt** on the keyboard.

Ⓐ Shortcut letters appear on the Ribbon.

Ⓑ Shortcut numbers appear on the Quick Access Toolbar.

3 Type a letter to select a tab on the Ribbon.

This example uses **P**, which activates the Layout tab.

The appropriate tab appears. In this example, the Layout tab appears.

Ⓒ Letters for each command on that tab appear.

4 Type the letter or letters to select the command you want to run.

For example, type **SA** to select the Space After box in the Paragraph group.

If appropriate, Word displays options for the command you selected.

5 Type a letter or use the arrow keys on the keyboard to select an option.

Word performs the command you selected, applying the option you chose.

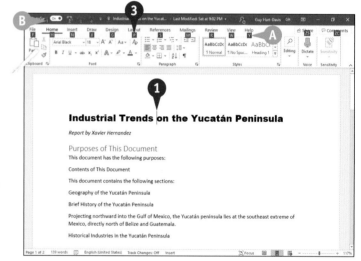

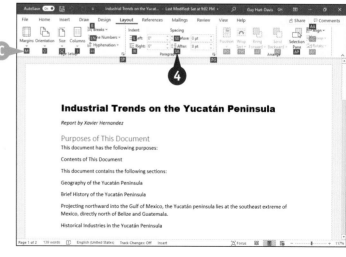

Give Commands with the Mouse

1 Click in or select the text or paragraph you want to modify.

2 Click the tab containing the command you want to use.

3 Move the pointer over the command you want to use.

D Word displays a ScreenTip describing the function of the button at which the pointer (⌖) is pointing.

4 Click the command. For example, click **Bold** (**B**).

E Word performs the command you selected. In this example, Word applies boldface to the selected text.

Note: If you selected text, click anywhere outside the text to continue working.

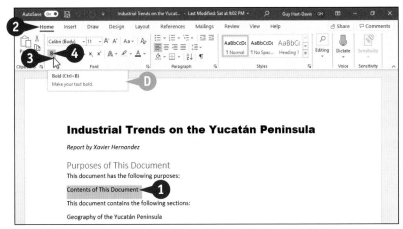

Can I toggle between the document and the Ribbon using the keyboard?

Yes. Each time you press **F6**, Word changes the focus of the program, switching among the document, the status bar, and the Ribbon, in that order. When the focus is on the status bar or the Ribbon, you can press **Tab** to move the focus to the next control, or press **Shift**+**Tab** to move the focus to the previous control.

What do the small down arrows below or beside buttons mean?

The small arrow (▾) on a button means several choices are available. Click the button directly to apply a default choice. Click ▾ to view additional options. As you move the pointer (⌖) over the two parts of the button, Word highlights one or the other to alert you that you have more choices.

Using Word on Tablets and Phones

You can use Word and the main Office apps on many tablets and phones as well as on PCs. Windows 10 tablets can run the full versions of the apps, and you can switch to Touch mode to make the interface easier to use with your fingers.

Microsoft also provides versions of Office for the iPad as well as the iPhone and iPod touch, and for Android phones and tablets. These versions of the apps look substantially different but provide most key features, including OneDrive connectivity, enabling you to continue your work no matter where you are.

Using Word on Tablets and Phones

Start a Program

1 Tap **Start** (⊞).

A The Windows 10 Start menu for Tablet Mode appears.

Note: If Word (w) appears at the top of the Start menu, tap it.

2 Tap **All apps**.

The All Apps screen appears.

3 Tap **Word** (w).

Word opens.

4 Tap the document you want to open.

The document opens.

Using Touch/Mouse Mode

1 Tap **Customize Quick Access Toolbar** (⤓).

2 Tap **Touch/Mouse Mode**.

B Word adds the Touch/Mouse Mode button to the Quick Access Toolbar.

Note: By default, each Office program displays the screen in Mouse mode.

3 Tap **Touch/Mouse Mode** (▣▾).

The Touch/Mouse pop-up panel appears.

4 Tap **Touch**.

C Word enlarges the Ribbon, adding space between the controls and collapsing some groups into buttons, as needed to fit the screen.

5 Tap to position the insertion point.

D The on-screen keyboard appears.

You can then type on the on-screen keyboard.

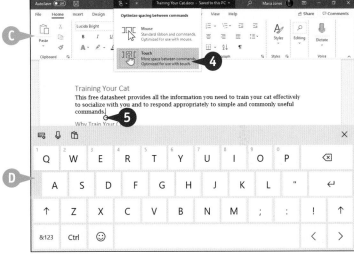

Where can I get Word for iOS, iPadOS, and Android devices?
You can get Word for iOS or iPadOS from the App Store. On your iPhone, iPod touch, or iPad, tap **App Store** on the Home screen, and then search for *Microsoft Word*. Similarly, you can get Word for Android on the Play Store. On your Android device, tap **Play Store** on the Home screen or the Apps screen, and then search for *Microsoft Word*.

You can use the basic features of these apps for free. But to use the apps' full capabilities, you must pay for a subscription.

Using Word in OneDrive and Microsoft Teams

From OneDrive, you can use the Word online app to open and edit Word documents with the same basic editing tools you use in Microsoft Word. Similarly, after signing in to Microsoft Teams, you can open a Word document for editing directly in Teams.

Both OneDrive and Teams provide a streamlined version of Word with fewer tools and commands than the full desktop version.

Using Word in OneDrive and Microsoft Teams

Using Word Online from OneDrive

1. Sign in to OneDrive at onedrive.live.com.

2. Open the folder containing the document you want to open.

3. Click the document you want to open.

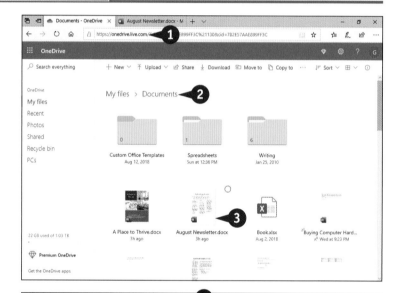

The document appears in the Word online app in another tab in the browser.

Ⓐ The insertion point appears, and you can edit as normal.

Ⓑ The Ribbon contains fewer tabs than in the desktop version.

Ⓒ You can click **Open in Desktop App** to open the document in Word, assuming Word is installed on the computer.

Note: The Word Online app automatically saves changes, so you do not need to save them explicitly.

4. When you finish working in the document, click **Close** (✕).

The document closes.

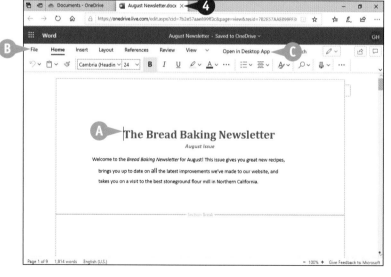

Using Word in Microsoft Teams

1 Open Teams as usual. For example, click **Start** (▦), and then click **Microsoft Teams** (▦).

Microsoft Teams opens.

2 Click **Teams** (▦) in the navigation bar.

The Teams list appears.

3 Click the appropriate team.

4 Click **Files**.

The Files pane appears.

5 Click the file you want to open.

The file opens, and you can work with it.

ⓓ For example, you can select a paragraph, and then apply a style to it.

Note: The Office Online apps inside Microsoft Teams automatically save changes, so you do not need to save them explicitly.

ⓔ You can click **Open in Desktop App** to open the document in Word, assuming Word is installed on the computer.

6 When you finish working with the file, click **Close**.

The document closes.

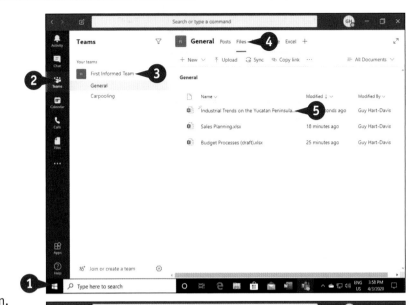

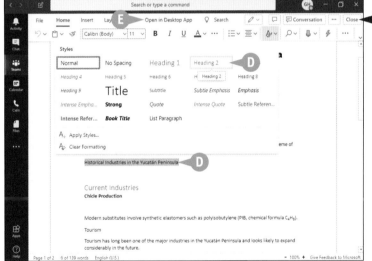

TIPS

What does the Conversation button in Microsoft Teams do?
Click **Conversation** to open the Conversation pane so that you can hold a conversation with fellow team members. For example, you can discuss the changes needed to a document as you work on it.

Work with the Mini Toolbar and Context Menus

Most of the formatting commands appear on the Home tab in Word, but you have alternatives to format text. Without switching to the Home tab, you can format text using the Mini Toolbar, which contains a combination of commands available primarily in the Font and Paragraph groups on the Home tab.

You also can use the context menu to format text without switching to the Home tab or the Review tab. The context menu contains the Mini Toolbar and a combination of commands available primarily in the Font group and the Paragraph group on the Home tab and on the Review tab.

Work with the Mini Toolbar and Context Menus

Work with the Mini Toolbar

1 Select text.

A The Mini Toolbar appears.

Note: If you slowly move the pointer (⬉) away from the selected text, the Mini Toolbar becomes transparent and then disappears.

2 Click any command or button to perform the actions associated with the command or button.

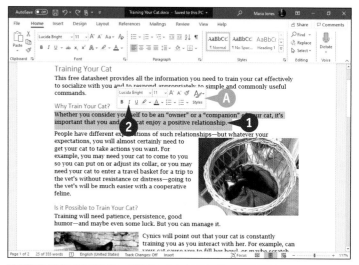

B Word performs the action on the selected text.

C The Mini Toolbar remains visible so that you can use it again if you want.

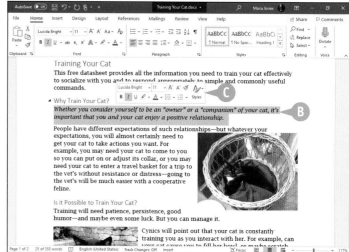

Work with Context Menus

1 Select text.

D The Mini Toolbar appears.

2 Right-click the selected text.

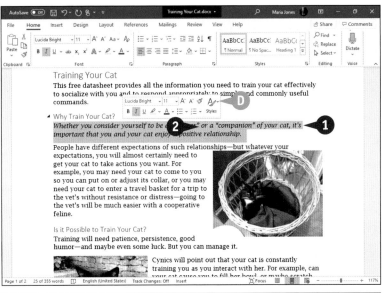

E The context menu opens.

Note: You can right-click anywhere in the document area, not just on selected text, to display the Mini Toolbar and the context menu.

3 Click a command or button to perform the associated action.

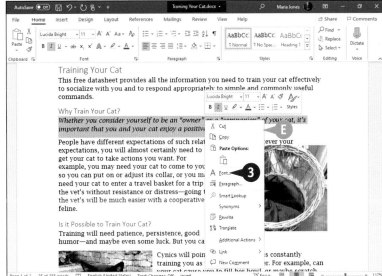

How do I turn off the Mini Toolbar?

Click **File** and then click **Options** to open the Word Options dialog box. Click **General** in the left pane to display the General category. Go to the User Interface Options section, and then click **Show Mini Toolbar on selection** (☐ changes to ☑). Click **OK**. The Word Options dialog box closes.

Enter Text in a Document

W ord makes text entry as easy as possible. By default, Word uses Insert mode, in which any text to the right of the insertion point moves along to accommodate the new text. When the text reaches the end of the line, Word automatically wraps it to a new line, so you need to press Enter only when you want to start a new paragraph.

When you want to use white space to align or position text, press Tab rather than Spacebar. See Chapter 6, "Formatting Paragraphs," for details on settings tabs.

Enter Text in a Document

Type Text

1 Type the text that you want to appear in your document.

A The text appears to the left of the insertion point as you type.

B As the insertion point reaches the end of the line, Word automatically starts a new one.

Press Enter only to start a new paragraph.

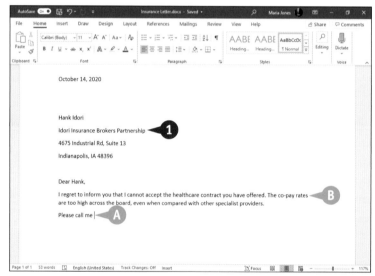

Separate Information Using Tabs

1 Type a word or phrase.

2 Press Tab.

To align text properly, you can press Tab to include white space between words.

Some white space appears between the last letter you typed and the insertion point.

3 Type another word or phrase.

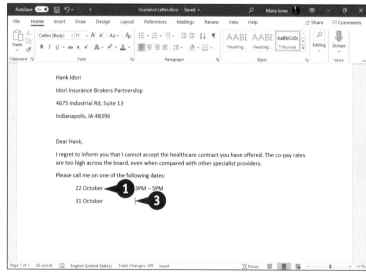

Enter Text Automatically

1 Begin typing a common word, phrase, or date.

C The AutoComplete feature suggests common words and phrases based on what you type.

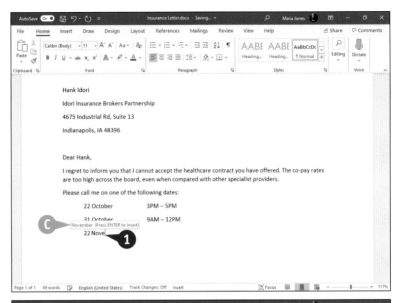

D You can press **Enter** to let Word finish typing the word, phrase, or month for you.

You can keep typing to ignore Word's suggestion.

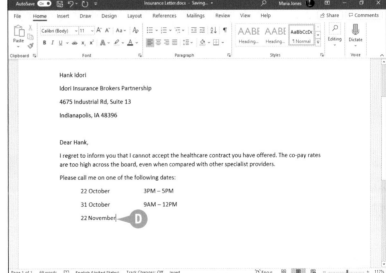

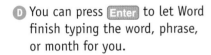

TIP

Why should I use Tab rather than Spacebar to include white space between words?
Typically, you include white space between words or phrases to align text in a columnar fashion. Most fonts are proportional, and each character takes up a different amount of space on a line, so using spaces does not usually align words exactly. Tabs, however, are set at specific locations on a line, so when you press Tab, the text will be aligned precisely with the next tab stop. For details on tab settings, see Chapter 6.

Move the Insertion Point Around a Document

You can move the insertion point around a document quickly by using either the keyboard or the mouse. Clicking with the mouse to place the insertion point works well when the new location is already on the screen, but using keyboard shortcuts is usually quicker for moving the insertion point longer distances. For example, pressing **Ctrl**+End is normally a faster way of moving the insertion point to the end of a long document than scrolling and then clicking.

Move the Insertion Point Around a Document

Move the Insertion Point by One Character

1 Note the location of the insertion point.

2 Press **→**.

A Word moves the insertion point one character to the right.

You can press **←**, **↑**, or **↓** to move the insertion point one character left, up, or down.

Pressing and holding any arrow key moves the insertion point repeatedly in the direction of the arrow key.

You can press **Ctrl**+**→** or **Ctrl**+**←** to move the insertion point one word at a time to the right or left.

Note: When the insertion point is inside a word, pressing **Ctrl**+**←** moves the insertion point to the beginning of that word.

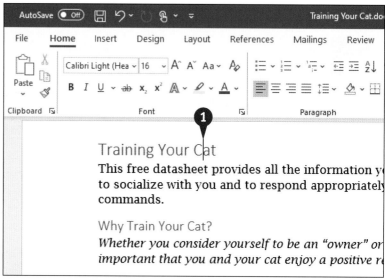

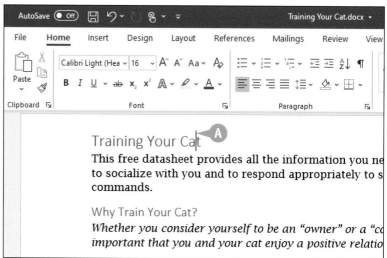

Move the Insertion Point by One Screen

1 Note the last visible line on-screen.

2 Press **Page down**.

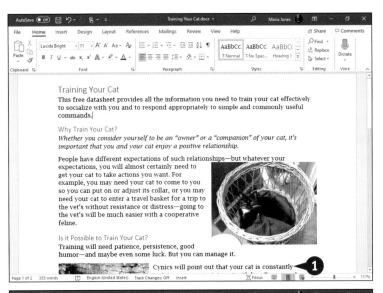

B Word moves the insertion point down one screen.

3 You can press **Page up** to move the insertion point up one screen.

C You can click ▲ to scroll up or ▼ to scroll down one line at a time in a document.

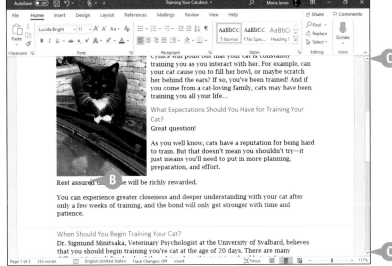

TIP

How do I quickly move the insertion point to the beginning or the end of a document or to a specific page?
Press **Ctrl**+**Home** or **Ctrl**+**End** to move the insertion point to the beginning or to the end of a document. To land on a specific page, press **F5** to display the Go To dialog box, type the number of the page, and press **Enter**. Press **Shift**+**F5** to move the insertion point to the last place you changed in your document. To move the insertion point to a specific location, use a bookmark; see the section "Mark and Find Your Place with Bookmarks" in Chapter 3, "Entering Text in Documents," for details.

Switch Document Views

Word provides five main views for viewing your document: Print Layout view, Web Layout view, Outline view, Draft view, and Read Mode view. The next section, "Understanding Document Views," explains the differences between the views, whereas this section shows you how to switch among the views by using the buttons on the status bar and on the View tab of the Ribbon.

Switch Document Views

1 Click **View**.

The View tab appears.

2 Click one of the buttons in the Views group on the Ribbon: **Read Mode**, **Print Layout**, **Web Layout**, **Outline**, or **Draft**.

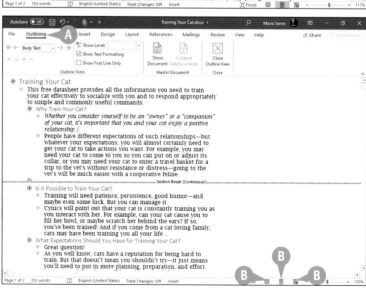

Word switches your document to the view you selected.

Note: In this example, the document switches from Print Layout view to Outline view, showing two outline levels.

Ⓐ In Outline view, the Outlining tab appears on the Ribbon.

Ⓑ Buttons for three of the views also appear at the right edge of the status bar; move the pointer (⌖) over each button to see its function, and click a button to switch views:

▥—Read Mode

▤—Print Layout

▨—Web Layout

Understanding Document Views

You can control the way that you view your document by choosing from five different views: Read Mode, Print Layout, Web Layout, Outline, and Draft.

Read Mode View

Read Mode view, which supports tablet motions, optimizes your document for easier reading and helps minimize eyestrain when you read a document on-screen. This view removes most toolbars. To return to another view, press **Esc**; alternatively, click **View**, and then click **Edit Document**.

Print Layout View

Print Layout view presents a "what you see is what you get" view of your document. In Print Layout view, you see elements of your document that affect the printed page, such as margins, headers, and footers.

Web Layout View

Web Layout view is useful when you are designing a web page because it displays a web page preview of your document.

Draft View

Draft view is designed for writing and editing text; it displays text formatting, but it does not display your document the way it will print. Instead, you can view elements such as the Style Area—which shows the formatting style for each paragraph—on the left side of the screen, but you cannot view certain document elements such as graphics or the document's margins, headers, and footers.

Outline View

Outline view helps you develop and edit the organization of a document. Word indents text styled as headings based on the heading number; you can move or copy entire sections of a document by moving or copying the heading. You also can display the Style Area to show the style names.

Work with the Navigation Pane

Word's Navigation pane helps you navigate through long documents. The Navigation pane appears on the left side of the Word window and contains three tabs: the Headings tab, the Pages tab, and the Results tab.

The Headings tab displays the document's headings in a collapsible view that works like a smaller version of Outline view. You can expand and collapse headings, as needed. The Pages tab displays page thumbnails that enable you to navigate quickly by eye. The Results tab enables you to navigate among search results and among objects, such as graphics, tables, or comments.

Work with the Navigation Pane

Navigate Using Headings

Note: To navigate using headings, your document must contain text styled with Heading styles. See Chapter 6 for details on styles.

1 Click **View**.

The View tab appears.

2 Click **Show**.

The Show pop-up panel appears.

3 Click **Navigation Pane** (☐ changes to ☑).

Ⓐ The Navigation pane appears.

Ⓑ Heading 1 styles appear at the left edge of the Navigation pane.

Ⓒ Word indents Heading 2 styles slightly and each subsequent heading style a bit more.

Ⓓ The Collapse icon (◢) represents a heading displaying subheadings; you can click it to hide the subheadings.

Ⓔ The Expand icon (▷) represents a heading hiding subheadings; you can click it to display the subheadings.

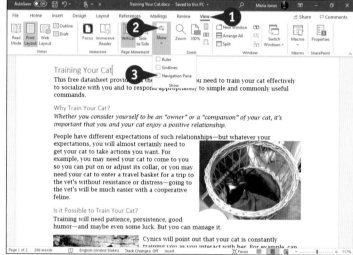

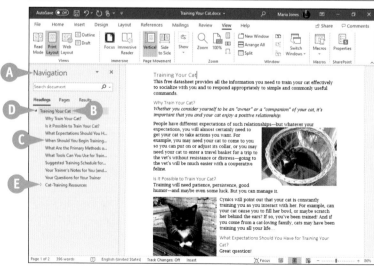

④ Click to select any heading you want to display.

Ⓕ Word moves the insertion point to that heading in your document.

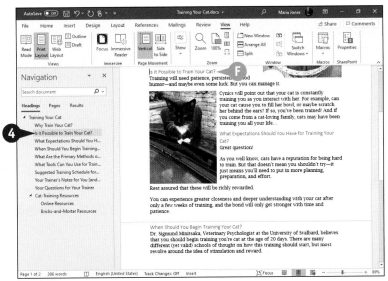

Navigate by Page

① Click **Pages**.

Ⓖ Word displays each page in your document as a thumbnail.

② Click a thumbnail.

Ⓗ Word selects that page in the Navigation pane and moves the insertion point to the top of that page. Word surrounds the current page's thumbnail with a heavy blue border.

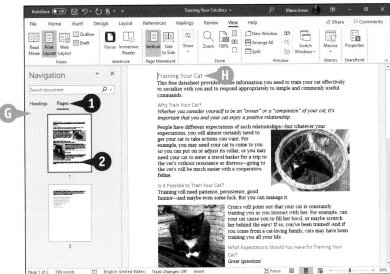

TIP

How do I control what headings appear?
On the Headings tab in the Navigation pane, right-click any visible heading to display the context menu. Click or highlight **Show Heading Levels** to display the Show Heading Levels submenu, and then click the lowest heading level you want to display. For example, click **Show Heading 3** to show Heading 1, Heading 2, and Heading 3 levels.

Using Focus Mode

When you need to concentrate on the contents of a document rather than its formatting or layout, you can switch on Focus mode from the Ribbon or from the status bar. Focus mode hides the title bar and window frame, the Ribbon, the status bar, and the scroll bars, leaving the document's contents displayed full screen.

When you need to use the Ribbon, you can display it temporarily by moving the mouse pointer up to the top of the screen. You can then issue a command as usual. Once you have done so, the Ribbon hides itself again.

Using Focus Mode

1 Click **View**.

The View tab appears.

2 Click **Focus**.

Note: If Focus Mode (🗔) appears on the status bar, you can click it to switch to Focus mode. To add this button, right-click the status bar, and then click **Focus** on the Customize Status Bar menu that opens.

Word displays the document in Focus mode, hiding almost all the controls.

3 When you need to use the Ribbon, move the pointer to the top of the screen.

The Ribbon reappears.

You can issue a command as usual.

4 When you want to stop using Focus mode, click **Restore Down** (🗗).

Note: You can also click **Focus Mode** (🗗) on the status bar to stop using Focus mode. Alternatively, press Esc.

Word switches back to the view you were using before.

Using Immersive Reader

When you need an even more focused reading experience than Focus mode provides, you can use Word's Immersive Reader feature. Immersive Reader provides a set of tools to help you focus on the document's text.

Immersive Reader enables you to narrow the focus to one line, three lines, or five lines. You can change the length of those lines by adjusting the column width setting, from Very Narrow through Narrow and Moderate to Wide. You can have Word add spacing between the characters, display syllable breaks, and even read the text aloud.

Using Immersive Reader

1 Click **View**.

The View tab appears.

2 Click **Immersive Reader**.

Word switches the document to Immersive Reader view.

Ⓐ The Immersive Reader tab appears on the Ribbon.

3 Click **Column Width**, and then click **Very Narrow**, **Narrow**, **Moderate**, or **Wide**.

4 Click **Page Color**, and then click the page color you want.

5 Click **Line Focus**, and then click **None**, **One Line**, **Three Lines**, or **Five Lines**, as needed.

Immersive Reader applies the settings you chose.

Ⓑ You can click **Text Spacing** to add spacing between letters and between lines.

Ⓒ You can click **Syllables** to display syllable breaks.

Ⓓ You can click **Read Aloud** to have Word read the text aloud.

6 Click **Up** (∧) to scroll up, or click **Down** (∨) to scroll down.

7 When you finish using Immersive Reader, click **Close Immersive Reader**.

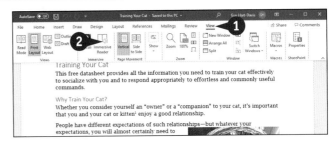

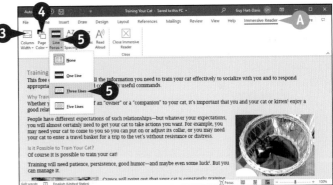

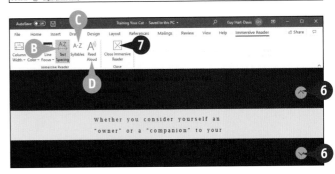

Word switches the document back to the view you were using before.

CHAPTER 2

Creating and Saving Documents

In this chapter, you learn how to create new documents and save them either to your computer or to OneDrive. You also explore how to work with different document formats, switch between open documents, and recover unsaved documents.

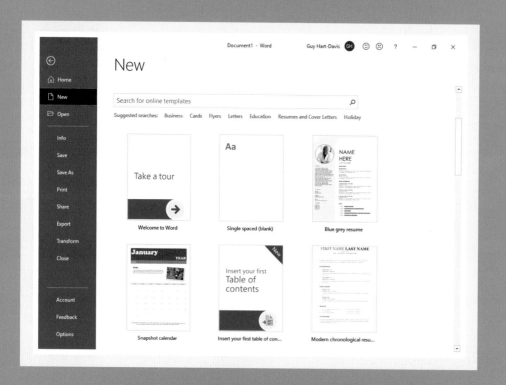

Start a New Document

Each time you open Word, the Word Start screen offers you a variety of choices, including several ways to begin a new document. But you can also start a new document while you are already working in Word.

You can use a *template*—a document containing predefined settings that saves you the effort of creating the settings yourself—as the foundation for a document. Word's Start screen and the New pane in Backstage View offer a variety of templates.

Start a New Document

1 With a document already open in Word, click **File**.

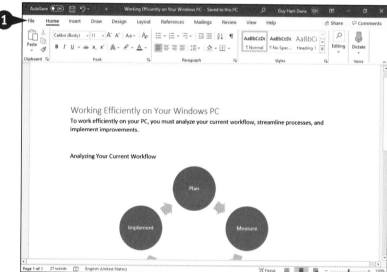

Backstage View appears.

2 Click **New**.

The New pane appears.

A Templates appear in the main part of the New pane.

B You can search for templates online at templates.office.com/en-US.

C You can click a button in the Suggested Searches list to search for templates in a particular category.

3 Click a template.

Note: This example uses **Blue grey resume**.

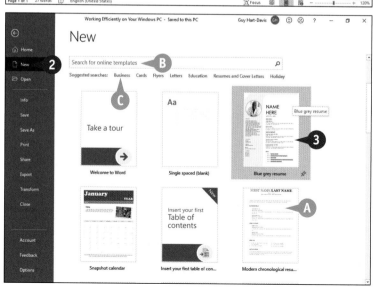

A preview of the template appears.

4 Click **Create**.

Note: If you change your mind about the template you chose in step **3**, click ✕ in the upper-right corner of the preview. Word redisplays Backstage View, showing the choices when you click New.

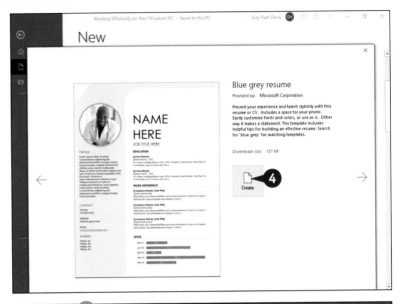

D The new document based on the template you chose appears.

You can edit this document any way you choose.

E Word gives the new document a generic name, such as Document2. When you save the document, as explained in the next section, you give the document a permanent name.

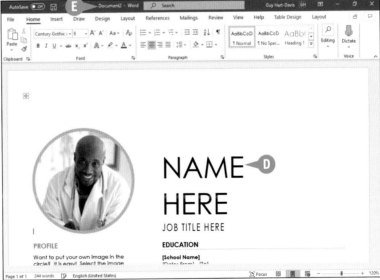

TIP

When I save the document, am I overwriting the settings in the template?
No. The document contains the settings found in the template, but saving the document has no effect on the template. The next time you choose to use that template, it will contain its original information. Think of it this way: a blank document is based on the Normal template, which contains no text, but it contains other settings such as fonts, font sizes, line spacing settings, and margins.

Save a Document to Your Computer

You save documents so that you can use them at another time in Microsoft Word. Word can save documents in various formats, but you will normally want to use the default format, which is called "Word Document (*.docx)." See the first tip in this section for brief details of the advantages of the Word Document format.

The first time you save a document, Word prompts you to specify a name for the document. Once the document has a name, you can click the Save button on the Quick Access Toolbar or press the `Ctrl`+`S` shortcut to save changes quickly.

Save a Document to Your Computer

Note: To avoid losing work, save each document immediately after you create it. After that, save the document whenever you have made changes that you would not want to have to make again.

1 Click **Save** (🖫).

The Save This File dialog box opens.

Note: The Save This File dialog box lets you save documents in only a few locations. Displaying the Save As pane in Backstage View gives you access to all your locations.

2 Click **More save options**.

The Save As pane in Backstage View appears.

A Locations where you can save files appear here.

Note: Once you select a location, folders available at that location appear on the right side of the screen.

3 Click the location where you want to save the file; this example uses **This PC**.

B If the folder in which you want to save the document appears here, click it and skip to step **5**.

4 Click **Browse**.

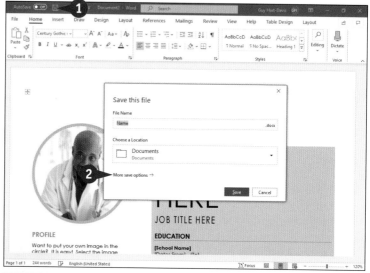

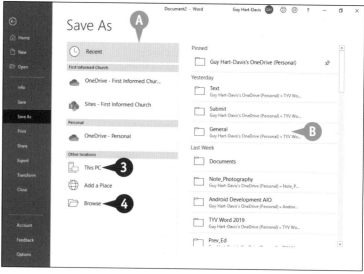

The Save As dialog box opens.

5 Type a name for the document here.

C You can click in the folder list to select a location on your computer in which to save the document.

D You can click **New folder** to create a new folder in which to store the document.

6 Click **Save**.

Word saves the document.

E The title bar shows the document's name.

F The title bar shows *Saved to this PC* to let you know the document is saved to your computer rather than to the Cloud.

G After making changes you want to keep, click **Save** (🖫) to save the changes.

Note: You can also press Ctrl+S to save the document.

TIPS

What are the advantages of the Word Document (*.docx) format?

The Word Document format has two main advantages. First, it reduces the amount of space needed to store a document. Second, it makes the document more resistant to corruption and improves your chances of recovering your work if a problem occurs, such as Word or your computer crashing. This format uses XML—the Extensible Markup Language—to provide structure and integrity for the file's contents.

How can I verify that the active document uses the Word .docx format?

Look at the document name in the title bar. The title of a document saved in a different format appears with "Compatibility Mode" in the title bar.

Save a Document to the Cloud

If you get Word through an Office 365 subscription, Microsoft gives you online storage space on its OneDrive cloud service. For example, an Office 365 Home subscription provides up to 1 TB—one terabyte, which is 1000 gigabytes—of space for each of up to six users.

OneDrive stores files in a folder on your PC and syncs that folder automatically to the OneDrive cloud. So each time you save a document in Word, the changes are saved first to your PC and then synced to the cloud.

Save a Document to the Cloud

1 Create a new document, as discussed in the section "Start a New Document," earlier in this chapter. For example, click **File**, and then click **New** to open the New pane in Backstage View; then click **Blank document** or a template of your choice.

Note: Alternatively, open an existing document that you want to save to the Cloud.

2 Enter any initial text needed, such as the document's title.

3 Click **File**.

Backstage View appears.

4 Click **Save As**.

5 Click your OneDrive.

A The list of folders appears.

6 If the folder where you want to save the document appears in these lists, click that folder; otherwise, click **Browse**.

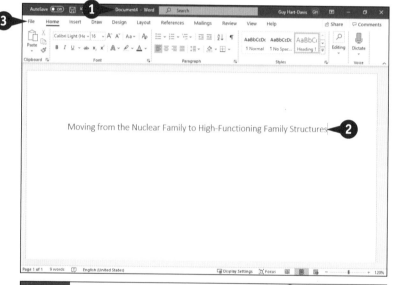

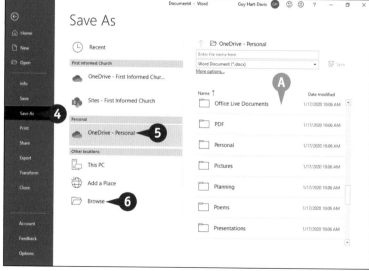

The Save As dialog box opens.

7 Click your OneDrive in the folder list.

8 Open the OneDrive folder where you want to place the document.

9 Type a filename.

Note: If you opened the document from your OneDrive space, you will be prompted to replace it; click **Yes**.

10 Click **Save**.

B Word saves the document and uploads it to OneDrive.

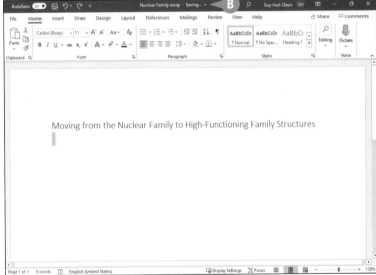

TIP

How do I prevent Word from automatically synchronizing with my OneDrive?

Perform the steps that follow: Click **File**, and then click **Options** to display the Word Options dialog box. Click **Save** in the left pane. Select **Save to Computer by default** (☐ changes to ☑), and then click **OK**.

Recover an Unsaved Document

You can open documents you created within the last seven days but did not save. Normally, it is best to save every document you create, but you may sometimes create a document, work in it, and then close it without saving because you think you will not need it again. And then, a few hours or days later, you find that you do need it.

You can reopen a document you created within the last seven days but did not save because Word automatically saves your documents in case problems occur.

Recover an Unsaved Document

1 With any document open, even a blank document, click **File**.

Note: See the section "Start a New Document" or "Open a Word Document" for details.

Backstage View appears.

2 Click **Info**.

The Info pane appears.

3 Click **Manage Document**.

The Manage Document pop-up menu opens.

4 Click **Recover Unsaved Documents**.

The Open dialog box appears, showing you available files that Word saved automatically but that you did not save as documents.

5 Click the unsaved file you want to open.

6 Click **Open**.

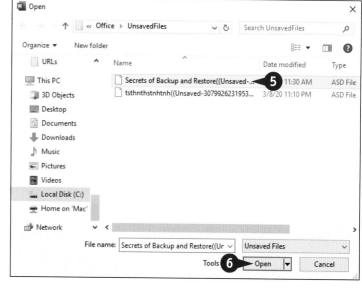

(A) The document opens.

(B) The gray Recover Unsaved File bar identifies the document as a recovered file temporarily being stored on your computer.

(7) Click **Save As**.

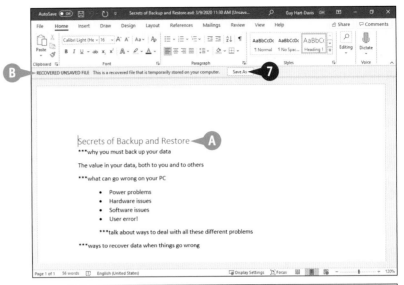

The Save As dialog box opens.

(8) Navigate to the folder in which you want to save the document. For example, click **OneDrive**, and then click the appropriate folder.

(9) Edit the suggested file name, or type a new filename over it.

(10) Click **Save**.

The Save As dialog box closes.

Word saves the document and removes the gray Recover Unsaved File bar.

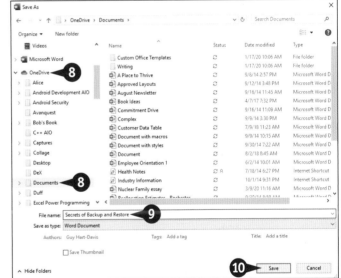

TIPS

How often does Word save a document while I work on it?
By default, Word automatically saves your work—even on documents you have not yet saved—every 10 minutes. If you work quickly, this is far too seldom. You can reduce the auto-save interval by changing the options for saving documents; see the section "Set Options for Saving Documents" for details.

Is there another way to open the dialog box that shows unsaved documents?
Yes. Click **File**, and then click **Open**. At the bottom of the Recent Documents list in Backstage View, click **Recover Unsaved Documents**.

Save a Document in a Different Format

You can save documents you create in Microsoft Word in a variety of other formats, such as Word templates, Word macro-enabled documents, OpenDocument Text files, or even plain-text files. One outdated format you may need to use is the Word 97–2003 format, which Word used by default up to Word 2003 for Windows and Word 2004 for Mac.

This section shows you how to save a document to Word 97–2003 format, but the steps for using any other file format that Word supports are similar.

Save a Document in a Different Format

1 With the document open, click **File**.

Backstage View appears.

2 Click **Save As**.

The Save As pane appears.

3 Click **This PC**.

A If the folder in which you want to save the document appears in this list, click it and skip to step **6**.

4 Click **Browse**.

The Save As dialog box opens.

5 Click the folder you want to save the document in.

6 Type a name for the document.

7 Click ⌄ to display the formats available for the document, and click **Word 97-2003 Document**.

8 Click **Save**.

Note: If you save a complex document, you might see the Compatibility Checker dialog box, which summarizes changes Word will make when saving your document. Click **OK**.

The Save As dialog box closes.

Word saves the document in the format you chose.

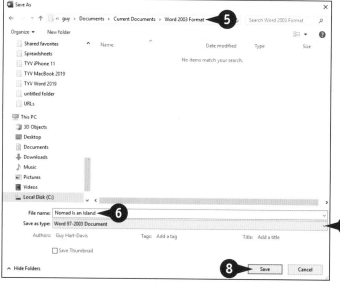

Save a Document in PDF or XPS Format

You can save Word documents in PDF or XPS formats. The PDF format is a universal format that any computer user can open using a PDF reader program. There are many free PDF reader programs; perhaps the most well-known one is Adobe Systems' free Acrobat Reader. Windows 8 and Windows 10 come with a built-in PDF reader.

XPS is Microsoft's alternative to PDF. Windows 10, Windows 8, and Windows 7 come with an XPS viewer; users of other versions of Windows can view XPS documents using Internet Explorer 7 or higher.

Save a Document in PDF or XPS Format

1 With the document open, click **File**.

Backstage View appears.

2 Click **Save As**.

The Save As pane appears.

3 Click **This PC**.

A If the folder in which you want to save the document appears in this list, click it and skip to step **6**.

4 Click **Browse**.

The Save As dialog box opens.

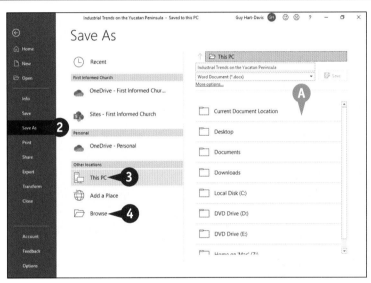

5 Click the folder in which you want to store the new file.

6 Click here and type a name for your document.

7 Click to select either **PDF (*.pdf)** or **XPS Document (*.xps)**.

Note: If you choose XPS format, you can opt to save and then open the document.

B If you plan to use your document online only, you can select **Minimum size** (○ changes to ●).

8 Click **Save**.

Word saves the document in the selected format.

Set Options for Saving Documents

By default, Word saves documents in the Word Document format, which uses the .docx file extension; automatically saves changes to the documents you store on OneDrive or the SharePoint Online services; and automatically saves your work every 10 minutes to help you recover from crashes and other problems.

You can configure Word's settings for saving documents by working in the Save category of the Word Options dialog box. For example, you may want to reduce the AutoRecover interval from 10 minutes to a shorter period.

Set Options for Saving Documents

1 Click **File**.

Backstage View appears.

2 Click **Options** at the bottom of the left pane.

Note: You may need to scroll down to see the Options button.

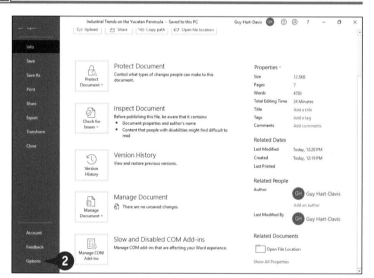

The Word Options dialog box opens.

3 Click **Save**.

4 Select **AutoSave OneDrive and SharePoint Online files by default on Word** (☑) if you want Word to save your Cloud files automatically.

5 Select **Save AutoRecover information every** (☑) and specify an interval for saving recovery information.

6 Select **Keep the last AutoRecovered version if I close without saving** (☑) to make sure Word saves unsaved documents.

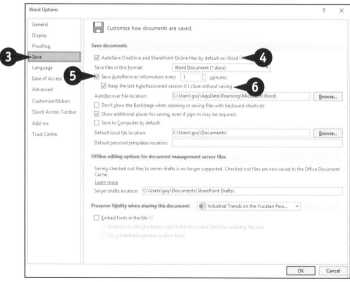

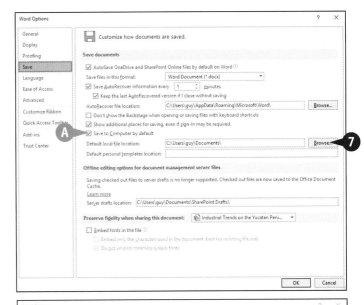

A If you want to save documents to your computer rather than to OneDrive, click **Save to Computer by default** (☐ changes to ☑).

7 Click **Browse** next to Default Local File Location.

The Modify Location dialog box opens.

8 Navigate to the folder where you want Word to save documents by default.

9 Click **OK**.

The Modify Location dialog box closes, returning you to the Word Options dialog box.

You can repeat steps **7** to **9** to set the AutoRecover File locations.

10 Click **OK**.

The Word Options dialog box closes.

Word saves your changes.

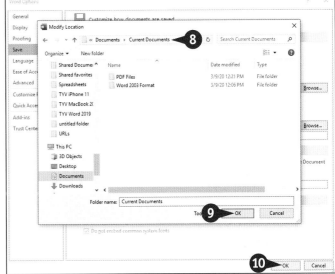

TIP

What happens if I select the Don't Show the Backstage When Opening or Saving Files option?
To take full advantage of this option, you need to add the Open button and the Save As button to the Quick Access Toolbar. When you opt not to show Backstage View, and then click the Open button or the Save As button, Word displays the Open dialog box or the Save As dialog box without showing Backstage View. If you are comfortable navigating folders, enabling this option saves you time. See Chapter 11, "Customizing Word," for instructions on customizing the Quick Access Toolbar.

Open a Word Document

You can open documents that you have created and saved previously to continue adding data or to edit existing data. Regardless of whether you store a file in a folder on your computer's hard drive or online, you can easily access files using the Open dialog box. If you are not sure where you saved a file, you can use the Open dialog box's Search function to locate it.

When you finish using a file, you should close it to free up processing power on your computer. See the second tip in this section.

Open a Word Document

1 Click **File**.

Backstage View appears.

2 Click **Open**.

A Word automatically selects Recent as the default location.

B Recently opened documents appear here. If you see the file you want to open, you can click it to open it and skip the rest of these steps.

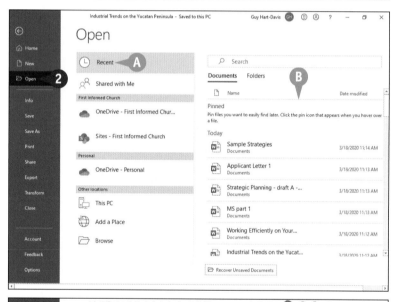

3 Click **Browse**.

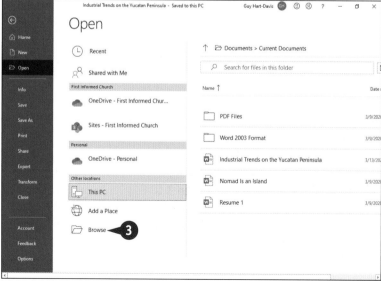

The Open dialog box appears.

④ Click the folder that contains the document you want to open.

ⓒ If you chose the wrong place, you can search for the file by typing part of the filename or content here.

⑤ Click the document you want to open.

⑥ Click **Open**.

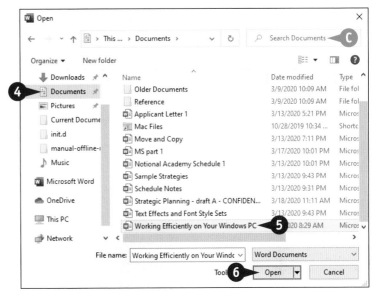

The document appears on-screen.

ⓓ To close a file, click ✕ in the upper-right corner. If you have not saved the file, the program prompts you to save it.

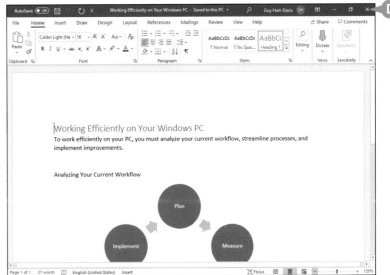

What if I cannot find my file?
You can use the search box in the upper-right corner of the Open dialog box to locate files. Complete steps **1** to **3** to display the Open dialog box. Locate and open the folder in which you believe the file was saved and type the file's name in the search box. Files containing the search term appear highlighted along with files containing a close match.

How do I close a document?
While viewing the document, click **File** to display Backstage View, and then click **Close**.

Open a Document That Uses a Different Format

You can open and edit documents created in other word processing apps or text editors. Word can open XML, web page, rich text, plain-text, OpenDocument, PDF, WordPerfect 5.x or 6.x, or Works 6–9 documents as well as documents created in earlier versions of Word.

Although you can open and edit PDF files, editing PDF files in Word works best if you used Word to originally create the PDF file. If you used a different program to create the PDF file, you may find that Word has difficulty maintaining the file's formatting.

Open a Document That Uses a Different Format

1 Click **File**.

Backstage View appears.

2 Click **Open**.

A You can click **Recent** to see a list of recently opened documents. If you see the file you want to open, you can click it to open it and skip the rest of these steps.

3 Click the place where you think the document is stored. This section uses **This PC**.

B If the folder containing the document appears here, click it and skip to step **5**.

4 Click **Browse**.

The Open dialog box appears.

5 Click in the folder list to navigate to the folder containing the file you want to open.

6 Click ∨, and then click the type of file you want to open.

The Open dialog box shows files of that type.

7 Click the file you want to open.

8 Click **Open**.

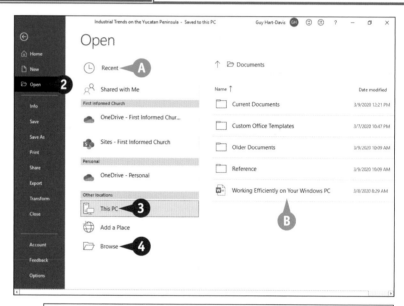

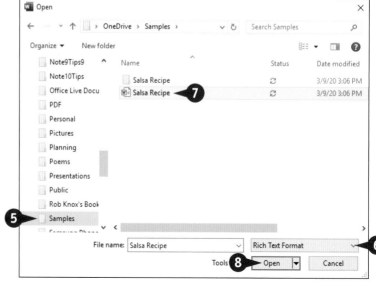

If you open a PDF file, Word displays a message indicating that it is converting your PDF file to an editable Word document; click **OK** to continue.

Note: You may be prompted to install a converter to open the file; click **Yes** or **OK** to install the converter and open the file.

Ⓒ Word opens the file.

Ⓓ The title bar shows *Compatibility Mode* to indicate that the file is not in Word Document format.

9 To save the file in Word Document format, click **File**.

Backstage View appears.

10 Click **Save As**.

The Save As pane appears.

11 Click ⋁, and then click **Word Document (*.docx)**.

12 Click **Save**.

Word saves the file in the Word Document format.

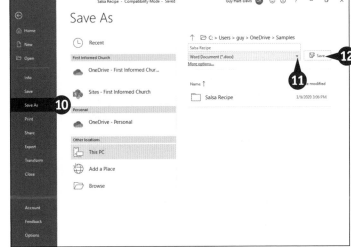

TIP

How do I open an XPS file?
Although you can create an XPS file in Word, you cannot open the file in Word. Instead, you can use an XPS viewer, or in Windows 10, you can use the Reader app. To open an XPS file, find it using File Explorer and double-click it.

Open a Document from the Cloud

*S*toring your documents on OneDrive enables you to access them from anywhere and makes it easy to work on the same documents on all your devices. For example, you can start a document on your PC, work on the document on your phone or tablet while out and about, and then resume work seamlessly on your PC.

Documents stored in your OneDrive folder are automatically synced with your cloud storage, keeping all versions up to date.

Open a Document from the Cloud

1 Make sure you have signed in to your Microsoft 365 subscription by looking for your name here.

2 Click **File**.

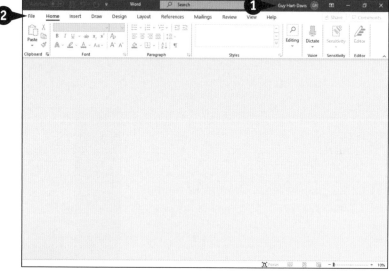

Backstage View appears.

3 Click **Open**.

A Word automatically selects Recent as the default location.

4 Click the appropriate OneDrive account. This example uses the personal OneDrive account.

B You may also have a business OneDrive account.

C You may also have access to one or more SharePoint servers.

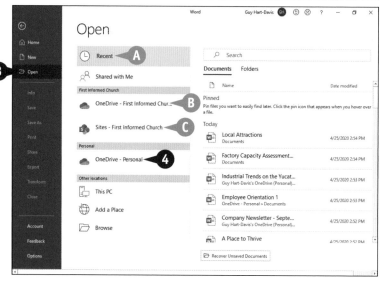

52

The contents of that OneDrive appear.

5 Navigate to the folder that contains the document you want to open.

D You can use the search box to search the current folder using keywords.

6 Click the document you want to open.

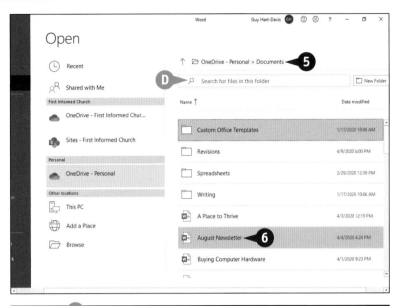

The document opens, and you can edit it as normal.

E By default, Word sets the AutoSave switch to On for a document stored on OneDrive or SharePoint. When AutoSave is On, you do not need to save changes manually.

TIP

What happens if I leave a OneDrive document open on my PC and then change the document on my phone?

As long as you leave the AutoSave feature enabled, OneDrive automatically synchronizes the changes you make across the different versions of the document. In this case, when you return to your PC, OneDrive will have updated the document with the changes you made on your phone.

Switch Between Open Documents

Word enables you to open as many documents as you need and to switch between them quickly. For example, you may need to copy information from one document to another, or you may simply need a change of focus.

You can switch between your open documents either by using the Switch Windows menu on the View tab of the Ribbon in Word or by using the Windows taskbar.

Switch Between Open Documents

Switch Documents Using Word

1 Click **View**.

The View tab appears.

2 Click **Switch Windows**.

A The menu displays a list of all open documents.

B A check mark (✔) appears beside the currently active document.

3 Click the document you want to view.

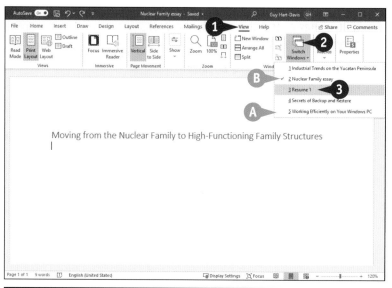

The selected document appears.

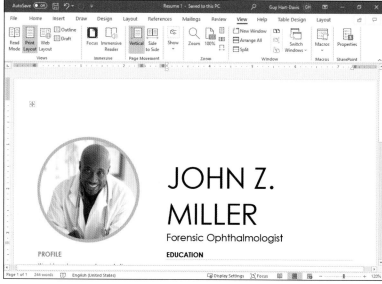

Switch Documents Using the Windows Taskbar

1 Position the mouse (⮲) over the Word button in the Windows taskbar.

C Preview thumbnails appear for each open document. The document over which you position the pointer (⮲) also previews in Word.

D You can close a document by moving the pointer over a thumbnail, and then clicking **Close** (✕).

2 Click the preview of the document you want to display.

The document appears.

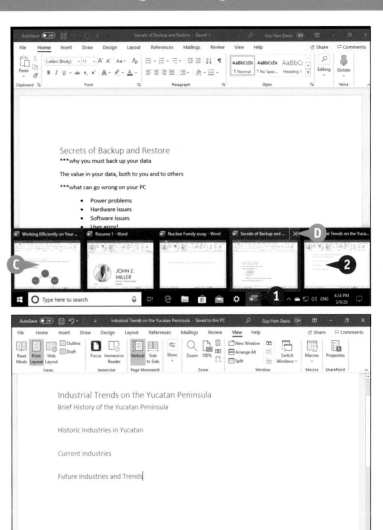

How can I keep the taskbar buttons separate from each other instead of stacked on top of each other?

Right-click the clock readout, and then click Taskbar Properties in the context menu that opens. The Taskbar screen in the Settings app appears. Click **Combine taskbar buttons** (⌄), and then click **Never**; alternatively, click **When taskbar is full** to stack the buttons only when the taskbar is full. Click **Close** (✕) to close the Settings app.

Compare Two Documents Side by Side

When you need to compare two documents, you can use Word's View Side by Side feature, which places the documents in equally sized windows alongside each other, making the contents easy to compare. The View Side by Side feature also provides two helpful features: First, it synchronizes the scrolling of the two windows, so when you scroll one window up or down, and the second window follows suit; and second, it synchronizes the zoom, enabling you to zoom both windows in or out together.

Compare Two Documents Side by Side

1 Open the two documents you want to compare and make one of the documents active.

2 Click **View**.

The View tab appears.

3 Click **View Side by Side** (⬛).

The Compare Side by Side dialog box opens, showing a list of your other open documents.

Note: If you have only two documents open, the Compare Side by Side dialog box does not open. Go to step **6**.

4 Click the second document for the comparison.

5 Click **OK**.

The Compare Side by Side dialog box closes.

Word displays the documents in two panes beside each other.

6 Drag either document's scroll bar.

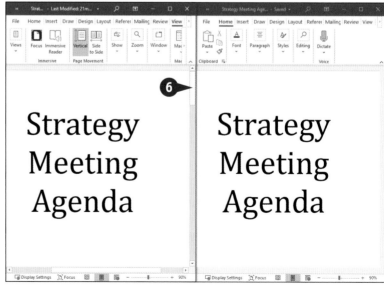

Word scrolls both documents simultaneously.

Note: You can also zoom both documents simultaneously by dragging the zoom slider on the status bar.

7 When you are ready to stop comparing the two documents, click **View** in the document that you want to keep viewing.

The View tab appears.

8 Click **Window**.

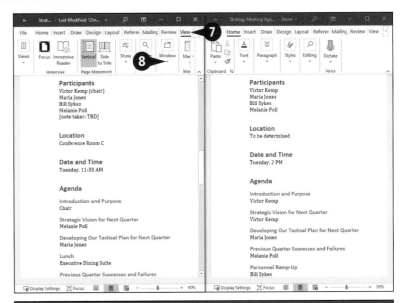

The Window panel appears.

9 Click **View Side by Side**.

Word expands the document to its previous size.

Note: The second document remains open.

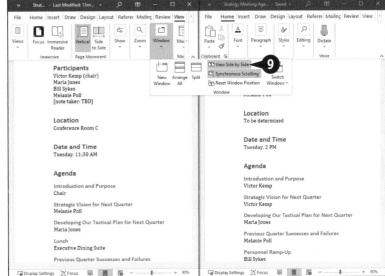

What does the Reset Window Position button do?
When you are comparing documents side by side, the **Reset Window Position** button has no effect. But you can use **Arrange All** to place one window above the other, each in its own separate pane. To return to side-by-side viewing, click **Reset Window Position**.

CHAPTER 3

Entering Text in Documents

Word provides easy-to-use but powerful tools for entering text in your documents. In this chapter, you learn to enter, delete, and select text; move or copy text within documents or between documents; and use bookmarks to mark places to which you want to return easily.

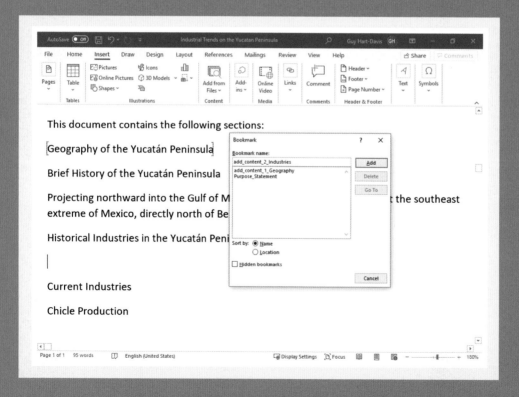

Insert and Add Text

Word has two modes for inserting text in a document: Insert mode and Overtype mode. By default, Word is set to Insert mode; when you start typing, Word moves any existing text to the right to accommodate the new text. By contrast, in Overtype mode, Word replaces existing text to the right of the insertion point, character for character.

You may find you prefer one mode to the other, or you may want to set Word up so that you can toggle quickly between the two modes.

Insert and Add Text

Insert Text Using Insert Mode

1 Click where you want to insert text.

The insertion point flashes where you clicked.

You can press ⬅, ➡, ⬆, or ⬇ to move the insertion point one character or line.

You can press `Ctrl`+➡ or `Ctrl`+⬅ to move the insertion point one word at a time to the right or left.

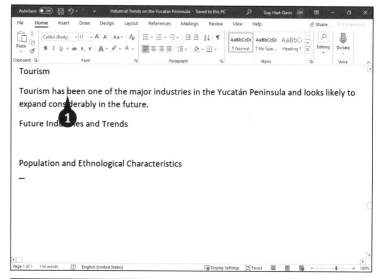

2 Type the text you want to insert.

A Word inserts the text to the left of the insertion point, moving existing text to the right.

Note: If you want to type over text in Insert mode, simply select the text and then type over the selection.

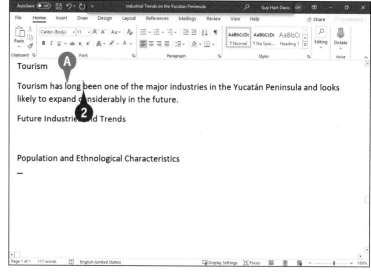

60

Insert Text Using Overtype Mode

1 Position the insertion point where you want to replace existing text.

2 Right-click the status bar.

The Customize Status Bar pop-up menu opens.

3 Click **Overtype** to display a check mark beside it.

B An indicator appears in the status bar.

4 Click the indicator to switch to Overtype mode.

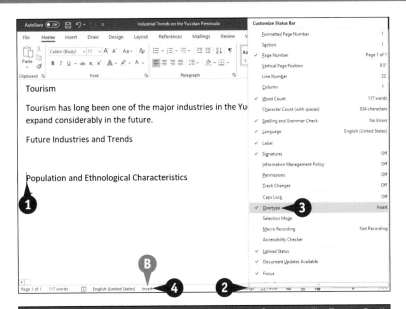

C The indicator switches to Overtype.

Note: Each time you click the indicator, you switch between Overtype mode and Insert mode.

5 Type the new text.

As you type, Word replaces the existing text with the new text you type.

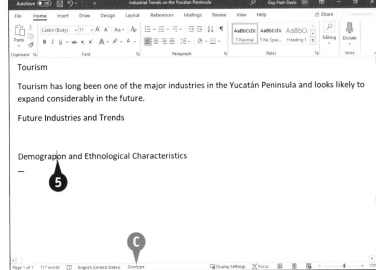

TIP

How can I use the keyboard to control switching between Insert mode and Overtype mode?
Click **File** to open Backstage View, and then click **Options** to display the Word Options dialog box. Click **Advanced** in the left pane, go to the Editing Options section of the Advanced pane, and then click **Use the Insert key to control overtype mode** (☐ changes to ☑). Click **OK** to close the Word Options dialog box. You can then press **Insert** to switch between Insert mode and Overtype mode.

Insert Symbols and Special Characters

Word provides a wide variety of symbols and special characters you can insert in your documents. Symbols include accented letters, Greek characters, mathematical symbols, and architectural symbols; special characters include em dashes and en dashes, nonbreaking spaces, paragraph symbols, and section symbols.

The Symbol gallery gives you access at first to common symbols and then to the symbols you use most frequently. To insert other symbols, and to insert special characters, you use the Symbol dialog box.

Insert Symbols and Special Characters

1 Click where you want the symbol to appear.

The insertion point appears.

2 Click **Insert**.

The Insert tab appears.

3 Click **Symbols**.

The Symbols panel opens.

4 Click **Symbol**.

Note: Depending on your screen resolution, you may or may not see the Symbols button.

A The Symbols gallery appears. If the symbol you need appears in the gallery, click it and skip the rest of these steps.

5 Click **More Symbols**.

The Symbol dialog box opens.

B The "[normal text]" item gives you symbols available in your current font.

C If you need to use a different font, click **Font** ✓ and select the symbol's font.

The available symbols change to match the font you selected.

D You can click ▲ and ✓ to scroll through available symbols.

6 Click the symbol you want to insert.

7 Click **Insert**.

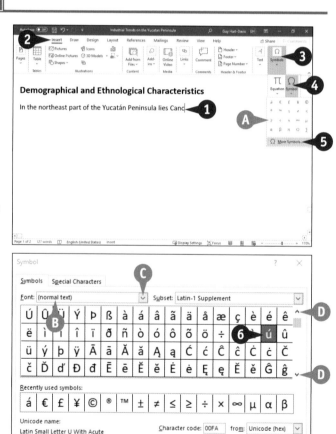

62

E Word inserts the symbol in the document.

F Word replaces the Cancel button with the Close button.

8 Click in the document.

Word moves the focus to the document.

The Symbol dialog box remains open.

9 Type any text needed.

10 When you want to insert a special character, click the Symbol dialog box.

The Symbol dialog box becomes active again.

11 Click **Special Characters**.

The Special Characters tab appears.

12 Click the special character you want to insert.

13 Click **Insert**.

G The special character appears in the document.

14 When you finish using the Symbol dialog box, click **Close**.

The Symbol dialog box closes.

Note: Windows includes the Character Map utility for inserting symbols and special characters in any app. To run Character Map, click **Start** (⊞), type **charmap**, and then press Enter.

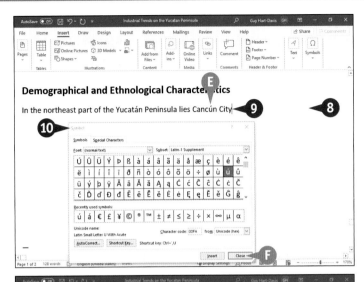

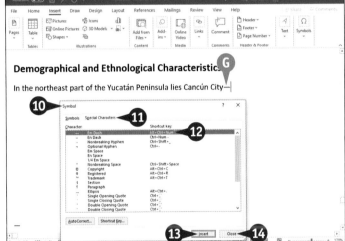

Create a Hyperlink

 ord enables you to create hyperlinks to connect text or graphical elements in a document to another file on your computer or on your company's network or to a web page on the Internet. Hyperlinks are useful for giving your readers direct access to other information they may want to view.

Hyperlinks you create in a Word document work much like the ones you use on web pages you browse. Pressing Ctrl while you click a hyperlink takes you to the linked location.

Create a Hyperlink

1 Select the text or graphic you want to use to create a hyperlink.

2 Click **Insert**.

The Insert tab appears.

3 Click **Links**.

The Links panel opens.

4 Click **Link**.

A The Recent Items list shows suggested items. If one is suitable, click it and go to step **6**.

5 Click **Insert Link**.

You can right-click the selection and click **Hyperlink** instead of performing steps **2**, **3**, and **4**.

The Insert Hyperlink dialog box opens.

6 Click **Existing File or Web Page**.

B Files in the current folder appear here.

C To link to a file, click ⌄ and navigate to the folder containing that file.

D You can click **Browsed Pages** to view a list of web pages you have browsed recently.

7 To link to a web page, click **Address** and type or paste the address.

8 Click **ScreenTip**.

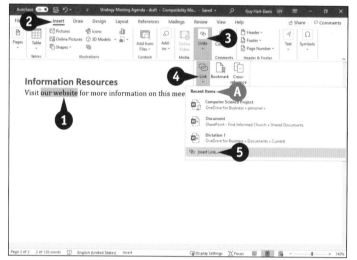

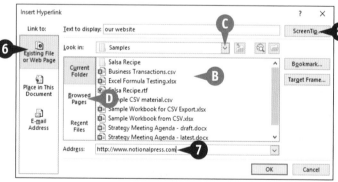

The Set Hyperlink ScreenTip dialog box opens.

9 Type text that should appear when a user moves the pointer ($\mathbb{R}$) over the hyperlink.

10 Click **OK**.

The Set Hyperlink ScreenTip dialog box closes.

11 Click **OK** in the Insert Hyperlink dialog box.

E Word creates a hyperlink shown as blue, underlined text in your document.

12 Move the pointer ($\mathbb{R}$) over the hyperlink.

F The ScreenTip text you provided in step **9** appears, along with instructions to the reader on how to use the hyperlink.

G The status bar shows the destination of the hyperlink.

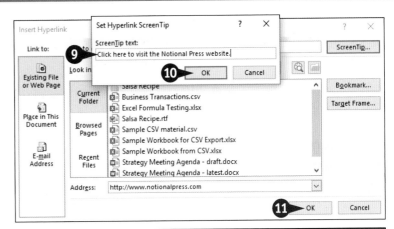

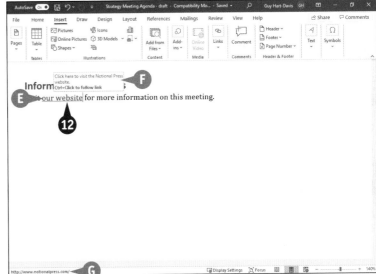

How do I use a hyperlink that appears in a Word document?

Press and hold Ctrl as you click the hyperlink. The linked document or web page will appear.

My hyperlink to a file does not work anymore. Why not?

Most likely, the file no longer exists at the location you selected in step **6**. If you moved the file to a new folder, edit the hyperlink to update the file location. To edit the hyperlink, move the pointer ($\mathbb{R}$) over it and right-click. From the menu that appears, click **Edit Hyperlink** to display the Edit Hyperlink dialog box, which works in a similar way to the Insert Hyperlink dialog box.

Delete Text

You can easily delete text from a document by pressing either **Delete** or **Backspace** on your keyboard. You can either delete a single character at a time or delete larger amounts of text, as needed.

Pressing **Delete** deletes text to the right of the insertion point, whereas pressing **Backspace** deletes text to the left of the insertion point.

Delete Text

Delete Text Using the Delete Key

1 Click to the left of the character you want to delete.

The insertion point flashes where you clicked.

You can press ←, →, ↑, or ↓ to move the insertion point one character or line.

You can press **Ctrl**+→ or **Ctrl**+← to move the insertion point one word at a time to the right or left.

2 Press **Delete** on your keyboard.

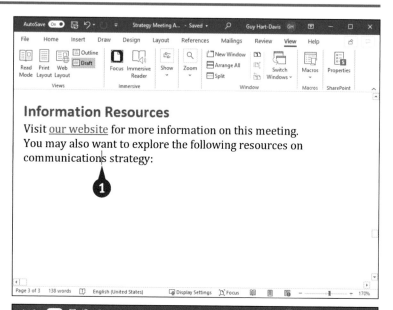

A Word deletes the character immediately to the right of the insertion point.

You can press and hold **Delete** to repeatedly delete characters to the right of the insertion point.

You can press **Ctrl**+**Delete** to delete the word to the right of the insertion point.

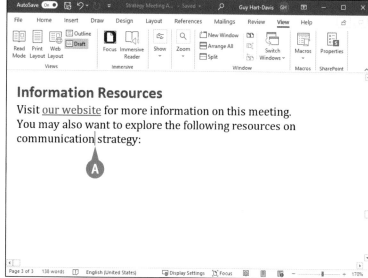

Using the Backspace Key

1 Click to the right of the character you want to delete.

The insertion point flashes where you clicked.

2 Press **Backspace** on your keyboard.

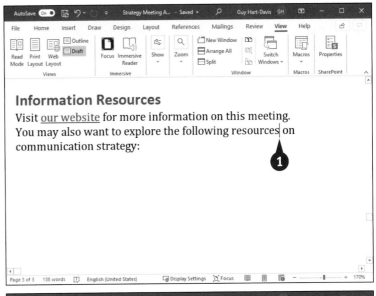

B Word deletes the character immediately to the left of the insertion point.

You can press and hold **Backspace** to repeatedly delete characters to the left of the insertion point.

You can press **Ctrl** + **Backspace** to delete the word to the left of the insertion point.

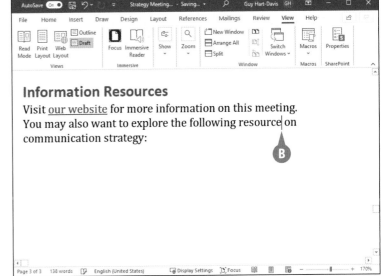

TIPS

How can I delete a large block of text quickly?
Select the block of text, and then press either **Delete** or **Backspace**; either key deletes selected text. See the section "Select Text," later in this chapter.

How can I recover text I deleted by accident?
Use the Undo feature in Word to restore the text you deleted. See the section "Undo, Redo, and Repeat Changes," later in this chapter.

Insert Blank Lines

You can insert blank lines in your text by inserting paragraph marks or line breaks. Word stores paragraph formatting in the paragraph mark, which you can display by clicking **Show/Hide** (¶) in the Paragraph group on the Home tab. When you start a new paragraph, you can change the new paragraph's formatting without affecting the preceding paragraph's formatting.

You use line breaks to start a new line without starting a new paragraph. For example, you might use line breaks for the inside address of a letter or to break lines of verse.

Insert Blank Lines

Display Paragraph Marks and Start a New Paragraph

1 Click **Home**.

The Home tab appears.

2 In the Paragraph group, click **Show/Hide** (¶).

Paragraph marks and other hidden characters appear.

3 Click where you want to start a new paragraph.

4 Press **Enter**.

Ⓐ Word inserts a paragraph mark and moves any text to the right of the insertion point into the new paragraph.

Note: For more information on styles and displaying paragraph marks, see Chapter 6.

Insert a Line Break

1 Click where you want to start a new paragraph.

2 Press **Shift** + **Enter**.

Ⓑ Word inserts a line break.

Note: Any text on the line to the right of where you placed the insertion point in step **1** moves onto the new line.

Note: Click **Show/Hide** (¶) in the Paragraphs group on the Home tab when you want to hide paragraph marks again. Alternatively, press **Ctrl** + **Shift** + **8**.

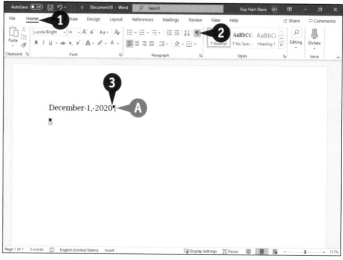

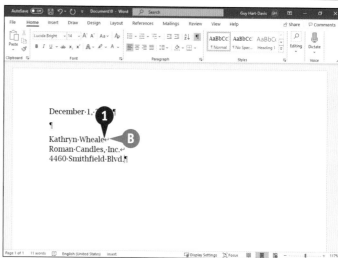

Undo, Redo, and Repeat Changes

You can use the Undo feature to reverse actions you take while working in a document. For example, if you accidentally delete text, you can use Undo to recover it. Or if you apply formatting and find it unsuitable, you can use Undo to remove the formatting.

You can undo either a single action or multiple actions. If you undo an action by mistake, you can use the Redo feature to restore what you have undone. You can also repeat an action quickly.

Undo, Redo, and Repeat Changes

Note: The position of the insertion point does not affect using the Undo feature.

1 Click ⌄ to the right of **Undo** (↩).

Note: To undo only the last action, click **Undo** (↩). From the keyboard, press Ctrl + Z.

The Undo pop-up menu opens.

2 Click the action up to which you want to undo your recent actions.

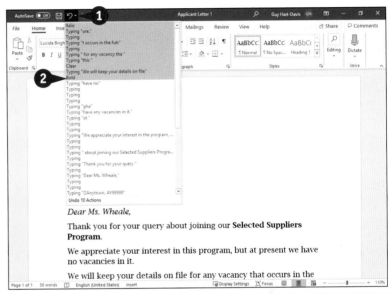

Ⓐ Word undoes those actions. In the example, among other changes, Word has removed the bold from the text that is selected.

Ⓑ If you change your mind after undoing one or more actions, click **Redo** (↪) to redo the last action. You can click **Redo** (↪) as many times as needed, up to the number of actions you have just undone.

Note: When there is no action you can redo, Repeat (↻) replaces Redo (↪) on the Quick Access Toolbar. Click this button to repeat the last action. If Redo is dimmed, there is no action you can repeat.

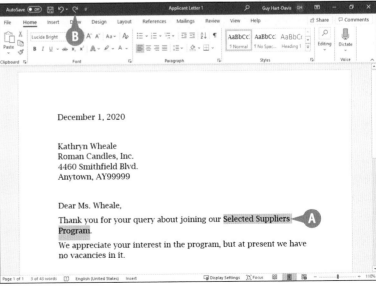

Select Text

Before performing many tasks in Word, you select the existing text on which you want to work. For example, you select existing text to underline it, align it, change its font size, or apply color to it.

You can use the keyboard and the mouse together to select a word, a sentence, or your entire document; you can even create a selection that contains text in different locations. If you like to keep your hands on the keyboard as much as possible, you can select text using only the keyboard.

Select Text

Select a Block of Text

1 Move the pointer (I) to the left of the first character you want to select.

2 Click and drag to the right and down over the text you want to select, and then release the mouse button.

Ⓐ The selection appears highlighted, and the Mini Toolbar appears.

Note: This example hides the Mini Toolbar so that you can see the beginning and end of the selection.

To cancel a selection, you can click anywhere on-screen or press ⬅, ➡, ⬆, or ⬇.

Select a Word

1 Double-click the word you want to select.

Ⓑ Word selects the word, and the Mini Toolbar appears.

You can move the pointer (↳) away from the Mini Toolbar to make it disappear.

Note: See Chapter 1 for details on using the Mini Toolbar.

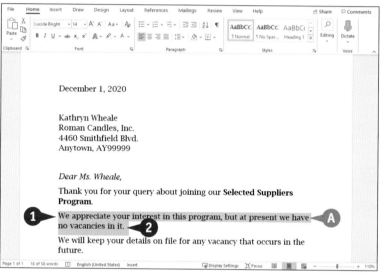

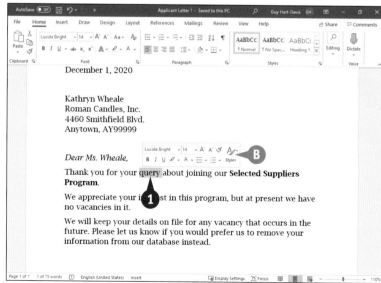

Select a Sentence

1 Press `Ctrl` while you click anywhere in the sentence you want to select.

C Word selects the entire sentence.

D The Mini Toolbar appears. You can move the pointer (⟨⟩) away from the Mini Toolbar to make it disappear.

Note: See Chapter 1 for details on using the Mini Toolbar.

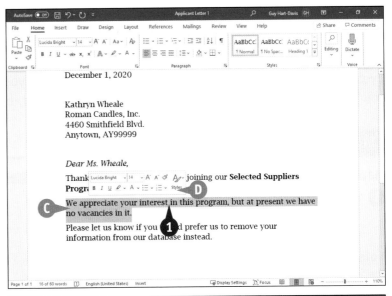

Select the Entire Document

1 Click **Home**.

The Home tab appears.

2 Click **Editing**.

The Editing panel opens.

3 Click **Select**.

The Select panel opens.

4 Click **Select All**.

E Word selects the entire document.

Note: You also can press `Ctrl`+`A` to select the entire document.

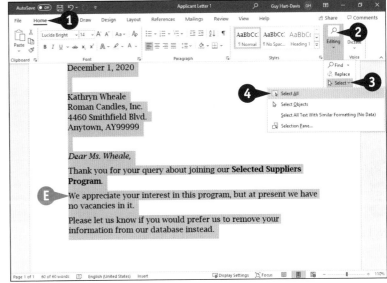

How can I select text using the keyboard?
Press and hold `Shift` while pressing ←, →, ↑, or ↓. You also can press `Shift`+`Ctrl` to select, for example, several words in a row. If you press and hold `Shift`+`Ctrl` while pressing → five times, you select five consecutive words to the right of the insertion point.

How can I select noncontiguous areas of text?
Select the first area using any of the techniques described in this section. Then press and hold `Ctrl` as you select the additional areas. Word selects all areas, even if text appears between them.

Move or Copy Text

You can move information in your document by cutting it to the Clipboard, a temporary storage area, and then pasting it elsewhere, either in the same document or in another document. You also can repeat text by copying it to the Clipboard and then pasting it elsewhere.

Another way of moving or copying information is by using drag and drop. You can drag and drop information either within the same document or to another document. Drag and drop does not use the Clipboard.

Move or Copy Text

Move or Copy Text Using Ribbon Buttons

1 Select the text you want to move or copy.

Note: To select text, see the section "Select Text," earlier in this chapter.

2 Click **Home**.

The Home tab appears.

3 To move text, click **Cut** (✄); to copy text, click **Copy** (▯▯).

Note: If you cut text, it disappears from the screen.

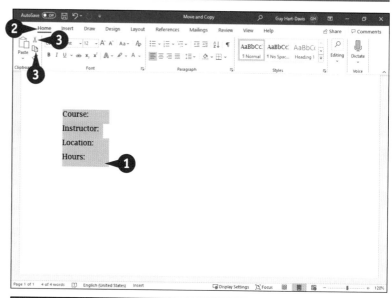

4 Click to place the insertion point where you want the text to appear.

5 Click **Paste** (▯).

Ⓐ The text appears at the new location.

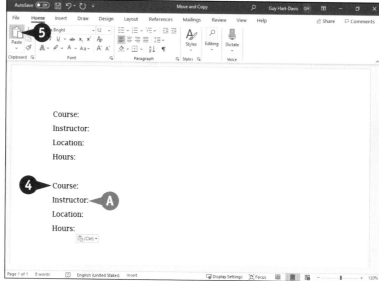

Select a Sentence

1 Press **Ctrl** while you click anywhere in the sentence you want to select.

C Word selects the entire sentence.

D The Mini Toolbar appears. You can move the pointer (⇱) away from the Mini Toolbar to make it disappear.

Note: See Chapter 1 for details on using the Mini Toolbar.

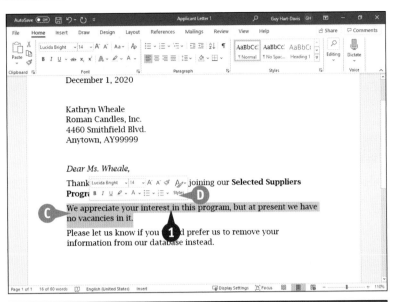

Select the Entire Document

1 Click **Home**.

The Home tab appears.

2 Click **Editing**.

The Editing panel opens.

3 Click **Select**.

The Select panel opens.

4 Click **Select All**.

E Word selects the entire document.

Note: You also can press **Ctrl** + **A** to select the entire document.

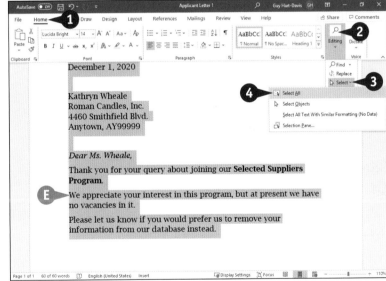

<div class="tips">

TIPS

How can I select text using the keyboard?
Press and hold **Shift** while pressing ⬅, ➡, ⬆, or ⬇. You also can press **Shift** + **Ctrl** to select, for example, several words in a row. If you press and hold **Shift** + **Ctrl** while pressing ➡ five times, you select five consecutive words to the right of the insertion point.

How can I select noncontiguous areas of text?
Select the first area using any of the techniques described in this section. Then press and hold **Ctrl** as you select the additional areas. Word selects all areas, even if text appears between them.

</div>

Mark and Find Your Place with Bookmarks

ord's Bookmark feature enables you to mark places in a document so that you can easily return to them later. A bookmark can mark a point in text, such as a point between words; a range of text, such as a word or a sentence; or a graphical object, such as a shape or a picture.

By default, Word does not display bookmark indicators, but you can set Word to display them so that you can see where your bookmarks are. Even when displayed, bookmark indicators do not print.

Mark and Find Your Place with Bookmarks

Mark Your Place

1 Select the item you want to mark. This example uses a placeholder word.

Note: To select a point in text, position the insertion point there by clicking or by pressing ➡, ⬅, ⬆, or ⬇, as needed. To select a graphical object, click it.

2 Click **Insert**.

The Insert tab appears.

3 Click **Links**.

The Links panel opens.

4 Click **Bookmark**.

The Bookmark dialog box opens.

5 Type a name for the bookmark.

Note: Each bookmark name must start with a letter. After that, the bookmark name can contain letters, numbers, and underscores, but not spaces, up to 40 characters maximum.

6 Click **Add**.

Word creates the bookmark.

The Bookmark dialog box closes.

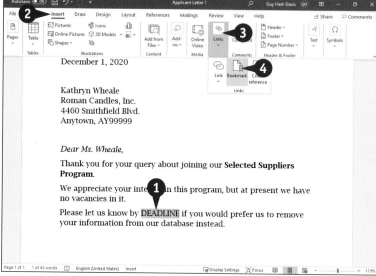

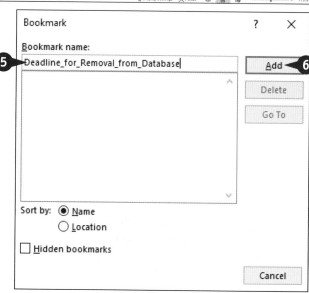

Go to a Bookmark

1 Click **Insert**.

The Insert tab appears.

2 Click **Links**.

The Links panel opens.

3 Click **Bookmark**.

The Bookmark dialog box opens.

4 Click the bookmark you want to go to.

5 Click **Go To**.

A Word selects the bookmark.

Note: If the bookmark is a single point in text, Word moves the insertion point to that point.

6 Click **Close**.

The Bookmark dialog box closes.

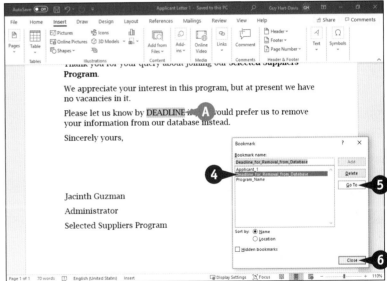

TIP

How can I display bookmarks in my document?

Click **File** to display Backstage View, and then click **Options** to open the Word Options dialog box. In the left pane, click **Advanced**. In the Show Document Content section, click **Show bookmarks** (☐ changes to ☑). Click **OK** to close the Word Options dialog box. Word displays open and close brackets representing a bookmark that has contents. A bookmark that marks a point looks like an I-beam (I).

Move or Copy Text

You can move information in your document by cutting it to the Clipboard, a temporary storage area, and then pasting it elsewhere, either in the same document or in another document. You also can repeat text by copying it to the Clipboard and then pasting it elsewhere.

Another way of moving or copying information is by using drag and drop. You can drag and drop information either within the same document or to another document. Drag and drop does not use the Clipboard.

Move or Copy Text

Move or Copy Text Using Ribbon Buttons

1 Select the text you want to move or copy.

Note: To select text, see the section "Select Text," earlier in this chapter.

2 Click **Home**.

The Home tab appears.

3 To move text, click **Cut** (✂); to copy text, click **Copy** (⧉).

Note: If you cut text, it disappears from the screen.

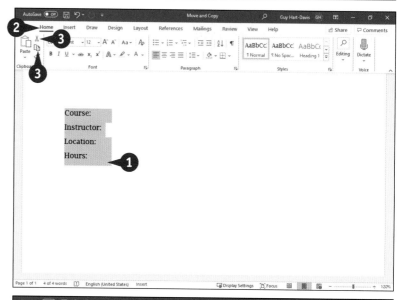

4 Click to place the insertion point where you want the text to appear.

5 Click **Paste** (📋).

Ⓐ The text appears at the new location.

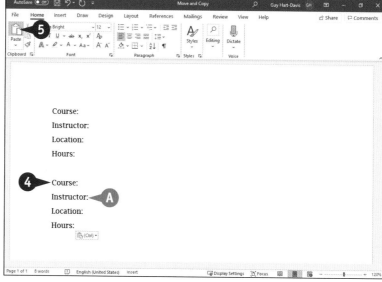

Move or Copy Text Using Drag and Drop

1 Select the text you want to move or copy.

2 To copy the text, press **Ctrl** while you drag the selected text to where you want the copy to be. Word displays the Copy pointer (⬚) as you drag.

To move the text, simply drag the text to its destination. Word displays the Move pointer (⬚) as you drag.

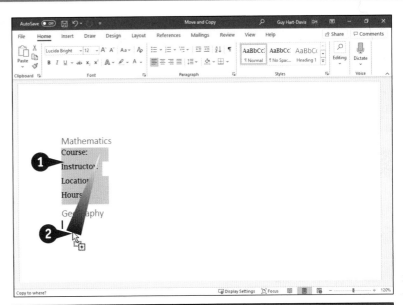

B The copied or moved text appears at the new location.

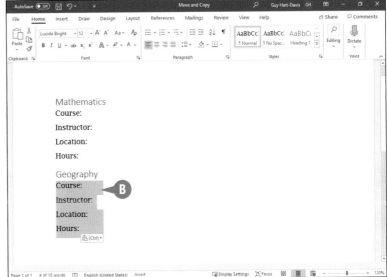

TIPS

Can I can move or copy text using the menus?
Yes. Select the text that you want to move or copy, and then right-click it. The context menu and the Mini Toolbar appear; click **Cut** or **Copy** on the context menu. Then place the insertion point at the location where you want the text to appear, and right-click again. From the context menu, click **Paste**.

Can I copy or move information other than text?
Yes. You can copy or move any element that you can select, such as text, pictures, tables, graphics, and so on. You also can copy or move text from one Word document to another; see the next section, "Share Text Between Documents."

Share Text Between Documents

You can move or copy information both within the current document and between two or more documents. For example, suppose that you are working on a marketing report and some colleagues provide you with background information for your report. You can copy and paste the information from the colleagues' documents into your document.

Any text that you cut disappears from its original location. Text that you copy continues to appear in its original location and also appears in the new location you choose.

Share Text Between Documents

1 Open the documents you want to use to share text.

2 Select the text you want to move or copy.

Note: For details on selecting text, see the section "Select Text," earlier in this chapter.

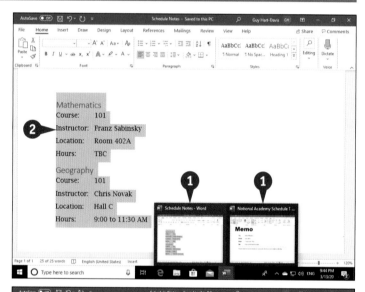

3 Click **Home**.

The Home tab appears.

4 Click **Cut** (✕) if you want to move the text, or click **Copy** (▣) if you want to copy the text.

5 Switch to the other document by clicking its button in the Windows taskbar.

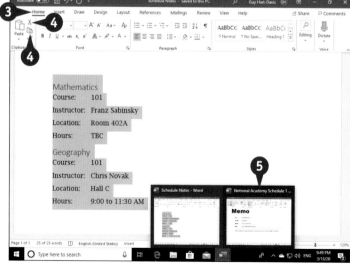

The other document appears.

6 Place the insertion point where you want the text you are moving or copying to appear.

7 Click **Paste** (📋).

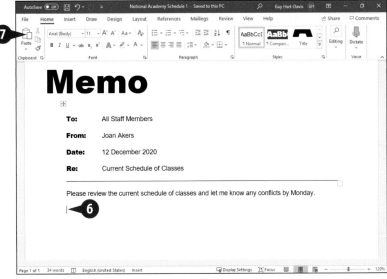

Ⓐ The text appears in the new location.

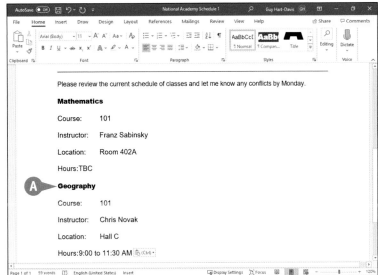

What is the button that appears temporarily after I paste?

Word displays the Paste Options button (📋(Ctrl)▾) to let you control the formatting of the selection you are pasting. See the section "Take Advantage of Paste Options," later in this chapter, for details on how to use Paste options.

How do I control the default format Word uses when I paste text?

After pasting something, click **Paste Options** (📋(Ctrl)▾), and then click **Set Default Paste** to display the Word Options dialog box. Go to the "Cut, Copy, and Paste" section, and choose options there. Click **OK** when you finish.

Move or Copy Several Selections

For regular cut, copy, and paste operations, Word shares the Windows Clipboard with all your PC's other apps. The Windows Clipboard stores only a single item at a time, so each item you copy or cut replaces the existing item.

Microsoft Office includes an enhanced clipboard called the Office Clipboard, which can save up to the last 24 items that you cut or copied. You can use the Office Clipboard to paste multiple items into a Word document or into another Office file, such as an Excel workbook or a PowerPoint presentation.

Move or Copy Several Selections

1 Click **Home**.

The Home tab appears.

2 Click the Clipboard group dialog box launcher (🔽).

Ⓐ The Office Clipboard pane appears.

Ⓑ The top item is the newest item and is the item on the Windows Clipboard.

Ⓒ Other items are ones you have previously cut or copied. These items are no longer on the Windows Clipboard.

Ⓓ The icon to the left of an item indicates the app it came from.

3 Select the text or information you want to move or copy.

4 Click **Cut** (✂) or **Copy** (🗐).

Note: This example uses Cut (✂), so the selected item disappears from the document's text.

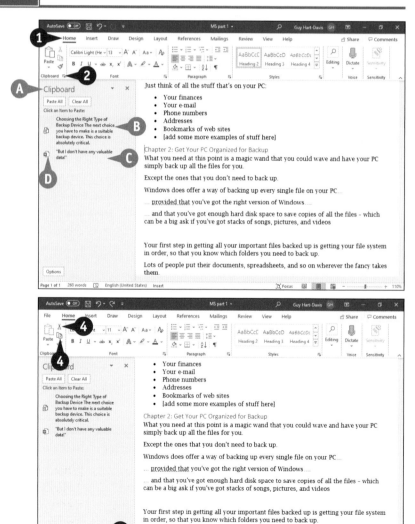

E An entry for the cut or copied material appears at the top of the Clipboard pane.

Note: Repeat steps **3** and **4** for each selection you want to move or copy. Word adds each cut or copied item to the Clipboard pane, with the newest item at the top.

5 Click in the document or in a different document where you want to place text you cut or copied.

6 Click a selection in the Clipboard pane to place it in the document.

F The entry appears in the document.

7 Repeat steps **5** and **6** to paste other items from the Clipboard, as needed.

G If you want to place all the items in one location, and the items appear in the Clipboard pane in the order you want them in your document, you can click **Paste All**.

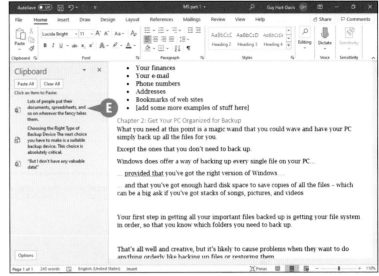

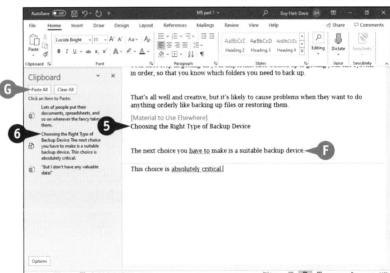

TIPS

Why does a down arrow appear when I point at an item in the Clipboard pane?

If you click ▾, a menu appears. From this menu, you can click **Paste** to add the item to your document, or you can click **Delete** to remove the item from the Clipboard pane.

Must I display the Office Clipboard to collect copied elements?

No. Click the **Options** button at the bottom of the Clipboard pane, and then click **Collect Without Showing Office Clipboard**. As you cut or copy, a message appears in the lower-right corner of your screen, telling you how many elements are stored on the Office Clipboard. You must display the Office Clipboard to paste any item except the one you last cut or copied.

Take Advantage of Paste Options

Word's Paste Options feature enables you to choose what formatting Word applies to a selection you paste into a document. For example, when you paste text that you cut or copied from a different document, you can keep the text's original formatting, make the text pick up the formatting of the location into which you paste it, or paste only unformatted text.

The paste options available depend on what you're pasting and where you're pasting it. This section shows how to paste information from an Excel workbook into a Word document.

Take Advantage of Paste Options

1 Make a selection. This example uses an Excel spreadsheet selection, but you can select text in a Word document.

2 Click **Home**.

The Home tab appears.

3 Click **Copy** (⟐).

Note: If you want to cut the selection from the source, click **Cut** (✂) instead of Copy (⟐).

4 Position the insertion point in your Word document where you want to paste the information.

5 Click **Home**.

The Home tab appears.

6 In the Clipboard group, click ⌄ below **Paste** (📋).

Ⓐ Buttons representing paste options appear.

7 To preview formatting for the selection, point at the **Keep Source Formatting** button (📋).

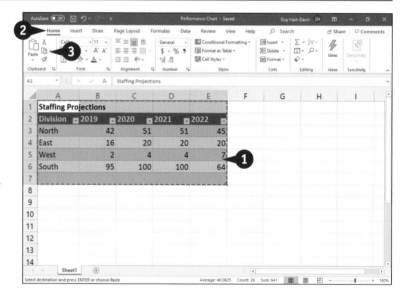

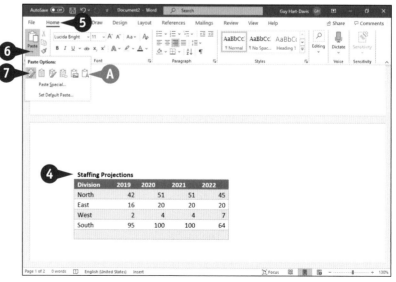

⑧ To preview formatting for the selection, point at the **Use Destination Styles** button (📋).

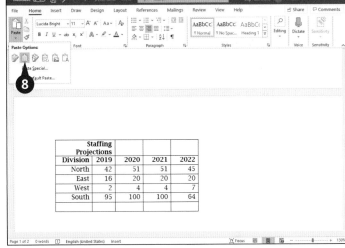

⑨ To preview formatting for the selection, point at the **Keep Text Only** button (📋).

⑩ Click a **Paste Options** button to paste the selection and specify its format in your Word document.

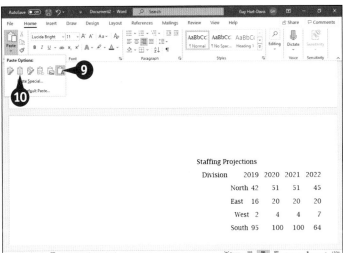

TIP

What do the various Paste Options buttons mean?

These are the five most widely useful Paste Options buttons:

• Click **Keep Source Formatting** (📋) to make the pasted material retain its original formatting.

• Click **Use Destination Styles** (📋) to make the pasted material take on the formatting of the location where you paste it.

• Click **Merge Formatting** (📋) to merge the formatting of the pasted material into the formatting of the location where you paste it.

• Click **Picture** (📋) to paste the material as a picture, not as text.

• Click **Keep Text Only** (📋) to paste text with no formatting.

CHAPTER 4

Editing and Proofing Text

In this chapter, you learn to use Word's features for editing and proofreading documents. After starting with Read Mode view, you move on to zooming in and out, translating text, and using additional actions. Next, you see how to search for and replace text, count the words in a document, correct mistakes automatically, and automatically insert frequently used text items. Finally, you learn how to check grammar and spelling and how to find synonyms, antonyms, and definitions for words.

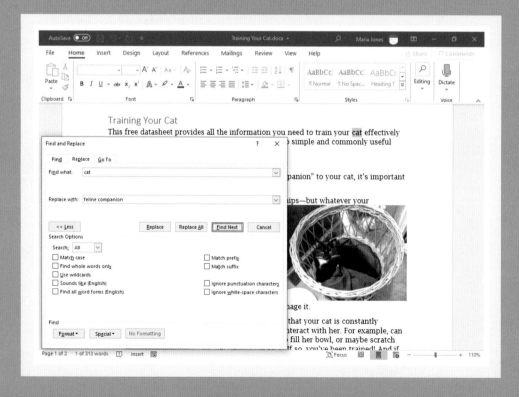

Work in Read Mode View

Read Mode view optimizes your document for easier reading by removing most of the Ribbon controls and some other interface elements. Read Mode view supports mouse, keyboard, and tablet motions.

To move from one page to another, click the arrows (◉ and ◉) on the left and right sides of the pages, by scrolling if your mouse has a scroll wheel, or by using the keyboard: press Page up, ↑, ←, or Backspace to move to the previous page, or press Page down, ↓, →, or Spacebar to move to the next page. On a tablet, swipe left or right with your finger.

Work in Read Mode View

Look Up Information

1 Click **Read Mode** (📖) on the status bar.

Word switches the document to Read Mode view.

Word hides the Ribbon.

2 Select the word you want to look up, and then right-click.

The contextual menu opens.

3 Click **Smart Lookup**.

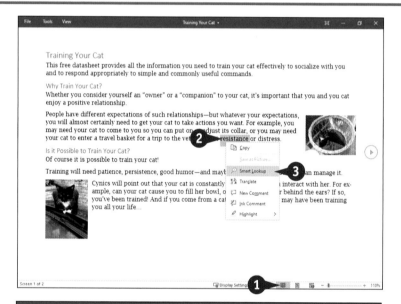

Ⓐ The Search pane appears.

Ⓑ If there is a primary definition, it appears at the top.

Ⓒ You can click **Show more** to display other definitions.

4 Click **Close** (✕) when you are ready to close the Search pane.

Translate a Word or Phrase

1 In Read Mode view, select the word or phrase you want to translate, and then right-click.

The contextual menu opens.

2 Click **Translate**.

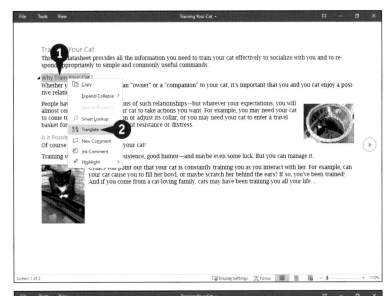

D The Translator pane opens, displaying a translation of the word or phrase you selected in step **1**.

E You can click ▼ to the right of the current language, and then click a different language on the drop-down menu.

3 To close the Translator pane, click ✕ in the upper-right corner of the pane.

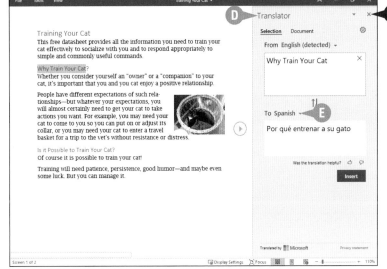

TIP

Can I change the color of the page in Read Mode view?

Yes. Click **View** to open the View menu; click **Page Color** to display the Page Color submenu; and then click **None**, **Sepia**, or **Inverse**, as needed.

continued ▶

In Read Mode view, you can look up words in the dictionary, translate a word or phrase, highlight important text, and insert comments in documents.

When you are viewing a long document in Read Mode view, you can also use the Navigation pane to move around the document. You can open the Navigation pane from the Tools menu in Read Mode view; for details on using the Navigation pane, see Chapter 1.

Work in Read Mode View (continued)

Highlight Important Text

1 In Read Mode view, select the text you want to highlight, and then right-click.

The contextual menu opens.

F To highlight the text with the current color, click **Highlight** and skip the remaining steps.

2 Click ＞.

The Highlight panel opens.

3 Click the highlight color you want to apply.

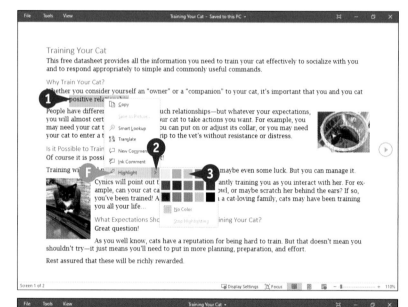

G Word highlights the selected text in the color you chose.

Note: The highlight color you chose becomes the color on the Highlight item on the contextual menu, so you can apply the same color more quickly next time.

4 Click anywhere outside the highlight to see its full effect and continue working.

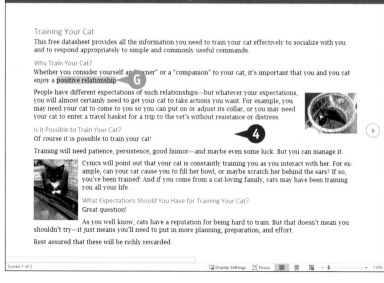

Insert a Comment

1 In Read Mode view, select the text the comment will reference, and then right-click.

The contextual menu opens.

2 Click **New Comment**.

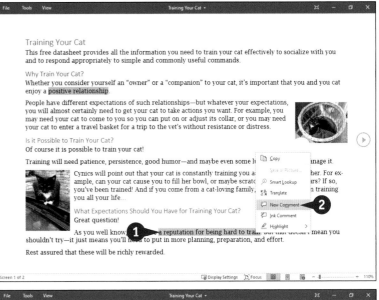

H Word changes the color used to select the text and displays a comment window containing the insertion point.

3 Type your comment.

4 Click ✕ to close the comment window.

I The comment marker (💬) represents your comment. Click it at any time to view the comment.

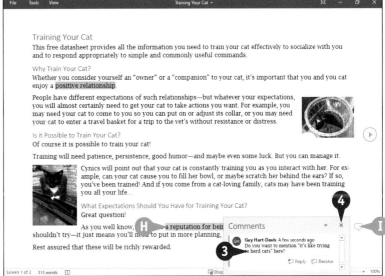

What are some of the different view commands available in Read Mode?

To display all comments in the document, click **View** and then click **Show Comments**. To view your document as if it were printed on paper, click **View** to open the View menu, click **Layout** to open the Layout submenu, and then click **Paper Layout**.

Can I change the column width?

Yes. Click **View** to open the View menu, click **Column Width** to display the Column Width submenu, and then either click **Narrow** or **Wide** to set the width or click **Default** to return to the original column view. On a standard monitor, Default and Wide look the same; Wide takes effect on widescreen monitors.

Zoom In or Out

The Zoom feature controls the magnification of your document on-screen. Zooming in enlarges text; zooming out reduces text, providing more of an overview of your document. Zooming affects only the display on screen—it does not affect the printed size of your document.

To use the full range of zoom options, use the Zoom dialog box. For quick zooming, you can use the Zoom slider bar located in the lower-right corner of the Word window.

Zoom In or Out

1 Click **View**.

The View tab appears.

2 Click **Zoom**.

The Zoom dialog box opens.

3 Click a zoom setting.

A You can click **Many pages** and click an arrangement on the pop-up panel to display multiple pages.

B A preview of the settings you choose appears here.

4 Click **OK**.

The Zoom dialog box closes.

Word zooms the document in the way you specified.

C You can drag the Zoom slider to zoom quickly.

D You can click + to zoom in.

E You can click – to zoom out.

F You can click **Zoom Level**—which shows a figure, such as 100% or 200%—to open the Zoom dialog box.

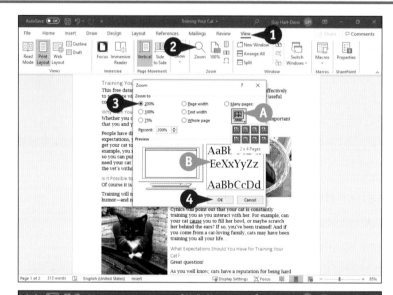

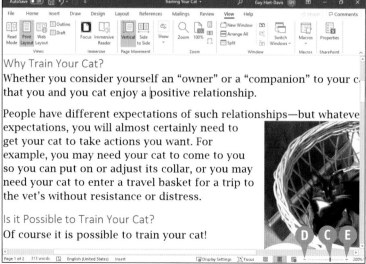

Translate Text

You can translate a word from one language to another using language dictionaries installed on your computer. If you are connected to the Internet, the Translation feature searches the dictionaries on your computer as well as online dictionaries.

You can choose Translate Document from the Translate drop-down menu to send the document over the Internet for translation, but be aware that Word sends documents as unencrypted HTML files. If security is an issue, do not choose this route; instead, consider hiring a professional translator.

Translate Text

1 Select the text you want to translate.

2 Click **Review**.

The Review tab appears.

3 Click **Language**.

The Language pop-up panel opens.

4 Click **Translate**.

The Translate pop-up panel opens.

5 Click **Translate Selection**.

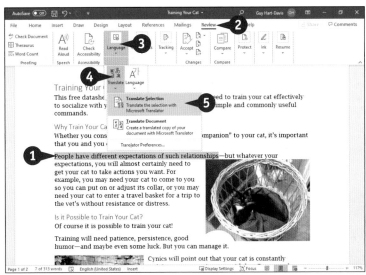

A The Translator pane appears.

B The phrase you selected appears here.

C The current translation language appears here.

You can click the boxes beside each language to display available translation languages.

D The translation appears here.

E You can click ▼ to the right of the current language, and then click a different language on the drop-down menu.

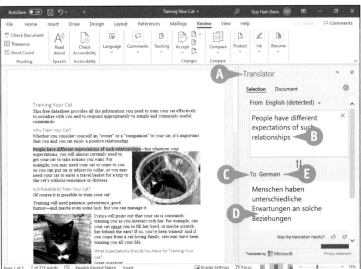

Set Options for Additional Actions

The Additional Actions feature lets Word recognize certain types of context-sensitive information, such as an address or a date, enabling you to use the information to take extra steps. For example, for an address, you can display a map or driving directions or add the information to Outlook contacts; for a date, you can display your Outlook Calendar.

You can control the kinds of information Word recognizes and identifies for additional actions that can save you time. You also can turn off additional action recognition entirely.

Set Options for Additional Actions

1 Click **File**.

Backstage view appears.

2 Click **Options**.

The Word Options dialog box opens.

3 Click **Proofing**.

The Proofing category appears.

4 Click **AutoCorrect Options**.

The AutoCorrect dialog box opens.

5 Click **Actions**.

The Actions tab appears.

6 Select **Enable additional actions in the right-click menu** (☑) to enable recognition of additional actions.

7 Select (☑) for each additional action you want to use.

8 Click **OK**.

The AutoCorrect dialog box closes.

9 Click **OK**.

The Word Options dialog box closes.

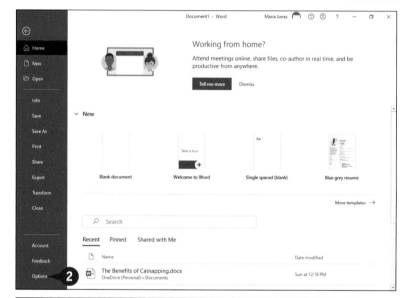

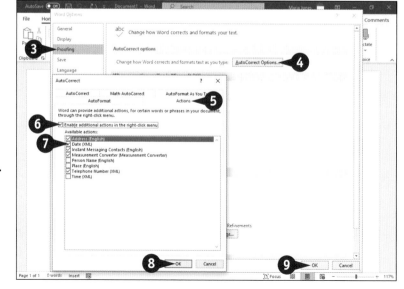

Using Additional Actions

You can use the Additional Actions feature to save time. Additional Actions recognizes certain context-sensitive information and provides extra information. Additional Actions can convert measurements, add a person or telephone number to Outlook Contacts, schedule a meeting, display a map of a location, or get you driving directions to that location.

You may need to enable Additional Actions, as explained in the previous section, "Set Options for Additional Actions." This section shows you how to use the Additional Actions feature.

Using Additional Actions

1 Right-click text of a type for which you have enabled additional actions. This example uses a date.

A The contextual menu appears.

2 Click **Additional Actions**.

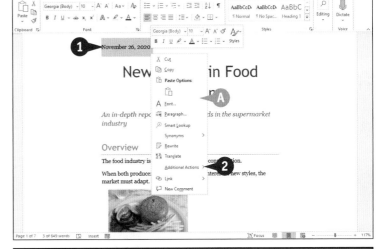

B Word displays the selected action.

3 Click an action in the list of available actions.

Word performs the action, or the program that performs the action you selected appears on-screen.

Search for Text

Word includes a powerful Find feature that enables you to quickly locate occurrences of specific words, phrases, or other items in your documents. You can search for all occurrences simultaneously—for example, to see how often you have used a particular word or phrase—or search for individual instances to review each in its context.

Word also enables you to replace text and other objects. See the next section for details.

Search for Text

Search for All Occurrences

1 Click **Home**.

The Home tab appears.

2 Click **Editing**.

The Editing pop-up panel opens.

3 Click **Find**.

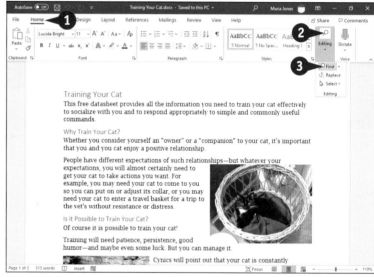

A The Navigation pane appears.

4 Type the word or phrase for which you want to search.

B Word highlights all occurrences of the word or phrase in yellow.

5 Click ✕ to clear the search and results.

6 Click ✕ to close the Navigation pane.

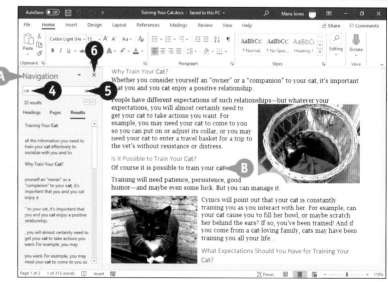

Search for One Occurrence at a Time

1 Press `Ctrl` + `Home` to position the insertion point at the beginning of your document.

2 Click **Home**.

The Home tab appears.

3 Click **Editing**.

The Editing pop-up panel opens.

4 Click ▾ to the right of **Find**.

The Find pop-up panel opens.

5 Click **Advanced Find**.

The Find and Replace dialog box opens.

6 Click **More**.

The Find and Replace dialog box expands, displaying more options.

7 Type the word or phrase for which you want to search.

C You can click **Reading Highlight** and then click **Highlight All** to highlight each occurrence.

D You can click **Find in** to limit the search to the current selection, the main document, or the headers and footers.

8 Click **Find Next** to view each occurrence.

Note: When Word finds no more occurrences, a dialog box opens telling you that the search is finished. Click **OK**.

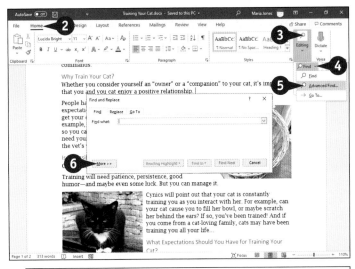

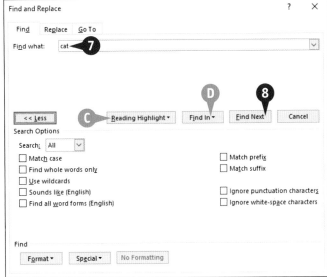

How can I set options to limit my search in the Navigation pane?
In the Navigation pane, click ▾ at the right end of the Search Document box, and then click **Options** to open the Find Options dialog box.

How do I search for elements other than words?
In the Navigation pane, click ▾ at the right end of the Search Document box to display the menu. You can then specify what you want to search for by clicking **Graphics**, **Tables**, **Equations**, **Footnotes/Endnotes**, or **Comments**; if you click **Comments**, you can then click **All Reviewers** or a specific reviewer.

Replace Text or Other Items

Often, you want to find a word or phrase because you need to substitute some other word or phrase for it. For example, suppose you complete a long report, only to discover that you have misspelled the name of a product you are reviewing. You can quickly fix the problem by using the Replace tool to substitute a word or phrase for all occurrences of the original word or phrase.

Alternatively, you can selectively substitute one word or phrase for another—a particularly useful tool when you have overused a word.

Replace Text or Other Items

1 Press **Ctrl**+**Home** to position the insertion point at the beginning of your document.

2 Click **Home**.

The Home tab appears.

3 Click **Editing**.

The Editing pop-up panel opens.

4 Click **Replace**.

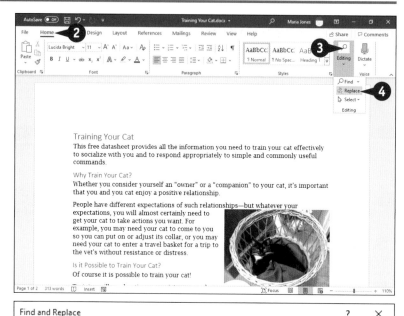

The Find and Replace dialog box opens, with the Replace tab displayed.

5 In the Find What box, type the word or phrase you want to find and replace.

6 Click **Replace with** and type the replacement word or phrase.

Ⓐ You can click **More** to display additional search and replace options (the Less button replaces the More button).

7 Click **Find Next**.

B Word highlights the first occurrence of the word or phrase that it finds.

C If you do not want to change the highlighted occurrence, you can click **Find Next** to ignore it.

8 Click **Replace**.

D To change all occurrences in the document, you can click **Replace All**.

E Word replaces the original word or phrase with the word or phrase you specify as the substitute.

9 Repeat steps **7** and **8** as needed.

When Word finds no more occurrences, a dialog box opens telling you that the search is finished.

10 Click **OK**.

The dialog box closes.

The Cancel button in the Find and Replace dialog box changes to Close.

11 Click **Close**.

The Find and Replace dialog box closes.

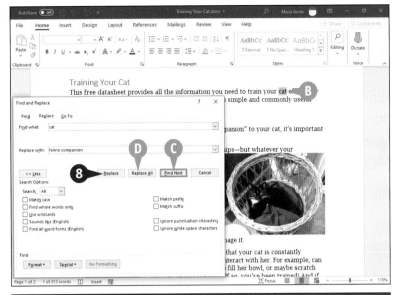

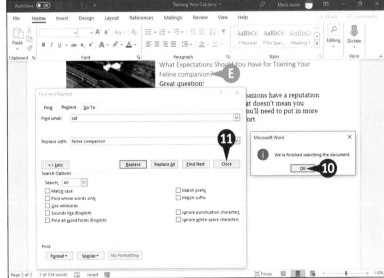

TIPS

How do I find italic text and change it to boldface text?
Open the Find and Replace dialog box, click **Replace** to display the Replace tab, and then click **More** to expand the dialog box. Click **Find what**, click **Format**, and then click **Font**. In the Font Style list of the Font dialog box that appears, click **Italic**, and then click **OK**. Click **Replace with**, click **Format**, and then click **Font**; click **Bold** in the Font Style list, and then click **OK**.

How can I search for special characters such as tabs or paragraph marks?
In the Find and Replace dialog box, click **More** to expand the dialog box. Click **Find what**, then click **Special** to display a menu of special characters; click the special character you want to insert.

Count Words in a Document

W ord includes a Word Count feature that enables you to count the number of words in a selection, a sentence, a paragraph, or the whole document. Word Count is useful both for monitoring your progress and for making sure you have not written too much—or too little—for a document that has a fixed length.

You can view the word count quickly by adding the Word Count readout to the status bar. For more information, including the number of sentences and paragraphs, you open the Word Count dialog box.

Count Words in a Document

Add the Word Count to the Status Bar

1 Right-click the status bar.

A The Customize Status Bar menu appears.

B The number of words in the selection or the document appears here.

2 If no check mark appears beside Word Count, click **Word Count**.

3 Click anywhere outside the menu.

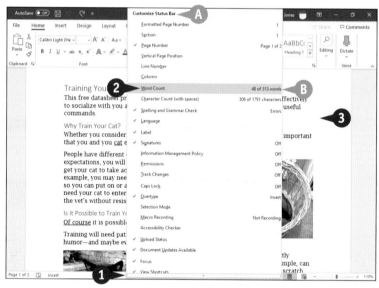

The Customize Status Bar menu closes.

C The word count appears on the status bar.

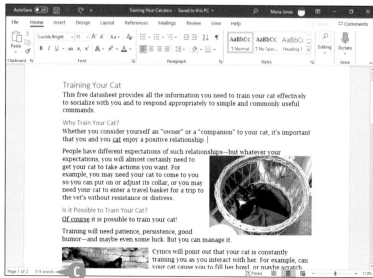

Display Count Statistics

1 Click the word count on the status bar.

Note: You can also open the Word Count dialog box from the Ribbon. Click **Review** to display the Review tab, go to the Proofing group, and then click **Word Count**.

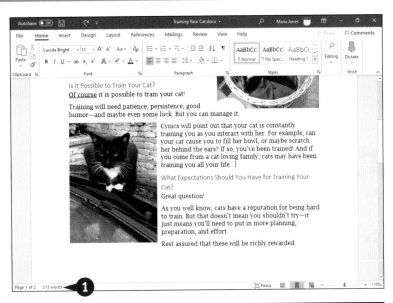

The Word Count dialog box opens.

The Word Count dialog box reports the number of pages, words, characters including spaces, characters excluding spaces, paragraphs, and lines in your document.

D Select **Include textboxes, footnotes and endnotes** (☑) if you want to include the words in text boxes, footnotes, and endnotes in the word count. If not, deselect (☐) this check box.

2 When you finish reviewing count statistics, click **Close**.

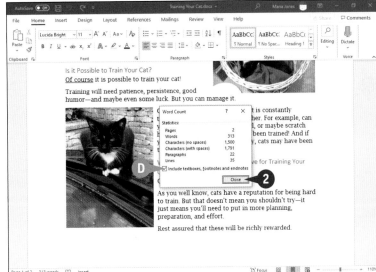

How do I count the number of words in just one paragraph?
Select the paragraph for which you want to count the words, and then look at the word count on the status bar or open the Word Count dialog box. You can select any amount of text—for example, a sentence or multiple paragraphs.

Automatically Correct Mistakes

ord's AutoCorrect feature automatically corrects typing and spelling mistakes as you type. AutoCorrect comes with a long list of preset misspellings, which you can customize by removing existing entries or adding new entries.

You can easily add AutoCorrect entries both for words you misspell or mistype and for words or phrases you want to enter quickly and consistently. You can also disable AutoCorrect entirely if you find it unhelpful.

Automatically Correct Mistakes

1 Click **File**.

Backstage view appears.

2 Click **Options**.

The Word Options dialog box opens.

3 Click **Proofing**.

The Proofing category appears.

4 Click **AutoCorrect Options**.

The AutoCorrect dialog box opens.

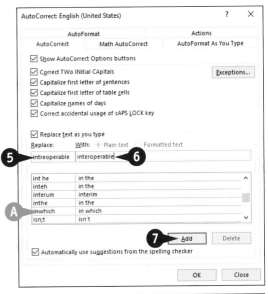

A The corrections Word already makes automatically appear in this area.

5 Click here and type the word you typically mistype or misspell.

Note: You can press `Tab` to move the insertion point from the Replace box to the With box.

6 Click here and type the correct version of the word.

7 Click **Add**.

B Word adds the entry to the list to automatically correct.

You can repeat steps **5** to **7** for each automatic correction you want to add.

8 Click **OK**.

The AutoCorrect dialog box closes.

9 Click **OK**.

The Word Options dialog box closes.

How does the automatic correction work?

As you type, if what you type matches an AutoCorrect entry, Word corrects the entry when you press `Spacebar`, `Tab`, `Enter`, or a punctuation key.

What should I do if Word automatically replaces an entry that I do not want replaced?

Position the insertion point at the beginning of the automatically corrected word and click the **AutoCorrect Options** button ( ). On the pop-up menu, click **Stop automatically correcting [*word*]**.

Automatically Insert Frequently Used Text

Suppose you repeatedly type the same text in your documents—for example, your signature block or your company name. You can add this text to Word's Quick Parts gallery; then, the next time you need to add the text to a document, you can select it from the gallery instead of retyping it.

In addition to creating your own Quick Parts for use in your documents, you can use any of the wide variety of preset parts included with Word. You access these preset Quick Parts from Word's Building Blocks Organizer window.

Automatically Insert Frequently Used Text

Create a Quick Parts Entry

1 Type the text that you want to store, including all formatting that should appear each time you insert the entry.

2 Select the text you typed.

3 Click **Insert**.

The Insert tab appears.

4 Click **Quick Parts** (▤ ▾).

The Quick Parts pop-up panel opens.

5 Click **Save Selection to Quick Part Gallery**.

The Create New Building Block dialog box opens.

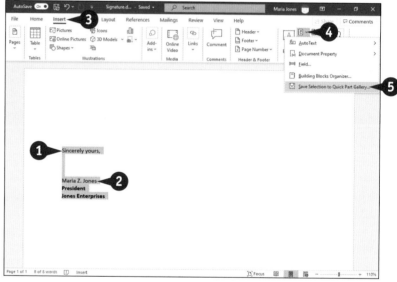

6 Type a name that you want to use as a shortcut for the entry.

Ⓐ You can specify what gallery to store the building block in.

Ⓑ You can specify the category for the building block.

7 Type a description for the building block.

8 Click **OK**.

The Create New Building Block dialog box closes.

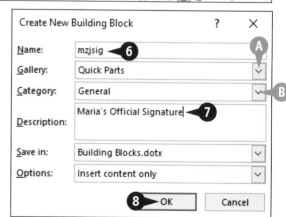

Insert a Quick Part Entry

1 Click in the text where you want to insert a Quick Part.

2 Click the **Insert** tab.

3 Click the **Quick Parts** button (▤ ▾).

All building blocks you define as Quick Parts appear in the Quick Part gallery.

4 Click the entry that you want to insert.

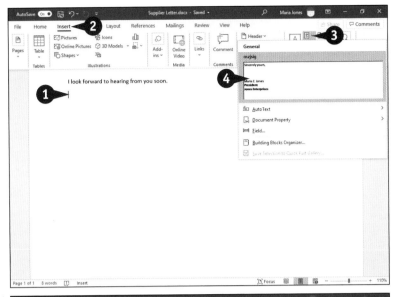

C Word inserts the entry into the document.

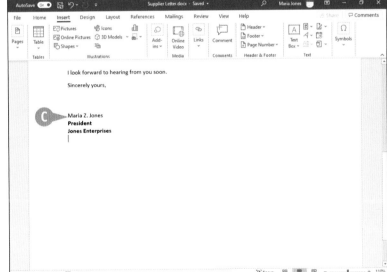

How can I find and use an AutoText entry?
Click the **Insert** tab, and then click **Quick Parts** (▤ ▾). In the menu that appears, point at **AutoText**. A gallery of all the AutoText entries appears.

How do I remove a Quick Parts entry?
To remove a Quick Parts entry, use the Building Blocks Organizer window. Click **Insert**, click the **Quick Parts** button (▤ ▾), and then click **Building Blocks Organizer**. In the Organizer window, locate and select the entry you want to remove, click **Delete**, and click **Yes** in the dialog box that appears.

Check Spelling and Grammar

ord automatically checks for spelling and grammar errors as you type. Misspellings appear underlined with a red wavy line, and grammar errors are underlined with a blue wavy line. If you prefer, you can turn off Word's automatic Spelling and Grammar Check features, as described in the first tip.

Alternatively, you can review your entire document for spelling and grammatical errors all at one time.

Check Spelling and Grammar

Correct a Mistake

1 When you encounter a spelling or grammar problem, right-click the underlined text.

The contextual menu opens.

2 If one of the suggested corrections is appropriate, click it.

A You can click **Ignore All** to ignore the supposed error.

B To make Word stop flagging a word as misspelled, click **Add to Dictionary**.

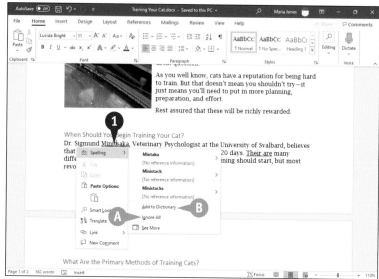

Check the Document

1 Click **Review**.

The Review tab appears.

2 Click **Check Document**.

The Editor pane appears.

C The Corrections list summarizes spelling and grammar issues.

D The Refinements list summarizes possible stylistic improvements.

3 Click **Review All Results**.

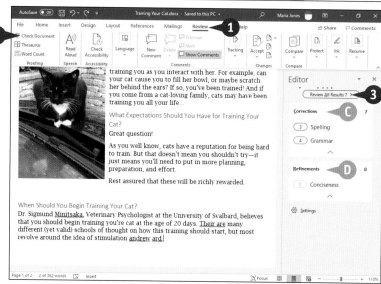

E Word selects the first spelling or grammar issue and displays the details of its objection, together with any suggestions it has.

4 Click the suggestion you want to use.

F You can click **Ignore Once** or **Ignore All** to leave the selected word or phrase unchanged.

5 Repeat step 4 for each spelling or grammar mistake.

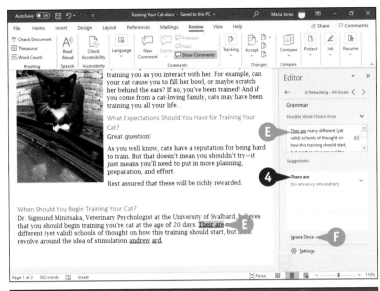

Word displays a dialog box when you finish reviewing Editor's issues and suggestions.

6 Click **OK**.

The dialog box closes.

7 Click ✕.

The Editor pane closes.

Note: To check only a section of your document, select that section.

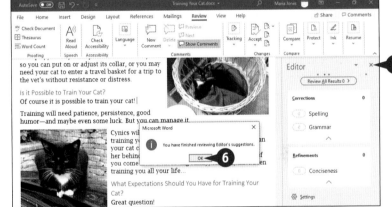

How do I disable spelling and grammar checking?
Click **File** to open Backstage view, and then click **Options**. In the Word Options dialog box, click **Proofing** in the left pane. Click **Check spelling as you type** (☑ changes to ☐) to disable automatic spell checking. Click **Mark grammar errors as you type** (☑ changes to ☐) to disable automatic grammar checking. Click **OK** to close the Word Options dialog box.

How can I exclude some text from spelling and grammar checking?
Select the text, then click **Review** to display the Review tab. Click **Language**, click **Language** again, and then click **Set Proofing Language** to open the Language dialog box. Click **Do not check spelling or grammar** (☐ changes to ☑), and then click **OK**.

Find Synonyms, Antonyms, and Definitions

Word includes a Thesaurus feature that you can use to find the words you need. The thesaurus provides both synonyms—words with a similar meaning to the word you look up—and antonyms, words with an opposite meaning.

You can access synonyms quickly from the contextual menu. If this menu does not supply a suitable word, you can open the Thesaurus pane, which provides a wider selection of words grouped by meaning. Word displays "(Antonym)" next to each antonym, so you can easily identify them.

Find Synonyms, Antonyms, and Definitions

1 Right-click the word for which you want to find a synonym or antonym.

The contextual menu opens.

2 Click or highlight **Synonyms**.

The Synonyms submenu opens.

A If the contextual menu displays a suitable word, click it to insert it in the document in place of the current word. Skip the remaining steps.

3 Click **Thesaurus**.

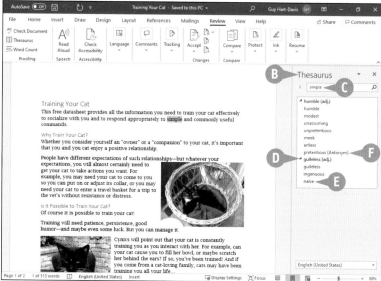

B The Thesaurus pane appears.

C The word you selected appears here.

D Each word with a triangle on its left and a part of speech on its right represents a major heading.

Note: You cannot substitute major headings for the word in your document. Instead, use the same word where it appears below the heading.

E Each word listed below a major heading is a synonym or antonym for the major heading.

F Each antonym is marked "(Antonym)."

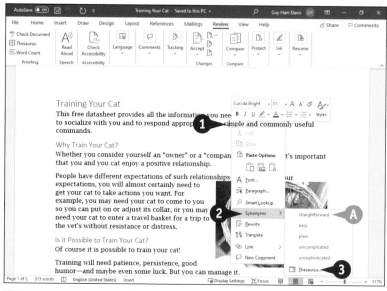

104

④ Move the pointer (▷) over the word you want to use in your document, and click the arrow (▾) that appears.

The pop-up menu opens.

Note: Clicking a word in the Thesaurus pane does not insert the word in the document. Instead, it displays the Thesaurus entry for that word.

⑤ Click **Insert**.

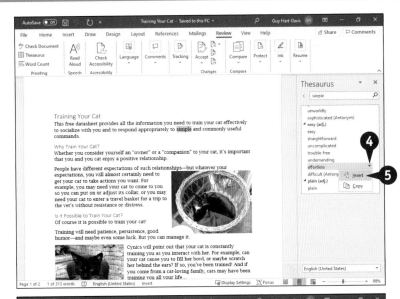

Ⓖ Word replaces the word in your document with the one in the Thesaurus pane.

⑥ Click ✕.

The Thesaurus pane closes.

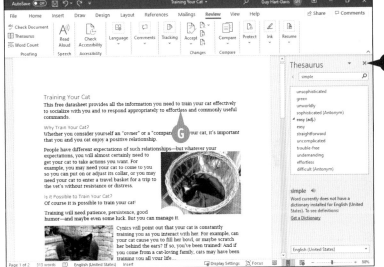

TIPS

How can I look up the definition for a word?

Right-click the word, and then click **Smart Lookup** on the contextual menu. The Search pane opens, showing a definition for the word, if one is available.

What does the Rewrite command on the contextual menu do?

Right-click a word or a selection, and then click **Rewrite** on the contextual menu to display the Editor pane with suggestions for rewriting the text. You can click a suggestion to insert it in the document, replacing the text you right-clicked.

CHAPTER 5

Formatting Text

You can format text to improve appearance, for emphasis, and for greater readability. And although the individual types of formatting are discussed separately, you can perform each of the tasks in this chapter on a single selection of text.

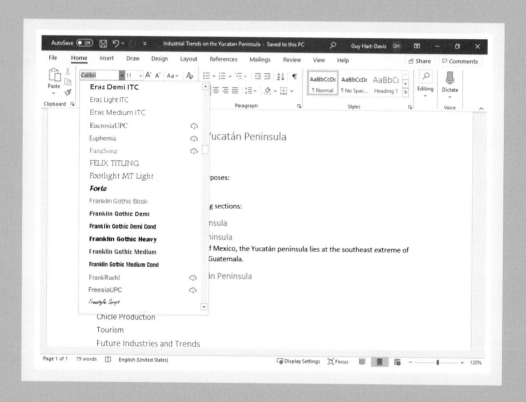

Understanding How Word's Formatting Works

Word enables you to format the text content of your documents in many ways, from formatting an individual character to formatting all the document's text at once. For example, you can apply boldface to a word, change line spacing for a paragraph, or apply the same font throughout a document.

Word's many formatting options make it easy to waste time and effort. To help you avoid such frustrations, this section briefly explains Word's formatting and tells you how to use *styles*—collections of formatting—to format your documents quickly, consistently, and easily, and how to use templates to manage styles.

Understanding What Direct Formatting Is

Direct formatting is formatting you apply to text directly, without using a style. For example, if you select two words and click **Bold** (**B**) in the Font group on the Home tab of the Ribbon, the italic formatting you apply is direct formatting.

Direct formatting is easy to use, but it is very inefficient, as you typically apply it separately to each instance of text that needs it. This chapter shows you how to use direct formatting first, because this is the way most people prefer to start using formatting in Word. But if you go directly to using styles, your work will be faster and more efficient.

Understanding Styles and Templates

A style is a collection of formatting that you can apply with a single click. Word has five different types of styles: paragraph styles; character styles; linked styles, which are both paragraph styles and character styles; table styles; and list styles.

Here is an example: You apply the Heading 1 paragraph style to each first-level heading in a document. The style contains all the formatting the first-level heading needs: font, such as Arial Black; font size, such as 24pt; font weight, such as Bold; space before the paragraph, such as 18pt; alignment, such as Center; and so on. By applying the style, you give each heading a consistent look.

You can create styles either by defining them formally, or by using direct formatting to format text the way you want it to appear, and then creating a style based on that formatting. If you change the formatting of the style, you can have Word instantly apply the change to all paragraphs formatted with that style.

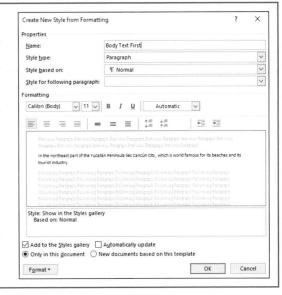

Using Templates to Manage Styles and Create Documents

A *template* is a predesigned document skeleton that you can use to create a particular type of document quickly. Each template contains styles—heading styles, body text styles, list styles, and so on—that give the document's text the intended look.

Word provides many templates as starting points, but you will likely want to create your own templates to save yourself the most time and effort. You typically choose a template when you create a document, but you can subsequently attach a different template to the document to change its look.

For example, say you create formal reports that undergo several review stages before publication. You might use two templates for the report: one template for writing and reviewing and the other for publication. The

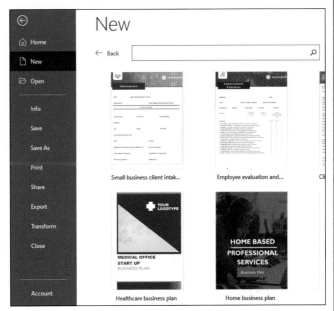

writing and reviewing template could have monospaced fonts and wide line spacing to allow easy editing and annotation, whereas the publication template could have a professional, polished look and design.

After finalizing the report's content, you would attach the publication template to the document, instantly switching all its contents to the publication format.

Change the Font

You can change the typeface that appears in your document by changing the font. Changing the font can help readers better understand your document.

Use *serif* fonts—fonts with short lines stemming from the bottoms of the letters—to provide a line that helps guide the reader's eyes along the line, making reading easier with less eyestrain. Use *sans serif* fonts—fonts without short lines stemming from the bottoms of the letters—for headlines.

Change the Font

1 Select the text you want to format.

Ⓐ If you drag to select, the Mini Toolbar appears, and you can use it by moving the pointer (⇖) toward the Mini Toolbar.

2 To use the Ribbon, click **Home**.

The Home tab appears.

3 Click ⌄ to the right of **Font** to display a list of the available fonts on your computer.

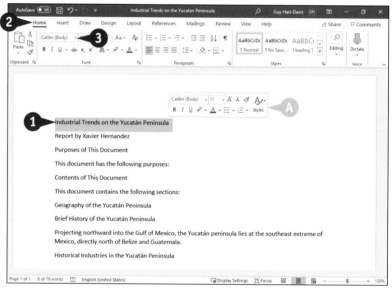

Note: Word displays a sample of the selected text in any font over which you position the pointer.

4 Click the font you want to use.

Ⓑ Word assigns the font to the selected text.

This example applies the **Arial Black** font to the text.

5 Click anywhere outside the selection to continue working.

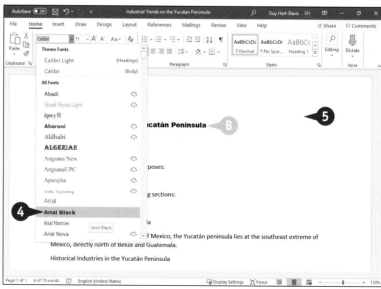

Change the Font Size

You can increase or decrease the size of the text in your document. Increase the size to make reading the text easier; decrease the size to fit more text on a page. You may also want to use a larger font size for more important text elements in a document, such as headings.

Font size is measured in *points*, where one point is ¹⁄₇₂ inch or ¹⁄₆ of a *pica*, a typesetting unit that is ¹⁄₁₂ inch.

Change the Font Size

1 Select the text that you want to format.

A If you drag to select, the Mini Toolbar appears in the background, and you can use it by moving the pointer (⇩) over the Mini Toolbar.

2 To use the Ribbon, click **Home**.

The Home tab appears.

3 Click ⌄ to the right of **Font Size** to display a list of the available sizes for the current font.

Note: Word displays a sample of the selected text in any font size over which you position the pointer.

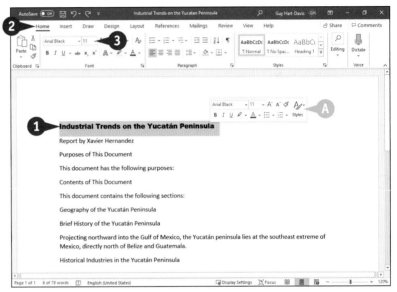

4 Click a size.

B Word changes the size of the selected text.

This example applies a 22-point font size to the text.

Note: You also can change the font size by clicking **Increase Font Size** (A^) and **Decrease Font Size** (A˅) in the Font group on the Home tab. Word increases or decreases the font size with each click of the button.

5 Click anywhere outside the selection to continue working.

Emphasize Information with Bold, Italic, or Underline

Y ou can apply italics, boldface, or underlining to add emphasis to text in your document.

Boldface changes the brightness of the text, making the text darker than the regular font. Italic applies a script-like appearance to text, slanting it the way handwriting slants. Underlining is not often used in printed material because it is considered to be too distracting to the reader; instead, you might find underlining appearing in handwritten materials to emphasize a point.

Emphasize Information with Bold, Italic, or Underline

1 Select the text you want to emphasize.

A If you drag to select, the Mini Toolbar appears in the background, and you can use it by moving the pointer ( ) toward the Mini Toolbar.

B If you want to use the Ribbon, click **Home** to display the Home tab.

2 Click **Bold** (**B**), **Italic** (*I*), or **Underline** (U̲) on the Ribbon or the Mini Toolbar.

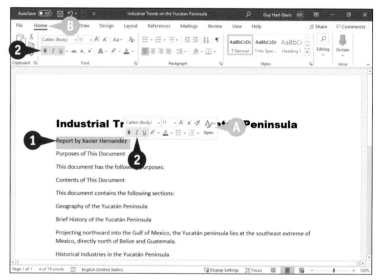

C Word applies the emphasis you selected.

This example shows the text after applying italic.

3 Click anywhere outside the selection to continue working.

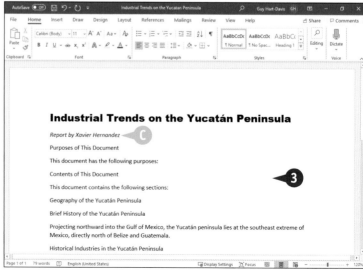

Create Superscripts and Subscripts

You can format text as a superscript or as a subscript. A superscript or subscript is a number, figure, or symbol that appears smaller than the normal line of type and is set slightly above or below it; superscripts appear above the baseline of regular text, whereas subscripts appear below the baseline. Subscripts and superscripts are perhaps best known for their use in formulas and mathematical expressions, but they are also used when inserting trademark symbols.

Create Superscripts and Subscripts

1 Type and select the text you want to appear in superscript or subscript.

A If you drag to select, the Mini Toolbar appears.

Note: To select multiple items, as in this example, select the first item using either the mouse or the keyboard, then press **Ctrl** while you drag over each subsequent item.

2 Click **Home**.

The Home tab appears.

3 Click **Superscript** (x^2) or **Subscript** (x_2).

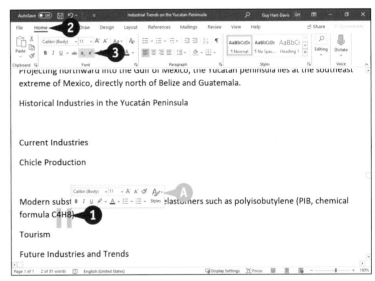

B Word applies superscript or subscript formatting to the selected text.

4 Click anywhere outside the selection to continue working.

Note: Before using superscripts and subscripts to create mathematical equations manually, see if Word's Equation feature can create the types of equations you need. Click **Insert** to display the Insert tab, click **Symbols** to open the Symbols panel, click **Equation**, and then click the type of equation.

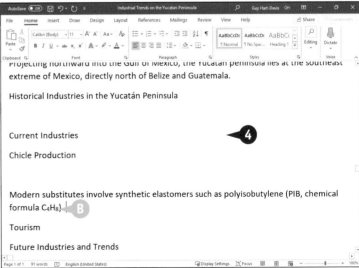

113

Change Text Case

You can change the case of selected text instead of retyping it with a new case applied. The Change Case feature offers four choices of case: Sentence Case, which capitalizes the first letter of the first word and applies lowercase to the other letters; Lowercase, which uses all lowercase letters; Uppercase, which uses all capital letters; or Capitalize Each Word, which capitalizes the first letter of each word.

The Change Case feature also offers the Toggle Case command, which changes uppercase letters to lowercase and lowercase letters to uppercase in selected text.

Change Text Case

1 Select the text to which you want to assign a new case.

The Mini Toolbar appears in the background if you drag to select text.

2 Click **Home**.

The Home tab appears.

3 Click **Change Case** (Aa⌄).

The Change Case panel opens.

4 Click the case you want to use.

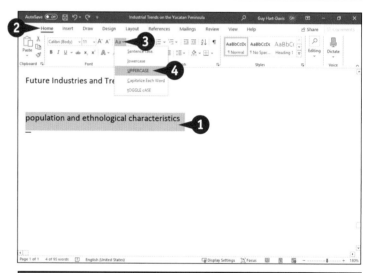

A The selected text appears in the new case.

5 Click anywhere outside the selection to continue working.

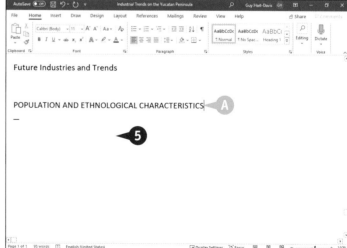

Change Text Color

You can change the color of selected text for emphasis. For example, if you are creating a report for work, you might make the title of the report a different color from the information contained in the report or even color-code certain data in the report.

Color is effective when you view your document on-screen, save it as a PDF or an XPS file, or print it using a color printer.

Change Text Color

1 Select the text that you want to change to a different color.

A If you drag to select, the Mini Toolbar appears, and you can use it by moving the pointer (⊳) toward the Mini Toolbar.

2 To use the Ribbon, click **Home** to display the Home tab.

3 Click ⌄ to the right of **Font Color** (A), and move the pointer (⊳) over a color.

Word displays a preview of the selected text.

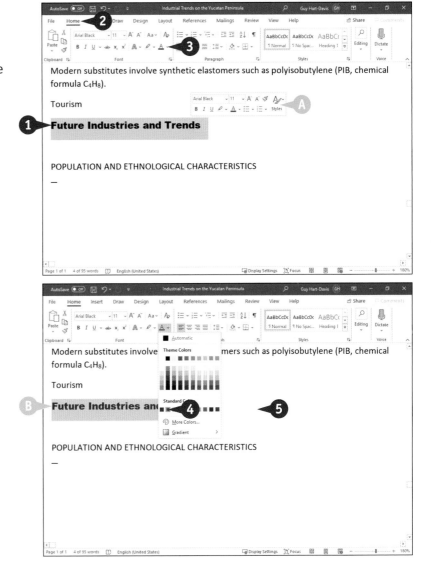

4 Click a color.

B Word assigns the color to the text.

This example applies a red color to the text.

5 Click anywhere outside the selection to continue working.

Apply Text Effects

When you need to draw the reader's eye to particular text strongly, you can apply Word's text effects, which include outlines, shadows, reflections, and glows. You can use text effects on either regular text or on WordArt objects.

Use text effects sparingly in your documents. If you overuse text effects, your documents will look "busy," and the reader may come to ignore the effects.

Apply Text Effects

1 Type and select the text to which you want to apply an effect.

2 Click **Home**.

The Home tab appears.

3 Click **Text Effects** (𝐀 ▾).

Ⓐ The Text Effects gallery appears.

4 Move the pointer (⃕) over the type of text effect you want to apply.

Ⓑ Word displays a gallery of options available for the selected text effect. You can preview any text effect by moving the pointer (⃕) over it.

5 Click an option from the gallery to apply it.

Ⓒ Word applies your choice to the selected text.

6 Click anywhere outside the selection to continue working.

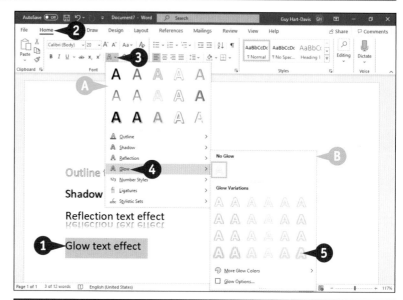

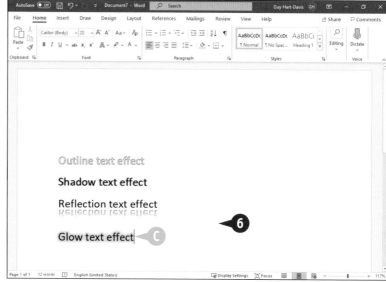

Apply a Font Style Set

You can use font style sets to enhance the appearance of OpenType fonts. Font style sets can add just the right mood to a holiday card by adding flourishes to the letters in the font set.

The OpenType font structure adds several options to its predecessor TrueType that enhance the OpenType font's typographic and language support capabilities. OpenType fonts use an extension of .otf or .ttf; the .ttf form typically includes PostScript font data. OpenType fonts store all information in a single font file and have the same appearance on Macs and PCs.

Apply a Font Style Set

1 Select an OpenType font.

This example uses Gabriola.

2 Type some text, and select it.

3 Click **Home**.

The Home tab appears.

4 Click **Text Effects** (A·).

Ⓐ The Text Effects gallery appears.

5 Move the pointer (⬚) over **Stylistic Sets**.

Ⓑ Word displays a gallery of options available for Stylistic Sets. You can preview any set by moving the pointer (⬚) over it.

6 Click an option from the gallery to apply it.

Ⓒ Word applies the font style set to the text you selected.

7 Click anywhere outside the selection to continue working.

Apply Highlighting to Text

You can apply color highlighting to draw attention to particular text. For example, you might highlight a keyword or a short phrase to help your reader grasp a key point. Highlighting works both on-screen and in color printouts but is wasted in monochrome printouts.

Use highlighting sparingly to keep it effective. If you highlight every other sentence or even all the headings in a document, your reader will learn to ignore the highlighting.

Apply Highlighting to Text

1 Drag to select the text that you want to highlight.

A The Mini Toolbar appears.

Note: If you prefer to use the keyboard to select the text, select it. Then click **Home** to display the Home tab, go to the Font group, and click ⌄ to the right of **Text Highlight Color** (✐ ⌄).

2 Click ⌄ to the right of **Text Highlight Color** (✐ ⌄).

B A palette of color choices appears.

You can move the pointer (⊹) over any color to make Word display a sample of the selected text highlighted in that color.

3 Click the color you want.

C Word highlights the selected text using the color you choose.

Note: When you apply highlighting, Word automatically deselects the selected text, moving the insertion point to its end.

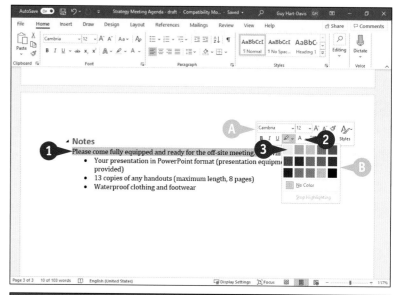

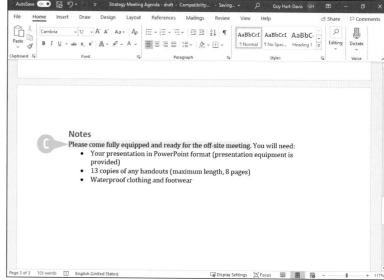

Apply Strikethrough to Text

Y ou can use the Strikethrough feature to draw a line through text you propose to delete or text that you want to show has been changed. Strikethrough formatting is often used in the legal community to identify text a reviewer proposes to delete; this formatting has developed a universal meaning and has been adopted by reviewers around the world. However, if you need to track both additions and deletions and want to update the document in an automated way, use Word's review tracking features as described in Chapter 8, "Reviewing and Finalizing Documents."

Apply Strikethrough to Text

1 Select the text to which you want to apply strikethrough formatting.

The Mini Toolbar appears if you drag to select text.

2 Click **Home**.

The Home tab appears.

3 Click **Strikethrough** (ab).

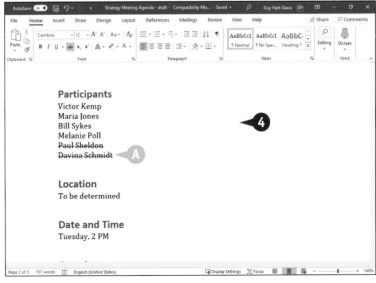

A Word applies strikethrough formatting to the selected text.

4 Click anywhere outside the selection to continue working.

Note: To remove strikethrough formatting, select the text and then click **Strikethrough** (ab) in the Font group on the Home tab.

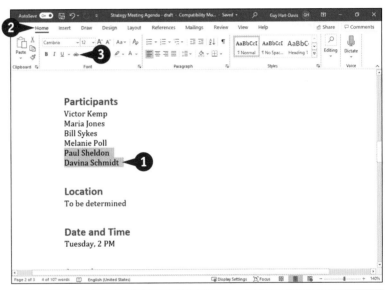

Copy and Paste Text Formatting

When you have formatted some text or a paragraph with formatting that you want to use elsewhere, you can use the Format Painter feature to copy the formatting and "paint" it on other text.

The Format Painter feature is great for reapplying custom formatting without having to create it again. But if you find yourself using Format Painter for many paragraphs, you may do better to create a style with that formatting instead. See Chapter 6, "Formatting Paragraphs," for information on creating and working with styles.

Copy and Paste Text Formatting

1 Select the text containing the formatting that you want to copy.

A If you select text with the pointer, the Mini Toolbar appears.

2 To use the Ribbon, click **Home**.

The Home tab appears.

3 Click **Format Painter** (🖌).

B The pointer (⌕) changes to the Format Painter pointer (🖌I) when you move it over your document.

4 Click and drag over the text to which you want to apply the same formatting.

C Word copies the formatting from the original text to the newly selected text.

To copy the same formatting multiple times, you can double-click **Format Painter** (🖌).

You can press Esc to cancel the Format Painter feature at any time.

Remove Text Formatting

Sometimes, you may find that you have applied too much formatting to your text, making it difficult to read. Instead of undoing all your formatting changes by hand, you can use Word's Clear Formatting command to remove any formatting you have applied to the document text. The Clear Formatting command removes all formatting applied to the text and restores the default settings.

Remove Text Formatting

1 Select the text from which you want to remove formatting.

Note: If you do not select text, clicking **Clear Formatting** (A◇) removes text formatting from the entire document.

2 Click **Home**.

The Home tab appears.

3 Click **Clear Formatting** (A◇).

A Word removes all formatting from the selected text.

4 Click anywhere outside the selection to continue working.

Set the Default Font for All New Documents

You can change the default font that Word uses for all new documents you create. Word's default font is Calibri, 11 point, a sans serif font, but you can change to any other font available on your PC. For example, you might prefer to use a serif font that gives your documents a more formal look and guides the reader's eye along the lines.

Changing the default font affects documents you create thereafter. It does not affect documents you have already created.

Set the Default Font for All New Documents

Note: This example begins with the default Word font, Calibri, and default size, 11 points. It changes the default font to Lucida Bright and the size to 12 points.

1. Click **Home**.

   The Home tab appears.

2. Right-click **Normal**.

   The context menu opens.

3. Click **Modify**.

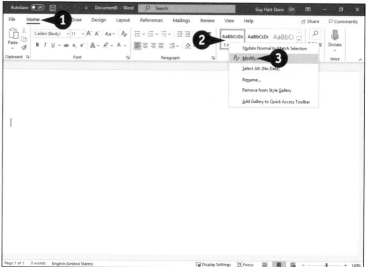

The Modify Style dialog box opens, with the Normal style selected in the Name box.

Note: While you have the Modify Style dialog box open, you can also make any other changes needed to the Normal style. See the tip for one possibility.

4. Click ⌄.

   The drop-down list opens.

5. Click the font you want to use for all new documents.

6 Click ⌄.

The drop-down list opens.

7 Click the font size you want to use for all new documents.

A A preview of the new selections appears here.

8 Click **New documents based on this template** (○ changes to ◉).

9 Click **OK**.

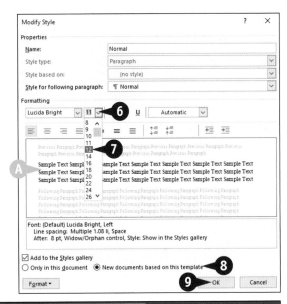

The Modify Style dialog box closes.

10 Press Ctrl+N.

Word creates a new blank document.

B The default font and font size are the font and font size you selected.

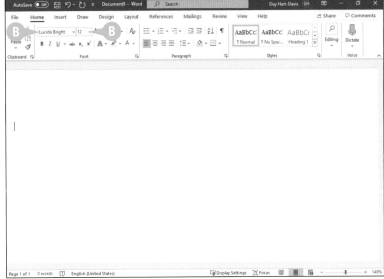

TIP

How can I indent the first line of each paragraph by default?
Open the Modify Style dialog box as explained in the main text. Click **Format** and then **Paragraph** to open the Paragraph dialog box in front of the Modify Style dialog box. In the Indentation section, click **Special** (⌄), and then click **First line**. In the **By** box, adjust the indent distance from the default 0.5", if needed. Click **OK** to close the Paragraph dialog box. Click **New documents based on this template** (○ changes to ◉), and then click **OK** to close the Modify Style dialog box.

CHAPTER 6

Formatting Paragraphs

To make your text appear the way you want, you can format its paragraphs. Word provides a wide range of paragraph formatting, from indents and line spacing to bullets, numbering, and borders. You can apply paragraph formatting manually, but it is better to apply it by using styles, which are collections of formatting.

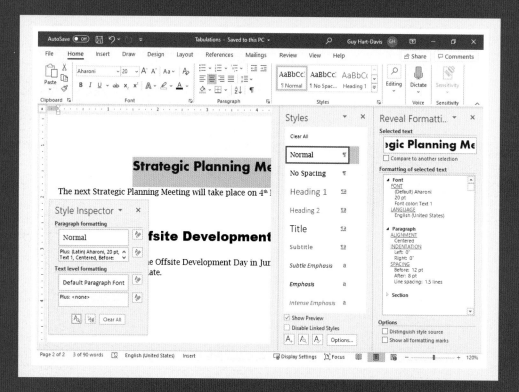

Change Text Alignment

You can use Word's alignment commands to change the way that your text is positioned horizontally on a page. By default, Word left-aligns text. You can align text with the left or right margins, center it horizontally between both margins, or justify text between both the left and right margins. You can change the alignment of all the text in your document or change the alignment of individual paragraphs and objects.

To align text vertically, see Chapter 7, "Formatting Pages." The example in this section centers a headline between the left and right margins.

Change Text Alignment

1 Click anywhere in the paragraph you want to align.

2 Click **Home**.

The Home tab appears.

3 Click an alignment button.

Click **Align Left** (≡) to align text with the left margin. Click **Center** (≡) to center text between the left and right margins. Click **Align Right** (≡) to align text with the right margin. Click **Justify** (≡) to align text between the left and right margins.

Word aligns the text.

Ⓐ This text is aligned with the left margin.

Ⓑ This text is centered between both margins.

Ⓒ This text is aligned with the right margin.

Ⓓ This text is justified between both margins.

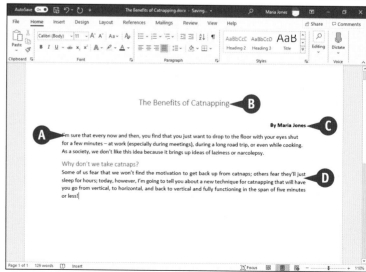

You can change the amount of space Word places between the lines of text within a paragraph. For example, you might set 1.5 spacing to make paragraphs easier to read. By default, Word assigns single spacing within a paragraph for all new documents that you create.

Word can measure line spacing in inches, but in keeping with typography tradition, line spacing is most often measured in points, specified as *pts*. Twelve pts equal approximately one line of space.

Set Line Spacing Within a Paragraph

1 Click in the paragraph for which you want to change line spacing.

2 Click **Home**.

The Home tab appears.

3 Click **Line Spacing** (≡▾).

The Line Spacing pop-up panel opens.

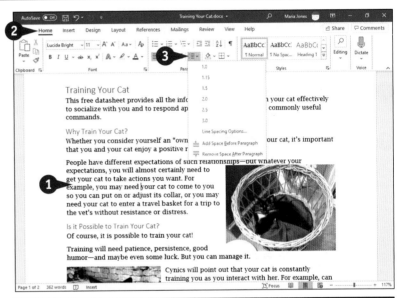

4 Move the pointer (◊) over the line spacing you want to preview.

Ⓐ Word displays the paragraph with a preview of the spacing.

A setting of 1 represents single spacing; 1.15 places a small amount of blank space between lines; 1.5 places half a blank line between lines of text; 2 represents double spacing; 2.5 places one and a half blank lines between lines of text; and 3 represents triple spacing.

5 Click the spacing you want.

Word applies the spacing to the paragraph.

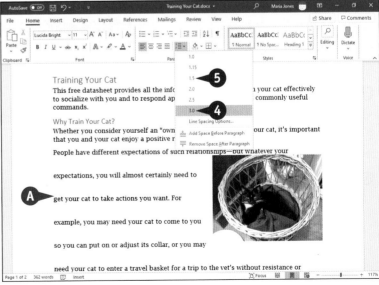

Set Line Spacing Between Paragraphs

In addition to changing the spacing between lines within a paragraph, you can change the amount of space Word places between paragraphs of text. For example, you can add space between single-spaced paragraphs so that there is a gap between them.

You can set spacing before a paragraph or after a paragraph. Word measures spacing between paragraphs in points (pts). For normal text size of about 12 pts, you can create one blank line between paragraphs by adding 6 pts before and 6 pts after the paragraph, or you can simply add 12 pts before or 12 pts after the paragraph.

Set Line Spacing Between Paragraphs

1 Select the paragraph or paragraphs for which you want to set line spacing.

2 Click **Home**.

The Home tab appears.

3 Click the dialog box launcher (⌐⊿) in the Paragraph group.

The Paragraph dialog box opens.

4 Click ⬆ to increase or decrease the space before the selected paragraph.

5 Click 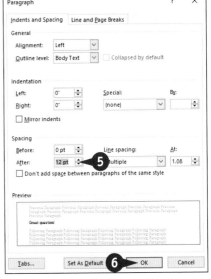 to increase or decrease the space after the selected paragraph.

6 Click **OK**.

The Paragraph dialog box closes.

Ⓐ Word applies the spacing before and after the selected paragraph.

7 Click anywhere outside the selection to continue working.

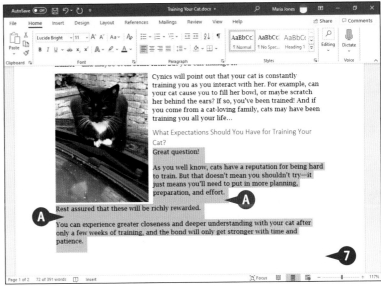

Create a Bulleted or Numbered List

You can use bulleted and numbered lists to organize your information. A bulleted list adds a dot or similar symbol in front of each list item, whereas a numbered list adds a sequential number or letter in front of each list item. You can create a list either as you type it or after you have typed list elements.

You can also create multilevel lists, such as the type of list you use when creating an outline. Word enables you to use numbering and bullets at different list levels to create the multilevel lists you need.

Create a Bulleted or Numbered List

Create a List as You Type

1. Type **1.** to create a numbered list or ***** to create a bulleted list.

2. Press **Spacebar** or **Tab**.

A Word automatically formats the entry as a list item and displays the AutoCorrect Options button (⬚▾) so that you can undo or stop automatic numbering.

3. Type a list item.

4. Press **Enter** to prepare to type another list item.

B Word automatically adds a bullet or number for the next list item.

5. Repeat steps **3** and **4** for each list item.

To stop entering items in the list, press **Enter** twice.

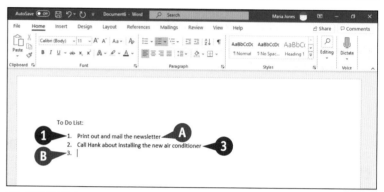

Create a List from Existing Text

1. Select the text to which you want to assign bullets or numbers.

2. Click **Home**.

The Home tab appears.

3. Click **Bullets** (⠿) or **Numbering** (⠿). This example uses Bullets (⠿).

C Word applies numbers or bullets to the selection.

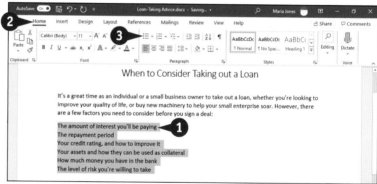

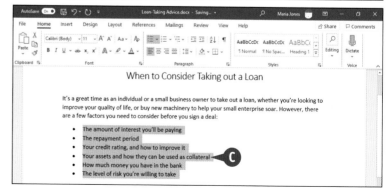

Create a Multilevel List

1 Position the insertion point where you want to create the list.

2 Click **Home**.

The Home tab appears.

3 Click **Multilevel List** (⌖).

The Multilevel List gallery opens.

4 Click the list type you want to use.

Ⓓ Word applies the list formatting to the paragraph in which you positioned the insertion point.

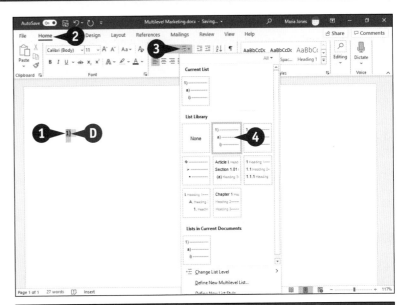

5 Type your list.

Ⓔ You can press Enter to enter a new list item at the same list level.

Ⓕ Each time you press Tab, Word indents a level in the list.

Ⓖ Each time you press Shift+Tab, Word outdents a level in the list.

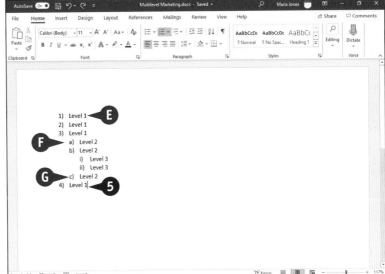

TIP

How do I change the numbering in a multilevel list?

Click **Home** to display the Home tab, then go to the Paragraph group and click **Multilevel List** (⌖). In the Multilevel List gallery, click **Define New Multilevel List** to open the Define New Multilevel List dialog box. In the Click Level to Modify box, click the list level you want to change; for example, click **1** to modify the top level of the list. Use the options in the Number Format area to specify the number format, number style, and font for the number. Then use the options in the Position area to specify the number alignment and indentation. Click **OK** when you finish.

Display Formatting Marks

Y ou can display formatting marks that do not print but that help you identify formatting in your document. Displaying formatting marks can often help you identify problems in your documents. For example, if you display formatting marks, you can visibly see the difference between a line break and a paragraph mark. You can see where spaces were used to attempt to vertically line up text, where you should have used tabs, as described in the section "Set and Use Tabs," later in this chapter. Word can display formatting marks that represent spaces, tabs, paragraphs, line breaks, hidden text, and optional hyphens.

Display Formatting Marks

1 Open any document.

2 Click **Home**.

The Home tab appears.

3 Click **Show/Hide** (¶).

Word displays all formatting marks in your document.

A Single dots (·) represent the spaces you insert each time you press **Spacebar**.

B A paragraph mark (¶) appears each time you press **Enter**.

C A line break (↵) appears each time you press **Shift** + **Enter**.

D An arrow (→) appears each time you press **Tab**.

E Hidden text appears underlined with dots.

F Optional hyphens, inserted by pressing **Ctrl** + **–**, appear as ¬.

4 Click **Show/Hide** (¶) again to hide formatting marks.

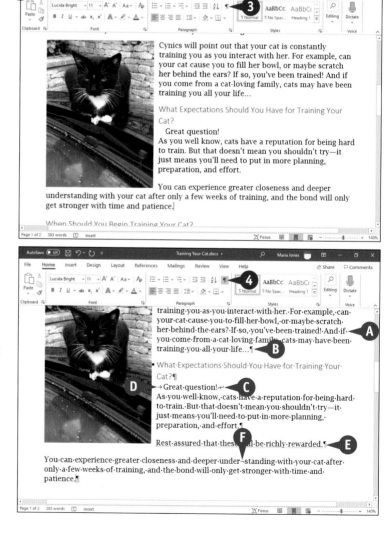

Hide or Display the Ruler

You can hide or display horizontal and vertical rulers while you work on a Word document in Print Layout, Web Layout, or Draft views. The rulers can help you position text and objects accurately on the page both horizontally and vertically. You also can use the rulers to align tables and graphic objects and to indent paragraphs or set tabs in your document, as described in the sections "Indent Paragraphs" and "Set and Use Tabs," later in this chapter.

Hide or Display the Ruler

1 Click **View**.

The View tab appears.

2 Click **Show**.

The Show pop-up panel opens.

3 Click **Ruler** (☐ changes to ☑).

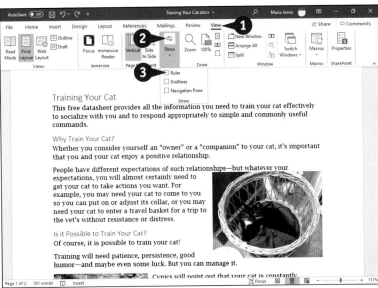

Ⓐ The horizontal ruler appears above your document and below the Ribbon.

Ⓑ The vertical ruler appears on the left side of your document.

Note: When you want to hide the rulers, click **View** to display the View tab, click **Show** to open the Show pop-up panel, and then click **Ruler** (☑ changes to ☐).

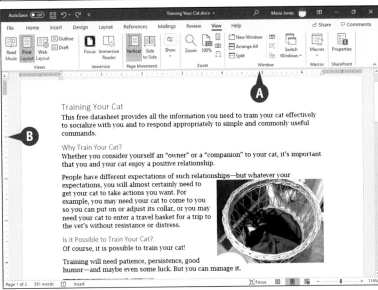

You can use indents as a way to control the horizontal positioning of text in a document. Indents are simply margin adjustments that affect individual lines or paragraphs. You might use an indent to distinguish a particular paragraph on a page—for example, a long quote.

You can indent paragraphs in your document from the left and right margins. You also can indent only the first line of a paragraph or all lines except the first line of the paragraph. You can set indents using buttons on the Ribbon, the Paragraph dialog box, and the horizontal ruler.

Indent Paragraphs

Set Quick Indents

1 Click anywhere in the paragraph you want to indent.

2 Click **Home**.

The Home tab appears.

3 Click an indent button:

A Click **Decrease Indent** (←≡) to decrease the indentation.

B Click **Increase Indent** (→≡) to increase the indentation.

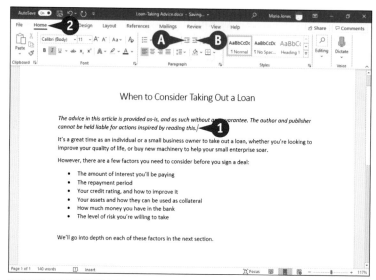

C Word applies the indent change.

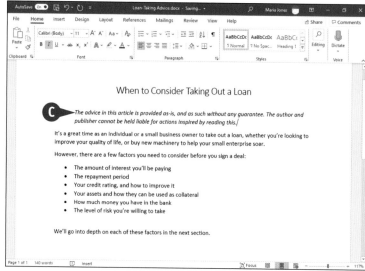

Set Precise Indents

1 Click in the paragraph or select the text you want to indent.

2 Click **Home**.

The Home tab appears.

3 Click the dialog box launcher (⌟) in the Paragraph group.

The Paragraph dialog box opens.

4 Optionally, click **Left** or **Right** and specify the distance to indent the left and right edges of the paragraph or selection.

5 Click **Special** (⌄) to select an indenting option.

First Line, shown in this example, indents only the first line of the paragraph, and Hanging indents all lines except the first line of the paragraph.

6 Click ⬍ to set the distance for the first line indent or the hanging indent.

D The Preview area shows a sample of the indent.

7 Click **OK**.

E Word applies the indent to the paragraph containing the insertion point.

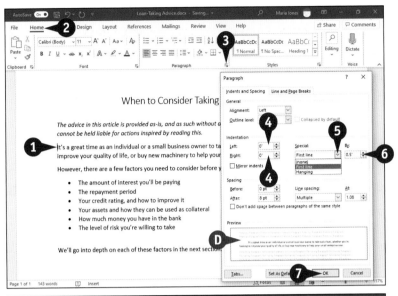

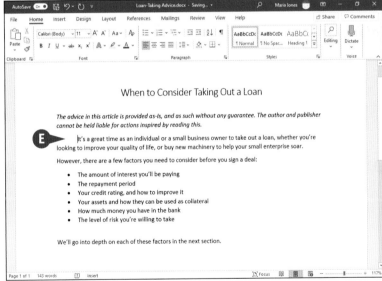

TIP

How do I set indents using the Word ruler?

The ruler contains markers for changing the left indent, right indent, first-line indent, and hanging indent. Click **View** to display the View tab, click **Show** to open the Show pop-up panel, and then click **Ruler** to display the ruler. On the left side of the ruler, drag **Left Indent** (◻) to indent all lines from the left margin, drag **Hanging Indent** (▽) to create a hanging indent, or drag **First Line Indent** (△) to indent the first line only. On the right side of the ruler, drag **Right Indent** (△) to indent all lines from the right margin.

Set and Use Tabs

You can use tabs to create vertically aligned columns of text. Using tabs as opposed to spaces ensures that information lines up properly. To insert a tab, press **Tab**; the insertion point moves to the next tab stop on the page.

By default, Word creates tab stops every 0.5 inch across the page and left-aligns the text on each tab stop. You can set your own tab stops using the ruler or the Tabs dialog box. You also can use the Tabs dialog box to change the tab alignment and to specify an exact measurement between tab stops.

Set and Use Tabs

Add a Tab

① Click **Tab** until the type of tab you want to add appears.

⌐—Left tab, which sets the starting position of text that then appears to the right of the tab.

⊥—Center tab, which aligns text centered around the tab.

⌐—Right tab, which sets the rightmost position of text aligned with the tab.

⊥—Decimal tab, which aligns values at the decimal point. Values before the decimal point appear to the left of the tab and values after the decimal point appear to the right of the tab.

▪—Bar tab, which inserts a vertical bar at the tab stop.

② Select the lines to which you want to add a tab.

③ Click the ruler where you want the tab to appear.

Word displays the type of tab you selected at the location you clicked on each selected line.

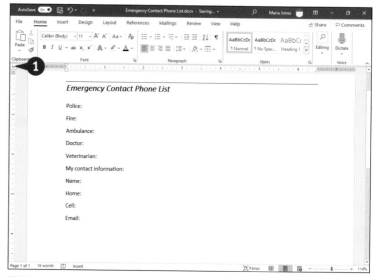

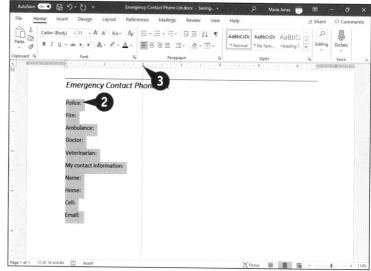

Using a Tab

1 Click to the left of the information you want to appear at the tab; in this example, immediately after the ":" after "Police" to add a tab followed by the phone number.

2 Press **Tab**.

A If you display formatting marks, Word displays an arrow (→) representing the tab character.

3 Type your text.

B The text appears aligned vertically with the tab.

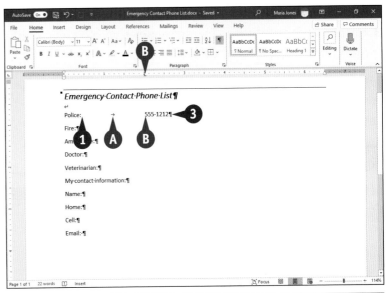

Move a Tab

1 Click the line using the tab or select the lines of text affected by the tab.

2 Drag the tab to the left or right.

C A vertical line marks its position as you drag.

When you click and drag a tab, the text moves to align vertically with the tab.

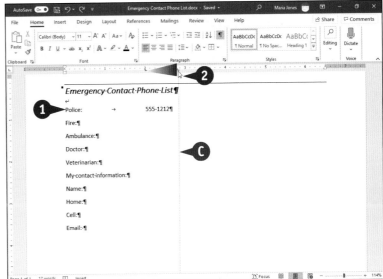

TIP

How can I delete a tab?
Click in the single paragraph containing the tab, or select all the paragraphs containing the tab. Then drag the tab off the ruler. When you delete a tab, text aligned at the tab moves to the first preset tab on the line.

continued ▶

Instead of setting tabs quickly using the ruler, you can use the Tabs dialog box, which offers further options for tabs and also enables you to clear all tabs quickly from the current paragraph or selection.

When you need to help the reader follow information across a page, you can use *dot leader tabs*— tabs that automatically insert the number of dots needed to bridge the tab's gap, as in the chapter-opening pages of this book.

Set and Use Tabs (continued)

Set Tabs Using the Tabs Dialog Box

1 Select the paragraphs for which you want to set tabs.

Note: To set tabs for a single paragraph, click in that paragraph.

2 Click **Home**.

The Home tab appears.

3 Click the dialog box launcher (⌐) in the Paragraph group.

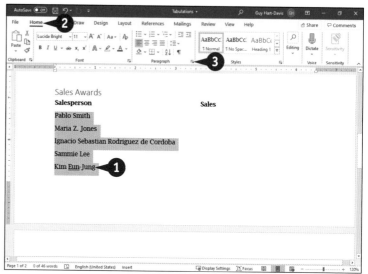

The Paragraph dialog box opens.

4 Click **Tabs**.

The Tabs dialog box opens.

5 Click **Tab stop position** and type the position, such as **4** for 4 inches.

6 In the Alignment area, click the appropriate option button, such as **Right** (○ changes to ◉).

7 In the Leader area, click the appropriate option button, such as **2. . . . . .** (○ changes to ◉).

8 Click **Set**.

9 Click **OK**.

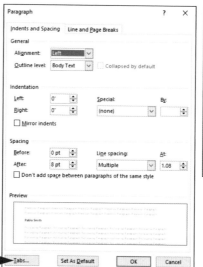

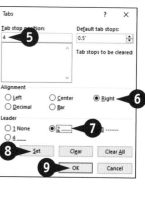

The Tabs dialog box closes.

D The new tab stop appears on the ruler for the selected paragraphs.

10 Click outside the selection to deselect it.

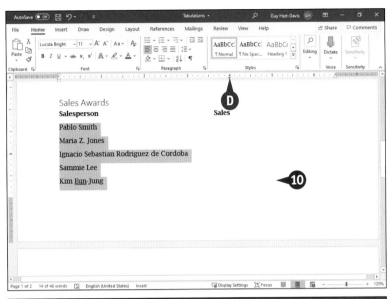

11 In the paragraphs for which you set the tab, enter tabs and text.

E The text appears with tab leaders.

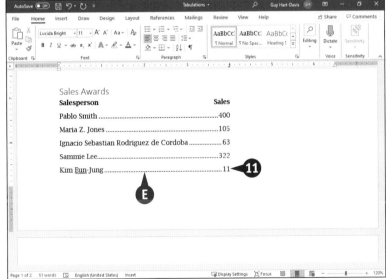

TIP

Is there a quicker way to open the Tabs dialog box?
Yes, if you can click precisely. Double-click an existing tab on the ruler to open the Tabs dialog box. This shortcut is handy, but if you double-click the lower part of the ruler where there is no tab, you place a tab of the current kind, and then open the Tabs dialog box. If you double-click the upper part of the ruler instead, you open the Page Setup dialog box.

Add a Paragraph Border

You can draw attention to a paragraph containing important information by adding a border to it. You can place a border around a paragraph or a page, and you can control the color, weight, and style of the border. You also can add shading to a paragraph, as described in the section "Add Paragraph Shading," later in this chapter. See Chapter 7 to learn how to add a border to a page.

Add a Paragraph Border

1 Select the text that you want to surround with a border.

Note: To surround all lines in a paragraph by a border, select both the text and the paragraph mark (¶). To display paragraph marks, click **Show/Hide** (¶) on the Home tab in the Paragraph group.

2 Click **Home**.

The Home tab appears.

3 Click ⌄ to the right of **Borders** (⊞ ⌄).

4 Click **Borders and Shading**.

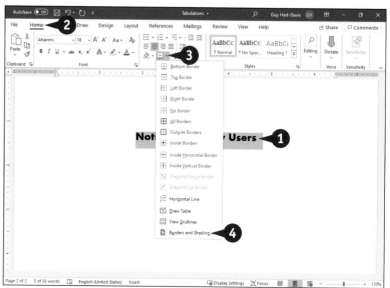

The Borders and Shading dialog box opens.

5 Click **Borders**.

The Borders tab appears.

6 Click in the Setting box to select a type of border.

This example uses Box.

7 Click in the Style box to select the style for the border line.

8 Click **Color** (⌄), and then click the color for the border line.

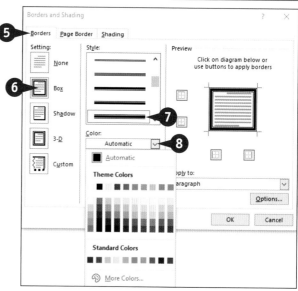

9 Click **Width** (🔽), and then click the thickness for the border line.

Ⓐ You can use the Apply To list to apply the border to an entire paragraph or to selected text.

Ⓑ The Preview area shows the results of the settings you select.

10 Click **OK**.

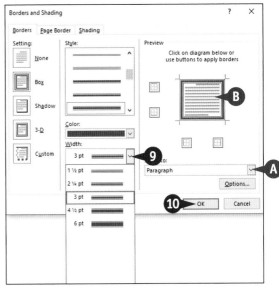

The Borders and Shading dialog box closes.

Ⓒ The border appears around the text you selected in step **1**.

11 Click anywhere outside the selection to continue working.

Note: You can apply a border using the same color, style, and thickness you established in these steps to any paragraph by completing steps **1** to **3** and clicking the type of border you want to apply in step **6**.

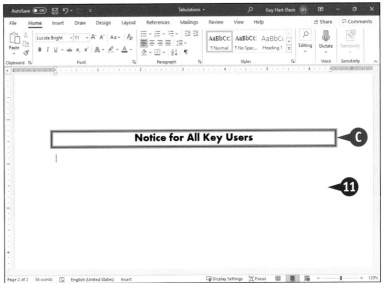

TIP

How do I remove a border?

Click anywhere in the text surrounded by a border. Then click **Home** to display the Home tab, go to the Paragraph group, and click 🔽 to the right of **Borders** (⊞ ▾). In the Borders pop-up panel, click **No Border**. Word removes the border.

Review and Change Formatting

To help you determine what formatting is applied to particular text or an object, Word provides the Reveal Formatting pane. This pane enables you to see all the formatting applied to the current selection without having to open various dialog boxes or peer at individual buttons on the Ribbon. You also can compare the formatting of two selections to see their differences, as described in the next section, "Compare Formatting."

You also can have Word display wavy blue underlines to mark text you have formatted inconsistently in your document and supply suggestions to correct the formatting inconsistencies.

Review and Change Formatting

1 Select the text containing the formatting you want to review.

2 Click **Home**.

The Home tab appears.

3 Click the dialog box launcher (⌐▾) in the Styles group.

The Styles pane appears.

4 Click **Style Inspector** (𝒜).

The Style Inspector pane appears.

5 Click **Reveal Formatting** (𝒜).

The Reveal Formatting pane appears.

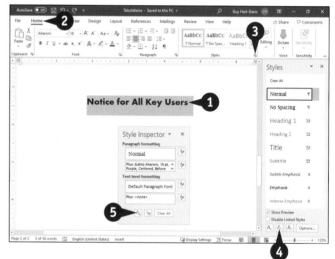

6 Click **Close** (✕).

The Style Inspector pane closes.

7 Click **Close** (✕).

The Styles pane closes.

Ⓐ A portion of the selected text appears here.

Ⓑ Formatting details for the selected text appear here.

Ⓒ You can click **Expand** (▷) to display details or click **Collapse** (◢) to hide details.

8 Click the link for the type of change you want to make. For example, click **ALIGNMENT**.

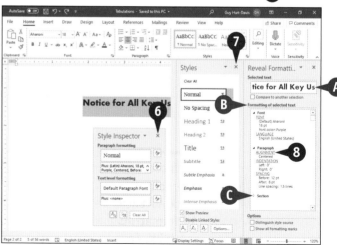

The Paragraph dialog box opens, showing the Indents and Spacing tab.

9 Change the appropriate options— for example, change the paragraph alignment.

10 Click **OK**.

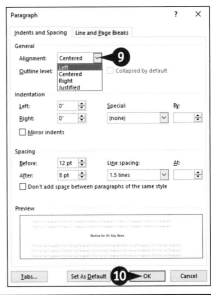

D Word applies the formatting changes.

E The Reveal Formatting pane shows the updated formatting.

11 Click ✕.

The Reveal Formatting pane closes.

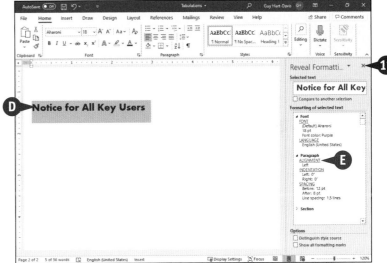

TIP

How can I view formatting inconsistencies?
To view wavy blue lines under formatting inconsistencies, click **File** and then click **Options** to display the Word Options dialog box. Click **Advanced** to display the Advanced category. Go to the Editing Options section, click **Keep track of formatting** (☐ changes to ☑) and **Mark formatting inconsistencies** (☐ changes to ☑), and then click **OK**. For suggestions to correct an inconsistency, right-click the underlined word and look at the context menu.

Compare Formatting

The Reveal Formatting feature enables you to compare the formatting of one selection to that of another selection. Reveal Formatting can be a great help in making your manual formatting consistent across similar selections. For example, if you format your document's headings manually, rather than using styles, you may get inconsistencies in the formatting. If Reveal Formatting finds such inconsistencies, it can update the formatting of the second selection to match that of the first selection.

Compare Formatting

1 Select the first text containing the formatting that you want to compare.

2 Click **Home**.

The Home tab appears.

3 Click the dialog box launcher (⌐) in the Styles group.

A The Styles pane appears.

4 Click **Style Inspector** (🔍).

B The Style Inspector pane appears.

5 Click **Reveal Formatting** (🔍).

C The Reveal Formatting pane appears.

6 Click ✕.

The Style Inspector pane closes.

7 Click ✕.

The Styles pane closes.

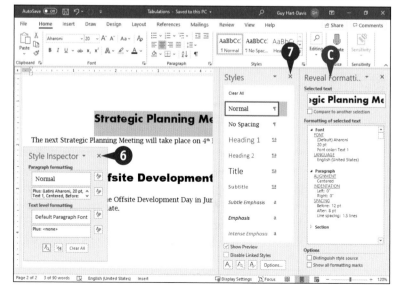

8 Click **Compare to another selection** (☐ changes to ☑).

D A second box for selected text appears.

9 Select the text that you want to compare to the text you selected in step **1**.

E Formatting differences between the selections appear here.

10 Move the pointer (◊) over the sample box for the second selection.

11 Click ▾.

The drop-down menu opens.

12 Click **Apply Formatting of Original Selection**.

Word applies the formatting of the first selection to the second selection.

Click anywhere to continue working.

13 Click ✕.

The Reveal Formatting pane closes.

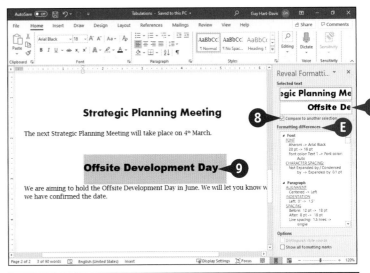

Apply Formatting Using Styles

To apply formatting quickly and consistently, you can use Word's styles. A *style* is a predefined set of formatting that can include font settings, paragraph settings, list settings, and border and shading settings. For example, to give all the first-level headings in a document the same formatting and ensure they look the same, you could apply the Heading 1 style to them.

You can access styles you use frequently through the Styles gallery. You can access all styles through the Styles pane and the Apply Styles pane.

Apply Formatting Using Styles

Using the Styles Gallery

1 Select the text to which you want to apply formatting.

2 Click **Home**.

The Home tab appears.

3 In the Styles group, click ▲ and ▼ to scroll through available styles.

4 Click **More** (▼).

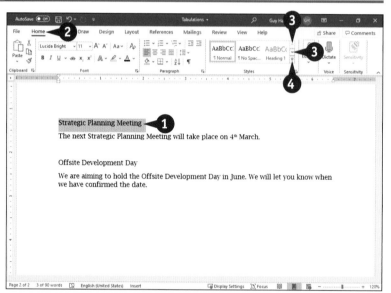

Ⓐ The Styles gallery opens.

Ⓑ The style of the selected text appears highlighted.

Ⓒ As you move the pointer (⌕) over various styles, Live Preview shows you the way the selected text would look in each style.

5 Click the style you want to apply.

The Styles gallery closes.

Word applies the style to the selected text.

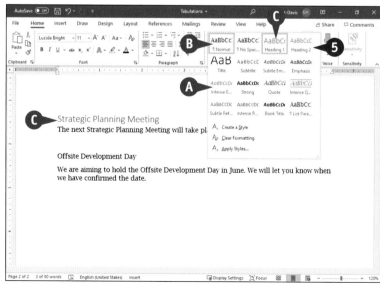

Using Other Styles

1. Select the text to which you want to apply the style.

2. Click **Home**.

   The Home tab appears.

3. In the Styles group, click **More** (⤓).

   The Styles gallery opens.

4. Click **Apply Styles**.

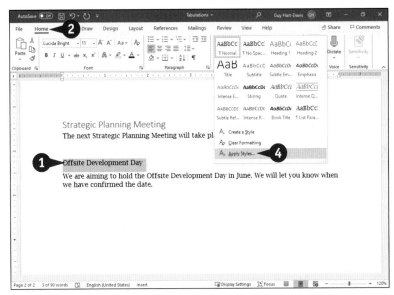

The Apply Styles pane appears.

5. Click ⌄ to the right of **Style Name**.

   The Style Name list opens.

6. Click the style you want to apply.

   D Word applies the style to the selected text.

7. Click ✕.

   The Apply Styles pane closes.

8. Click anywhere outside the selection to continue working.

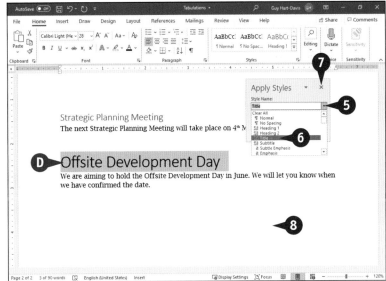

TIP

How can I easily view styles as they would appear in my document?

Click **Home** to display the Home tab, go to the Styles group, and then click the dialog box launcher (⤵) to display the Styles pane. In the Styles pane, click **Show Preview** (☐ changes to ☑). Word displays styles using their formatting in the Styles pane.

Switch Styles

Word enables you to easily change all text formatted with one style to another style. This technique can not only help you format your documents consistently but also help you work swiftly and efficiently.

For example, you might decide to change all the text that used a particular body text style to a different style. Rather than needing to work with each paragraph individually, you can change all the paragraphs in a single move by working in the Styles pane.

Switch Styles

1 Click in a paragraph formatted with the style you want to switch.

2 Click **Home**.

The Home tab appears.

3 Click the dialog box launcher (⌐) in the Styles group.

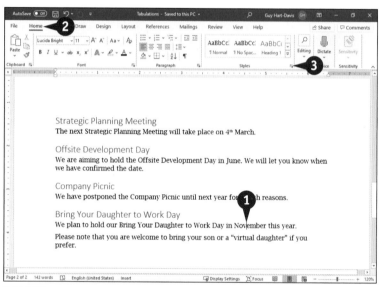

The Styles pane appears.

Note: If the Styles pane appears floating on-screen, you can dock it at the right side of the screen. Either double-click the Styles name at the top of the pane, or drag the pane past the right edge of the window. If the pane appears docked, you can undock it by dragging it toward the middle of the window.

A The style for the selected text appears highlighted.

B You can position the pointer (⋏) over any style to display its formatting information.

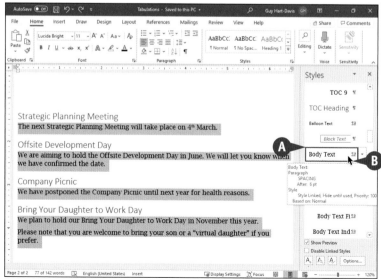

④ Position the pointer (⌖) over a style until ✲ appears.

⑤ Click ✲ to display a list of options.

⑥ Click **Select All *N* Instance(s)**.

Ⓒ Word selects all text in your document formatted using the style of the text you selected in step **1**.

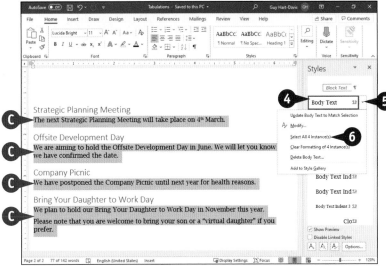

⑦ Click the style you want to apply to all selected text.

Ⓓ Word changes all selected text to the style you selected in step **7**.

Click anywhere to continue working.

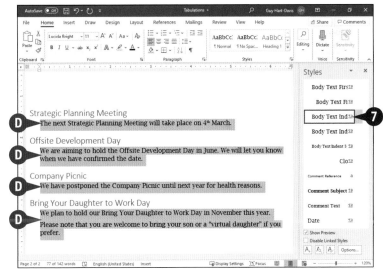

TIP

How do I sort styles alphabetically in the Styles pane?

By default, Word sorts styles using the As Recommended setting, but sorting in alphabetical order is a useful alternative. At the bottom of the Styles pane, click **Options** to display the Style Pane Options dialog box. Click **Select how list is sorted** (✲), click **Alphabetical**, and then click **OK**.

Save Formatting in a Style

In addition to the styles Word provides for you in the Styles gallery for headings, normal text, quotes, and more, you can easily create your own styles to store formatting information. Creating your own styles is particularly useful if you cannot find a built-in style that suits your needs.

You can create a new style by formatting text the way you want it to appear when you apply the style. You then use the example text to create the style and store it in the Styles gallery. You also can modify the style settings at the same time that you create the style.

Save Formatting in a Style

① Format text in your document using the formatting you want to save in a style.

② Select the text containing the formatting you want to save.

③ Click **Home**.

The Home tab appears.

④ In the Styles group, click **More** (▽).

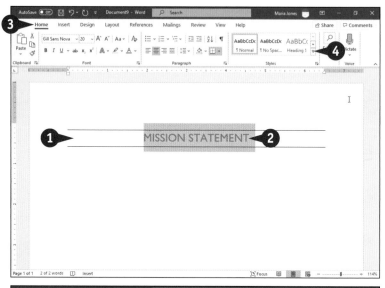

Ⓐ The Styles gallery appears.

⑤ Click **Create a Style**.

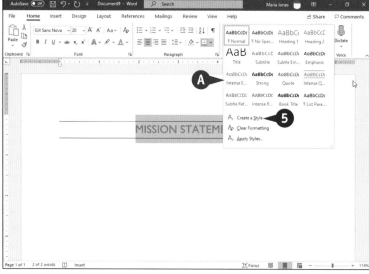

The Create New Style from Formatting dialog box opens.

6 Type a name for the style.

7 Click **Modify**.

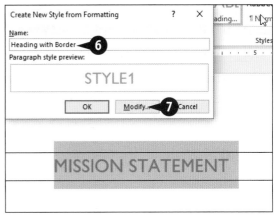

A larger version of the Create New Style from Formatting dialog box opens.

B You can click **Style for following paragraph** (⌄) and select the style for the following paragraph when you use the style you are creating.

C Use these options to select font formatting for the style.

D Use these options to set paragraph alignment, spacing, and indentation options.

E Click **New documents based on this template** (○ changes to ◉) to make your style available in new documents.

8 Click **OK**.

Word saves your newly created style.

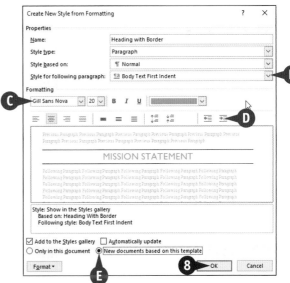

What happens if I click Format in the Create New Style from Formatting dialog box?
A menu appears that you can use to specify additional formatting. Select the type of formatting, and Word displays a dialog box where you can add more formatting characteristics to the style.

What does the Style Based On option do?
Every style you create is based on an existing Word style. Changing an existing style can result in many styles changing. For example, many styles are based on the Normal style. If you change the font of the Normal style, you change the font of all styles based on the Normal style.

If you format a document using heading styles, you can hide or display parts of the document's content by expanding or collapsing headings. Hiding or displaying content can be particularly helpful if you are working on a long, complicated document. For example, you can hide everything except the portion on which you want to focus your attention. If you send the document to others to review, you can help your reader avoid information overload if you display only the headings and let your reader expand the content of the headings of interest.

Expand or Collapse Document Content

1 In a document, apply heading styles such as Heading 1 or Heading 2.

2 Move the pointer (I) toward a heading.

A collapse button (◢) appears next to the heading.

3 Click ◢.

Ⓐ All text following the heading that is not styled as a heading disappears from view.

An expand button (▷) replaces 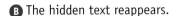.

④ Click ▷.

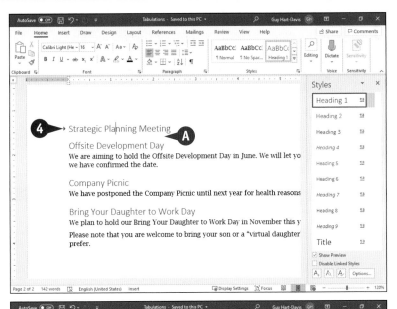

Ⓑ The hidden text reappears.

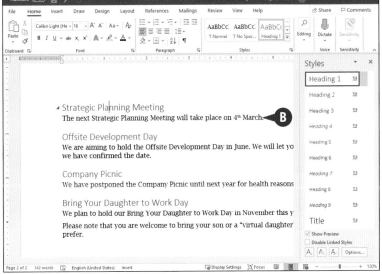

Modify a Style

You can modify any style to make it look the way you want. For example, you might want to change the font used for body text, or you might decide to add extra space before and after your Heading 1 paragraphs to give them some air.

When you change a style, you can add the style to the Styles gallery, and you can ensure that the style changes appear in new documents you create. You also can have Word update all the text in your document that currently uses the style you modify.

Modify a Style

1 Open a document containing the style you want to change.

2 Click **Home**.

The Home tab appears.

3 Click the dialog box launcher (⌐) in the Styles group to display the Styles pane.

4 Right-click the style you want to change.

5 Click **Modify**.

The Modify Style dialog box opens.

6 Make any changes needed. For example, use the controls in the Formatting section to make quick changes to font or paragraph settings.

7 Click **New documents based on this template** (○ changes to ◉).

8 Click **Add to the Styles gallery** (☐ changes to ☑).

9 Click **OK**.

The Modify Style dialog box closes.

Word updates all text in the document formatted with the style you changed.

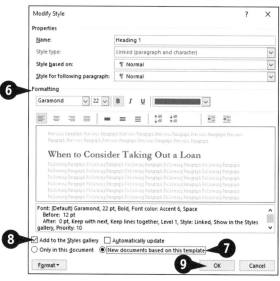

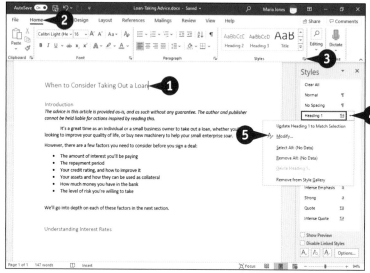

*S*hading is another technique you can use to draw your reader's attention. Shading appears on-screen and when you print your document; if you do not use a color printer, paragraph shading will be most effective if you select a shade of gray for your shading.

Add Paragraph Shading

1. Select the paragraph(s) that you want to shade.

2. Click **Home**.

   The Home tab appears.

3. Click ▼ to the right of **Borders** (⊞ ▾).

4. Click **Borders and Shading**.

   The Borders and Shading dialog box opens.

5. Click **Shading**.

   The Shading tab appears.

6. Click ▼.

7. Click a fill color.

8. Click **OK**.

9. Click anywhere outside the paragraph(s) you selected in step **1**.

Ⓐ Word shades the selection you made in step **1**.

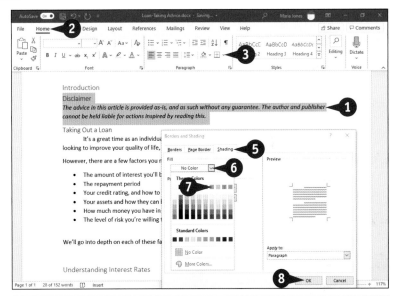

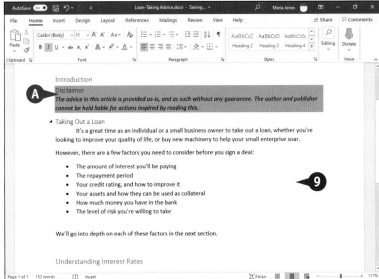

CHAPTER 7

Formatting Pages

Word provides a wide range of page formatting that you can use to make your documents look the way you want. In this chapter, you first learn to adjust margins, control text flow and pagination, and set page orientation. You then move on to adding page numbers, line numbers, headers and footers, and footnotes and endnotes. You finish by learning to create a table of contents, add a watermark or page border, and lay out a document in newspaper-style columns.

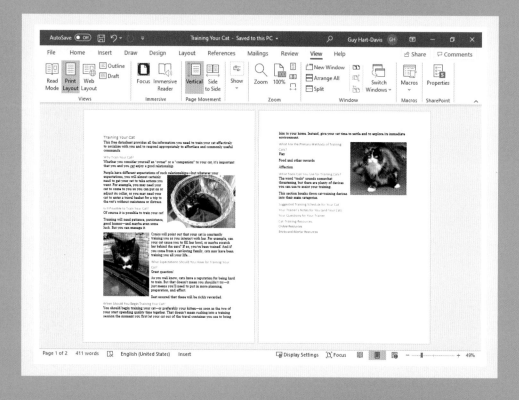

Adjust Margins

By default, Word assigns a 1-inch margin all the way around the page in every new document that you create. You can change these margin settings, as needed. For example, you can set narrower margins to fit more text on a page or set wider margins to fit less text on a page.

You can apply your changes to the current document only or set them as the new default setting, to be applied to all new Word documents you create.

Adjust Margins

Set Margins Using Layout Tools

1 Click anywhere in the document or section where you want to change margins.

2 Click **Layout**.

The Layout tab appears.

3 Click **Margins**.

Ⓐ The Margins gallery appears.

4 Click the margin setting you want.

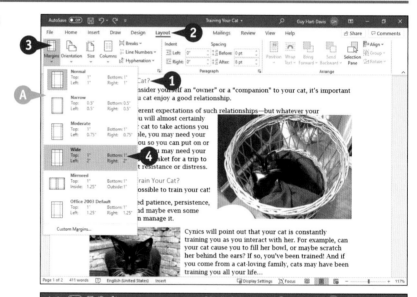

Ⓑ Word applies the new setting.

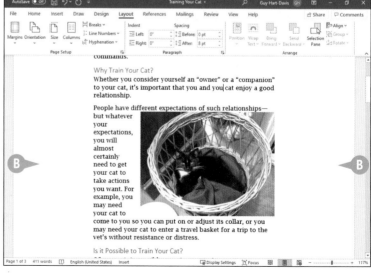

Set a Custom Margin

1. In the document or section you want to change, click **Layout**.

   The Layout tab appears.

2. Click **Margins**.

   Ⓒ The Margins gallery appears.

3. Click **Custom Margins**.

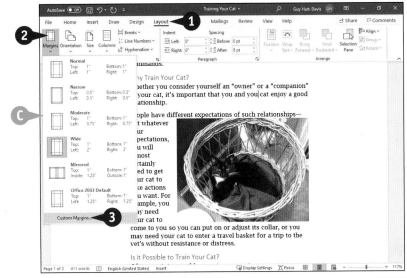

The Page Setup dialog box opens, displaying the Margins tab.

4. In the Margins area, enter a specific margin measurement in the **Top**, **Bottom**, **Left**, and **Right** boxes.

5. In the Orientation area, click **Portrait** or **Landscape** to set the page orientation.

6. Look at the Preview area to preview the margin settings.

7. Click **Apply to** (⌄), and then click **This section**, **This point forward**, or **Whole document**, as appropriate.

8. Click **OK**.

   The Page Setup dialog box closes.

   Word implements the margin settings you chose.

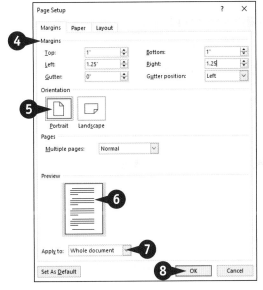

TIPS

How do I set new default margins?

To establish a different set of default margins for every new blank document that you create, make the desired changes on the Margins tab of the Page Setup dialog box, click **Set As Default**, and then click **OK**.

Why is my printer ignoring my margin settings?

Some printers have a minimum margin setting, and in most cases, that minimum margin is 0.25 inches. If you set your margins smaller than your printer's minimum margin setting, you place text in an unprintable area. Test the margins or check your printer documentation for more information.

Insert and Manage Page Breaks

ord automatically starts a new page when the current page becomes filled with text, but you can insert a page break to force Word to start a new page any place you want one. You can insert page breaks using the Ribbon or your keyboard.

You can insert a page break in any view except Read Mode view. Page breaks are visible in Print Layout view and, if you display formatting information as described in Chapter 6, "Formatting Paragraphs," page breaks are also visible in Draft, Web Layout, and Outline views.

Insert and Manage Page Breaks

Insert a Page Break

1 Click in the document where you want to insert a page break.

For example, place the insertion point before the paragraph you want to appear at the top of the new page.

2 Click **Insert**.

The Insert tab appears.

3 Click **Pages**.

The Pages pop-up panel opens.

4 Click **Page Break**.

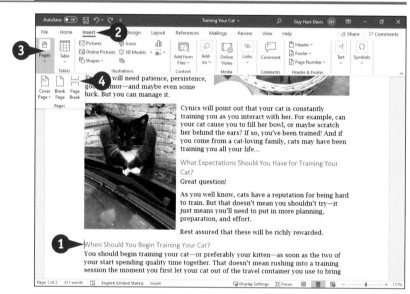

A Word inserts a page break and moves all text after the page break onto a new page.

B If you want to see more of the document's content at once in Print Layout view, move the pointer over the gray horizontal bar between the pages (➟ or I changes to ⬌), and then double-click. Word reduces the white space to a minimum and displays a gray bar between the pages; you can double-click this bar to restore the white space.

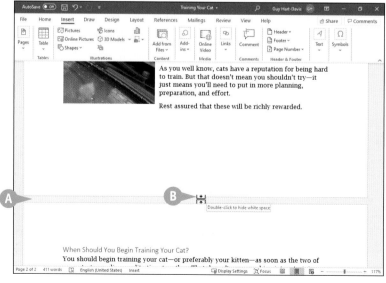

View and Delete Page Breaks

1 Click **Home**.

The Home tab appears.

2 Click **Show/Hide** (¶) to display formatting information.

3 Click **View**.

The View tab appears.

4 Click **Draft**.

The document appears in Draft view.

5 Select the page break.

6 Press Del.

Word deletes the page break.

C A dotted line shows where the automatic page break will fall using the document's current pagination.

Note: You can insert a page break from the keyboard by pressing Ctrl + Enter.

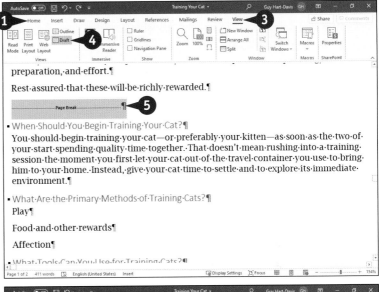

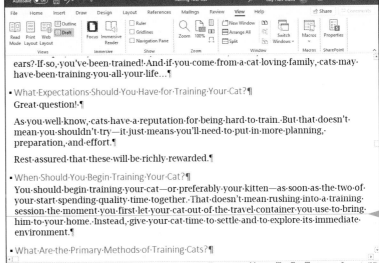

Why does Word put a Heading 1 paragraph at the top of a new page? There is no manual page break.
Most likely, the style has the Page Break Before setting enabled; another possibility is that the Keep with Next setting is enabled. See the following section, "Control Text Flow and Pagination," for details.

You can fix this problem for a single paragraph by opening the Paragraph dialog box and changing the Page Break Before setting or the Keep with Next setting on the Line and Page Breaks tab. If the problem is in the style, you must change the setting in the style. For example, you can make the change in the Paragraph dialog box, and then update the style.

Control Text Flow and Pagination

Y̲ou can configure several settings that influence where Word places page breaks. Used the right way, these settings can improve the document's layout and readability; used incorrectly, they can produce bizarre-looking layout problems.

You can eliminate widows and orphans. You can set Word to keep all the lines of a paragraph together on the same page. Similarly, you can mark a paragraph to be kept with the next paragraph. You can also set Word to insert a page break before a particular paragraph.

Control Text Flow and Pagination

1 Click in the paragraph whose flow and pagination you want to affect, or select multiple paragraphs.

This example uses a six-line paragraph of body text that is currently split across pages.

2 Click **Home**.

The Home tab appears.

3 Click the Paragraph group dialog box launcher (⌐🔲).

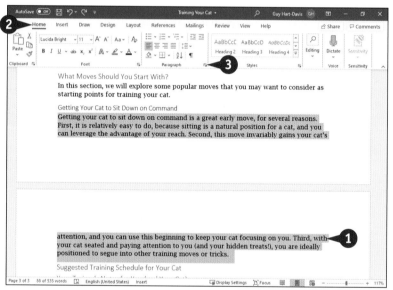

The Paragraph dialog box opens.

4 Click **Line and Page Breaks**.

The Line and Page Breaks tab appears.

A For typical body text styles, select **Widow/Orphan control** (☑) to prevent widow and orphan lines, discussed in the tips.

5 Click **Keep lines together** (☐ changes to ☑).

6 Click **OK**.

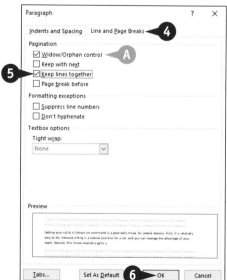

The Paragraph dialog box closes.

Ⓑ All the lines in the paragraph appear together.

Ⓒ However, the heading is now separated from the paragraph. Such separation is unhelpful to readers and gives designers and proofreaders conniptions.

⑦ Click anywhere in the heading paragraph.

⑧ Click the Paragraph group dialog box launcher (🔽).

The Paragraph dialog box opens again, now with the Line and Page Breaks tab at the front, because you used that tab last.

⑨ Click **Keep with next** (☐ changes to ☑).

⑩ Click **OK**.

The Paragraph dialog box closes again.

Ⓓ The heading paragraph appears with its text.

Note: A more direct method of controlling text flow and pagination is by inserting extra paragraphs to move lines or paragraphs from one page to another. The disadvantage to this approach is that, if you add or delete text early in the document, you may need to adjust all subsequent page breaks manually.

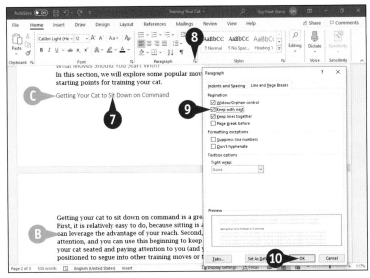

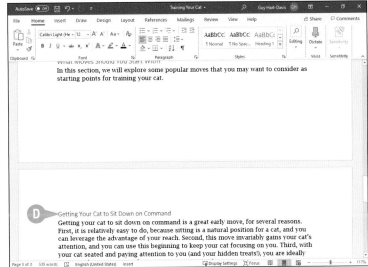

What is a widow?

A *widow* is the first line of a paragraph that appears at the bottom of a page, with the paragraph's remaining lines appearing on the next page. Widows are distracting to reading comprehension.

What is an orphan?

An *orphan* is the last line of a paragraph that appears on its own at the top of a new page, with all the paragraph's preceding lines appearing at the bottom of the previous page. Like widows, orphans are distracting to reading comprehension.

Align Text Vertically on the Page

You can control the vertical alignment of text between the top and bottom margins of a page. For example, you might want to center text vertically on a report cover page to improve its appearance.

By default, Word applies vertical alignment to your entire document, but you can limit the alignment by using sections. For example, before vertically centering the cover page of a report, put that page in its own section so that you do not vertically center the other pages too. See the section "Insert a Section Break," later in this chapter, for more information.

Align Text Vertically on the Page

1 After creating a separate section for the page you want to align, click anywhere on that page.

2 Click **Layout**.

The Layout tab appears.

3 Click the Page Setup group dialog box launcher (🖪).

The Page Setup dialog box opens.

4 Click **Layout**.

The Layout tab of the Page Setup dialog box appears.

5 Click **Vertical alignment** (∨), and then click the vertical alignment—for example, **Center**.

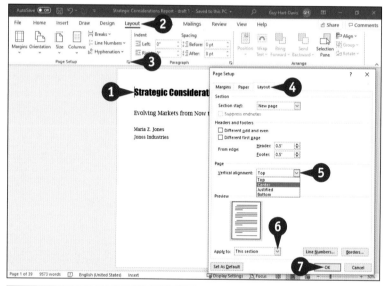

6 To make the change only for the current section, click **Apply to** (∨), and then click **This section**.

7 Click **OK**.

The Page Setup dialog box closes.

A Word applies vertical alignment.

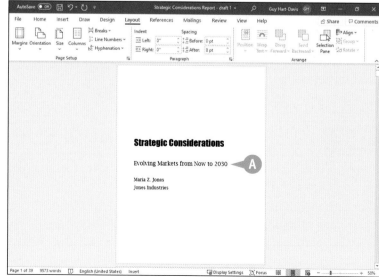

Change Page Orientation

You can change the direction that text prints from the standard portrait orientation, in which the page is taller than it is wide, to landscape orientation, in which the page is wider than it is tall. Changing orientation is particularly helpful on pages containing wide tables, where using landscape orientation may help you fit the table's full width on a single page.

Change Page Orientation

Note: To change the page orientation of a single page in a multipage document, first insert a Next Page section break before and after the page.

1. Click anywhere on the page whose orientation you want to change.

Note: If you want to change the orientation of the entire document, click anywhere in it.

2. Click **Layout**.

   The Layout tab appears.

3. Click **Orientation**.

   The Orientation pop-up panel opens.

A. The icon for the current orientation appears highlighted.

4. Click **Portrait** or **Landscape**, as appropriate. This example uses **Landscape**.

B. Word changes the orientation.

Note: By default, Word changes the orientation for the entire document. To limit orientation changes, divide the document into sections. See the next section, "Insert a Section Break."

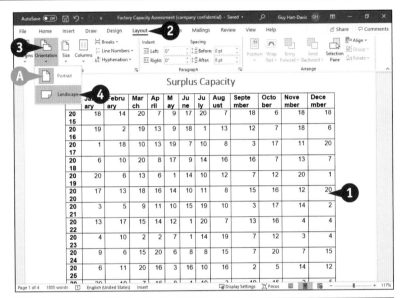

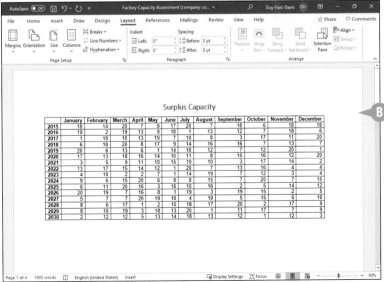

Insert a Section Break

You can create separate sections in a document to implement different page layouts. You use sections for formatting changes such as margins, headers and footers, newspaper-style columns, and vertical page alignment. For example, if a document includes both a one-column layout and a three-column layout, you need to create a separate section for each layout.

To create a section, you insert a section break of the appropriate type: Continuous, Next Page, Even Page, or Odd Page.

Insert a Section Break

1 Click in the location where you want to start a new section in your document.

2 Click **Layout**.

The Layout tab appears.

3 Click **Breaks**.

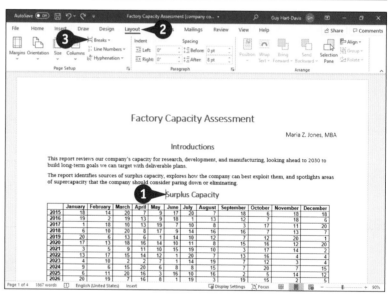

A The Breaks gallery appears, showing the Page Breaks list and the Section Breaks list.

4 Click the type of section break you want to insert. This example uses **Next Page**.

Word inserts the type of break you selected.

Ⓑ In this example, Word inserts a Next Page section break, which effectively adds a page break.

Note: In the example, the document is in Print Layout view, but the white space between pages has been hidden by double-clicking the gray bar between them.

⑤ Click **Home**.

The Home tab appears.

⑥ Click **Show/Hide** (¶).

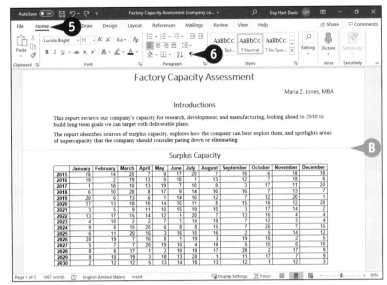

Word displays nonprinting characters, also called formatting marks.

Ⓒ The Section Break (Next Page) divider appears.

Ⓓ You can now implement different layouts in the different sections. In this example, the first section is in portrait orientation, whereas the second section is in landscape orientation.

Note: You can remove the section break by clicking the section break line and pressing Delete.

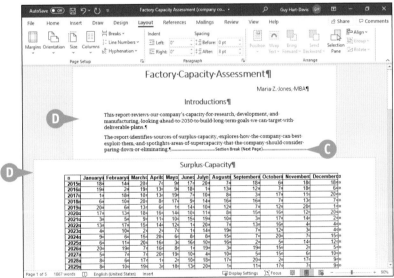

TIP

How do the four types of section breaks work?

After a Continuous section break, the document continues on the same page. For example, a page might have a single-column paragraph, then a Continuous section break, then a three-column section, and then another Continuous section break before resuming as a single column.

After a Next Page section break, the document continues on the next page. After an Even Page section break, the document continues on the next even page, leaving a blank odd page if necessary. Similarly, after an Odd Page section break, the document continues on the next odd page, leaving a blank even page if necessary.

Add Page Numbers to a Document

You can add page numbers to make your documents more navigable. You can add page numbers to the header or footer area at the top or bottom of a page or in the page margins, or you can add a single page number at the current position of the insertion point.

Page numbers in headers and footers appear on-screen only in Print Layout view. Read Mode view displays a single page number at the current position of the insertion point. Word updates page numbers automatically as you change your document.

Add Page Numbers to a Document

Note: To place a single page number at a specific location in the document, click that location.

1 Click **Insert**.

The Insert tab appears.

2 Click **Page Number** in the Header & Footer group.

Ⓐ The Page Number pop-up panel opens.

3 Click a placement option. This example uses **Top of Page**.

Note: If you choose **Current Position**, Word inserts a page number only at the current location of the insertion point.

Ⓑ A gallery of page number alignment and formatting options for that placement option appears.

4 Click the page number type you want.

Ⓒ The page number appears in the location and using the formatting you selected.

Ⓓ For page numbers placed anywhere except at the current position of the insertion point, Word opens the header pane or footer pane.

Ⓔ The Header & Footer tab appears on the Ribbon.

Ⓕ If you do not see the page number, click **Print Layout** (▤) on the status bar to display the document in Print Layout view.

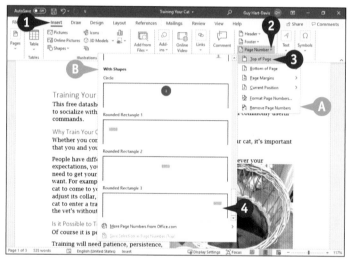

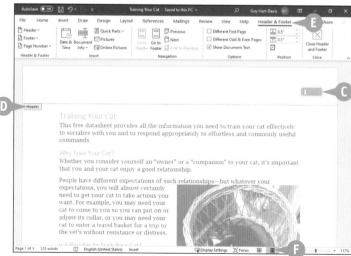

5 To control the way the page number appears, click **Page Number**.

The Page Number pop-up menu opens.

6 Click **Format Page Numbers**.

The Page Number Format dialog box opens.

7 To include a chapter number, click **Include chapter number** (☐ changes to ☑). Click **Chapter starts with style** (⌄), and then click the appropriate style. Click **Use separator** (⌄), and then click the appropriate separator.

8 In the Page Numbering area, click **Continue from previous section** (○ changes to ◉); or click **Start at** (○ changes to ◉), and then enter the starting number.

9 Click **OK**.

The Page Number Format dialog box closes.

10 Click **Close Header and Footer**.

The header and footer pane closes.

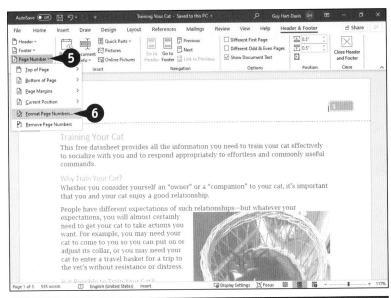

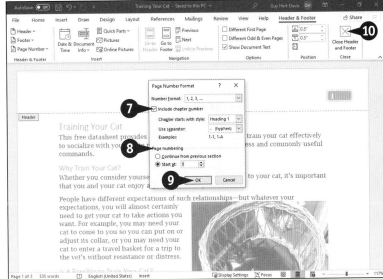

What does the Number Format pop-up menu in the Page Number Format dialog box do?
The Number Format pop-up menu enables you to change the numbering format from the default "1, 2, 3" format to a different format, such as "a, b, c" or "i, ii, iii". For example, you might choose the "i, ii, iii" format for the front matter in a book, before the main page numbering starts.

Add Line Numbers to a Document

You can add the line number to the left end of every line of your document. Line numbers are particularly useful for reviewing and reference, especially if you share hard copies of the documents. You can number lines continuously, have numbering restart on each page or at each new section, or suppress line numbers for selected paragraphs. Line numbers appear on-screen only in Print Layout view.

By default, line numbers appear beside every line in your document, but using line numbering options, you can display lines at intervals you establish.

Add Line Numbers to a Document

Add Line Numbers

1 Click **Print Layout** (📄).

Word displays the document in Print Layout view.

2 Click **Layout**.

The Layout tab appears.

3 Click **Line Numbers**.

The Line Numbers pop-up panel opens.

4 Click the line numbering option type you want to use. This example uses **Continuous**.

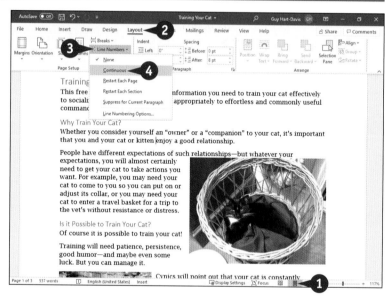

A Word assigns a line number to each line of your document.

Note: To remove line numbers, click **Layout** to display the Layout tab, click **Line Numbers** to open the Line Numbers pop-up panel, and then click **None**.

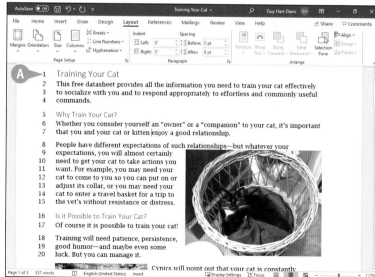

Number in Unusual Increments

1 With the document in Print Layout view, click **Layout**.

The Layout tab appears.

2 Click **Line Numbers**.

The Line Numbers pop-up panel opens.

3 Click **Line Numbering Options**.

The Page Setup dialog box opens, displaying the Layout tab.

4 Click **Line Numbers**.

The Line Numbers dialog box opens.

5 Click **Count by** and enter the increment you want to use.

6 Click **OK**.

The Line Numbers dialog box closes.

7 Click **OK**.

The Page Setup dialog box closes.

B Line numbers in the increment you selected appear on-screen.

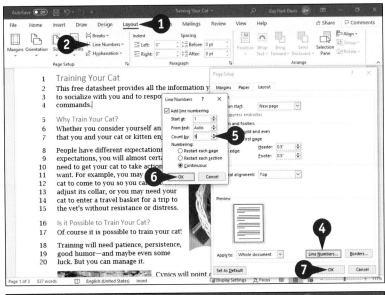

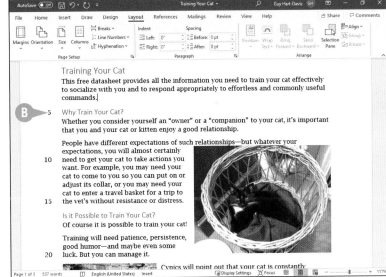

How can I skip numbering certain lines?

To skip numbering certain lines, such as a page title or introductory text, select the paragraphs for which you do not want to display line numbers. Click **Layout** to display the Layout tab, and then click **Line Numbers**. In the Line Numbers pop-up panel, click **Suppress for Current Paragraph**. Word removes line numbers from the selected paragraph or paragraphs and renumbers subsequent lines.

Using the Building Blocks Organizer

Building blocks are preformatted document components that you can add to quickly build your documents. Some building blocks appear by default as gallery options in Word. Many building blocks provide placeholder text that you replace to customize the building block in your document.

Word organizes building blocks into different galleries, such as cover pages, headers, footers, tables, and text boxes, so that you can sort the building blocks by gallery to easily find something to suit your needs. This section adds a text box building block to a document.

Using the Building Blocks Organizer

1 Open a document to which you want to add a building block.

Note: Depending on the type of building block you intend to use, you may need to position the insertion point where you want the building block to appear.

2 Click **Insert**.

The Insert tab appears.

3 Click **Text**.

The Text pop-up panel opens.

4 Click **Quick Parts** (▣ ▾).

The Quick Parts pop-up panel opens.

5 Click **Building Blocks Organizer**.

The Building Blocks Organizer dialog box opens.

Ⓐ The Building Blocks list shows the available building blocks.

Ⓑ The preview of the selected building block appears here.

6 Click the column heading by which you want to sort the building blocks. For example, click **Gallery** to sort to the building blocks by categories, such as Headers, Tables, and Text Boxes.

7 Click the building block you want to insert.

8 Click **Insert**.

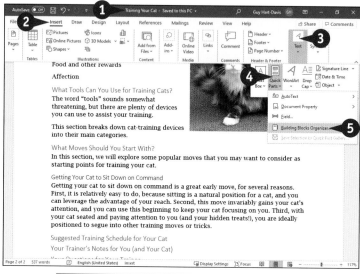

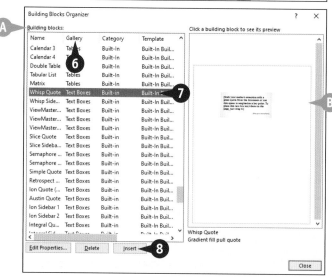

The Building Blocks Organizer dialog box closes.

C The building block appears in your document.

9 If necessary, drag the building block to where you want it to appear.

10 Click in the building block.

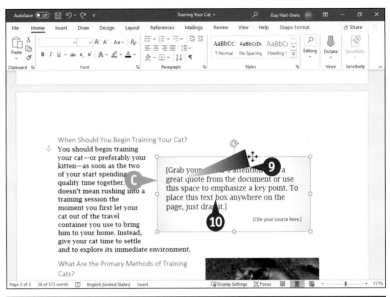

11 Fill in any information needed. For example, in a text box, replace the placeholder text with your text.

12 Click outside the building block to deselect it and continue working.

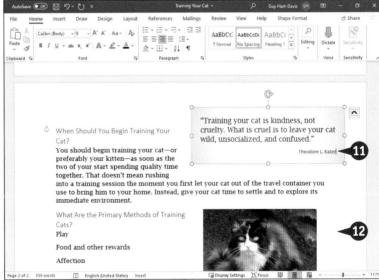

TIP

How do I know where in my document Word will insert a building block?
Word places a building block in your document based on the building block's properties. In the Building Blocks Organizer window, click a building block, and then click **Edit Properties** to display the Modify Building Block dialog box. To control where a building block will appear in the document, click the building block, click **Options** (⌄), and then click **Insert content only**, **Insert content in its own paragraph**, or **Insert content in its own page**, as needed.

Add a Header or Footer

Word's headers and footers make it easy to include text at the top or bottom of every page. Header text appears at the top of the page above the margin; footer text appears at the bottom of the page below the margin.

To view or edit the header or footer, you use Print Layout view. You can click **Print Layout** (▤) on the status bar to switch to Print Layout view manually. If you give a header or footer command, Word automatically switches the document to Print Layout view if it is in another view.

Add a Header or Footer

1 Optionally, click **Print Layout** (▤).

Word switches the document to Print Layout view.

Note: You do not have to switch to Print Layout view, but doing so makes it easier to see your work in the header or footer.

2 Click **Insert**.

The Insert tab appears.

3 Click the **Header** button to add a header, or click the **Footer** button to add a footer.

This example adds a header.

Ⓐ The header or footer gallery appears.

4 Click the header or footer style you want to use.

Ⓑ Word adds the header or footer.

Ⓒ The Header & Footer Tools tab appears on the Ribbon.

Ⓓ The text in your document appears dimmed.

Ⓔ The insertion point appears in the header area.

Ⓕ Some headers and footers, like the one shown here, contain placeholders and controls for adding information.

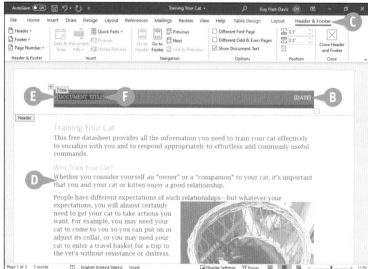

5 Click or select a placeholder or a control, and then enter the information needed for the header or footer.

G For a control such as a date picker, click the control, and then click the appropriate information.

6 Click **Close Header and Footer**.

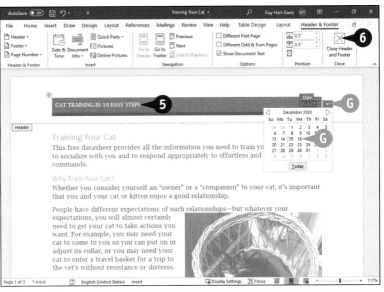

Word closes the header and footer areas.

H The header or footer appears in the document. It is dimmed to indicate that you need to open the header or footer area to edit it.

Note: To open a header or footer for editing, double-click in it. Alternatively, click **Insert** on the Ribbon to display the Insert tab; click **Header** or **Footer**, as appropriate; and then click **Edit Header** or **Edit Footer** on the pop-up panel.

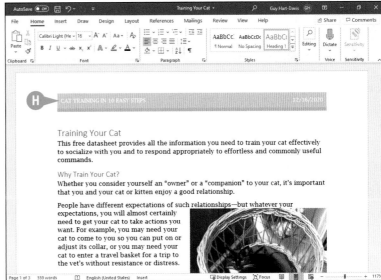

TIPS

Can I format text in a header or footer?
Yes. You can apply boldface, italics, underlining, and other character formatting the same way that you apply them in the body of a document, and you can use styles. Also, the header area and footer area each contain two predefined tabs so that you can center or right-align text you type.

How do I remove a header or footer?
Click the **Insert** tab, click the **Header** or **Footer** button, and then click **Remove Header** or **Remove Footer**. Word removes the header or footer from your document.

Vary Headers or Footers Within a Document

You can use different headers or footers in different portions of your document. For example, suppose that you are preparing a business plan and you intend to divide it into chapters. You could create separate headers or footers for each chapter.

If you plan to use more than one header or footer in your document, insert section breaks before you begin. See the section "Insert a Section Break," earlier in this chapter, for details.

Vary Headers or Footers Within a Document

1 Click in the first section for which you want to create a header.

2 Click **Insert**.

The Insert tab appears.

3 Click **Header**.

The Header gallery appears.

4 Click a header.

A Word inserts the header in the First Page Header-Section 1 box.

B The text in your document appears dimmed.

The insertion point appears in the header.

C To make all headers for a section the same, you can click **Different First Page** (☑ changes to ☐).

Note: This example uses different first page headers.

5 Type any necessary text in the header.

6 Click **Next** to move the insertion point to the next page of the first section, Header-Section 1.

7 Click **Next** again.

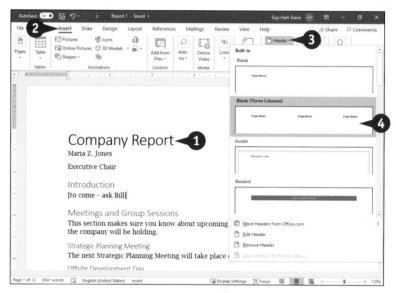

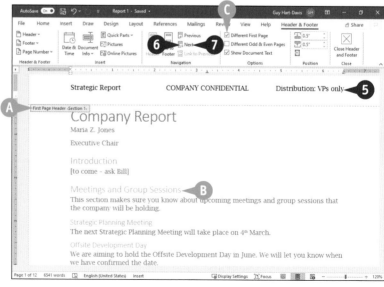

D Word moves the insertion point into the header for Section 2.

E The Header-Section 2 box appears.

F Word identifies the header or footer as "Same as Previous."

Click Link to Previous to deselect it and unlink the headers of the two sections.

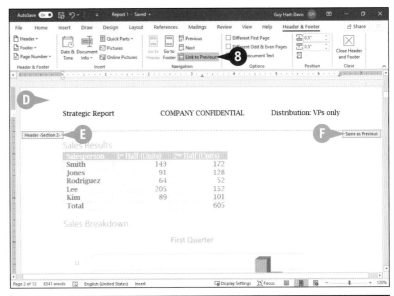

G Word removes the "Same as Previous" marking from the right side of the header box.

8 Either repeat steps **2** to **5** to insert a new header in the second section, or create a new header manually.

9 Repeat these steps for each section for which you want a different header.

10 Click **Close Header and Footer**.

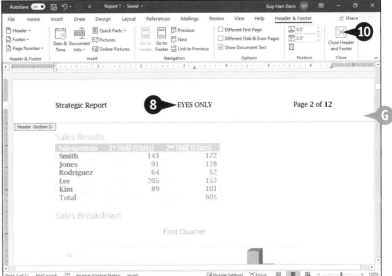

TIP

How do I create different headers or footers for odd or even pages?

Open the header or footer area of the document. Then, on the Header & Footer tab, click **Different Odd & Even Pages**. Each header or footer box is renamed to Odd Page or Even Page. Click **Next** to display the Even Page Header box or the Even Page Footer box and type text.

You do not need to create separate sections to have different headers and footers on odd and even pages. However, if you want the headers or footers on odd pages or even pages to change through the document, you do need to create sections.

Add a Footnote

You can include footnotes in your document to identify sources or references to other materials or to add explanatory information. When you add a footnote, a small superscript number appears alongside the associated text, and footnote text appears at the bottom of a page. As you add, delete, and move text in your document, Word also adds, deletes, moves, or renumbers associated footnotes.

Footnotes appear within your document in Print Layout view and Read Mode view. Footnote references appear in the body of your document in all views.

Add a Footnote

1 Click where you want to insert the footnote reference.

2 Click **References**.

The References tab appears.

3 Click **Insert Footnote**.

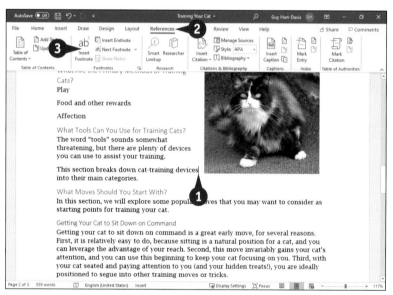

A Word displays the footnote number in the body of the document and in the note at the bottom of the current page.

4 Type the footnote text.

5 Double-click the footnote number in the footnote area.

Word returns the insertion point to where you inserted the footnote.

Note: You can also press Shift + F5 to return the insertion point to where you inserted the footnote.

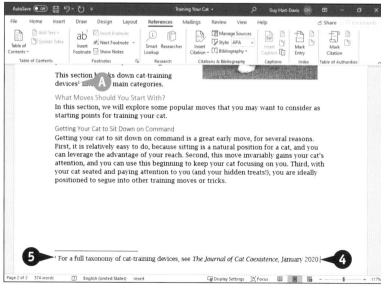

Add an Endnote

An *endnote* is similar to a footnote, but it appears at the end of the section, or at the end of the document, rather than at the bottom of the page. You can include endnotes in your document to identify sources or references to other materials or to add explanatory information.

Word automatically numbers endnotes i, ii, iii, and so on, and deletes, moves, or renumbers any associated endnotes as you add, delete, and move text in your document.

Add an Endnote

1 Click where you want to insert the endnote reference.

A In this example, the endnote number appears on page 1.

2 Click **References**.

The References tab appears.

3 Click **Insert Endnote**.

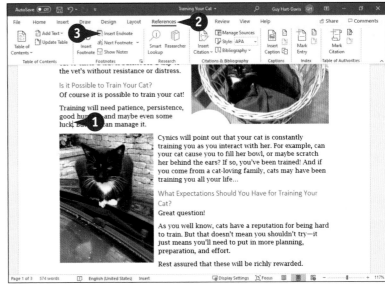

Word inserts the endnote number in the body of your document.

B Word inserts the endnote number at the end of the section or the document and displays the insertion point in the endnote area at the bottom of the last page of the section or document.

4 Type your endnote text.

5 Double-click the endnote number to return the insertion point to the place in your document where you inserted the endnote. Alternatively, press Shift + F5.

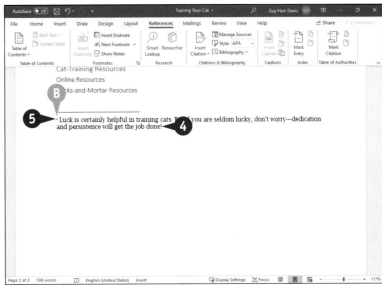

Find, Edit, or Delete Footnotes or Endnotes

On the References tab of the Ribbon, Word provides tools that enable you to quickly locate the footnotes and endnotes in your documents. You can either move quickly through the footnote references or endnote references in the document, or display the footnote area or endnote area to work directly with the notes.

As you delete or rearrange footnotes or endnotes, Word automatically renumbers the remaining ones for you, so you do not need to change them manually.

Find, Edit, or Delete Footnotes or Endnotes

Find Footnotes or Endnotes

1 Press Ctrl+Home to move the insertion point to the top of the document.

2 Click **References**.

The References tab appears.

Ⓐ To find the next footnote, you can click **Next Footnote**.

3 Click ⌄ to the right of **Next Footnote**.

4 Click **Next Footnote**, **Previous Footnote**, **Next Endnote**, or **Previous Endnote**, as needed.

Word moves the insertion point to the reference number of the next note or previous note.

Edit Footnotes or Endnotes

Note: To easily edit endnotes at the end of a document, skip steps **1** and **2**. Instead, press Ctrl+End to move the insertion point to the end of the document.

1 Select the footnote reference number in your document.

2 Double-click the selection.

Ⓑ In Print Layout view, Word moves the insertion point into the footnote.

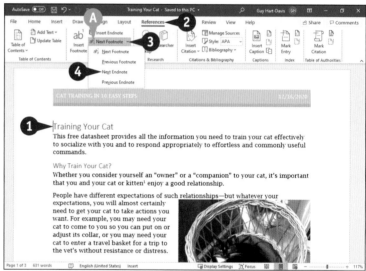

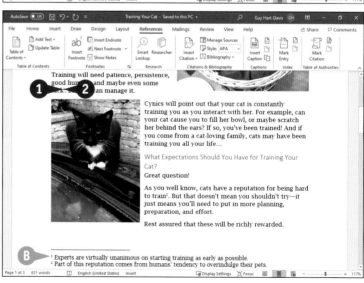

C In Draft view, Word displays footnotes in the Footnotes pane.

3 Edit the text of the note as needed.

4 In Draft view, click **Close** (✕) when you finish editing.

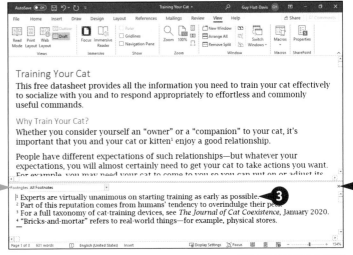

Delete a Footnote or Endnote

1 Select the reference number of the footnote or endnote you want to delete.

2 Press Delete.

Word removes the footnote or endnote number and related information from the document and automatically renumbers subsequent footnotes or endnotes.

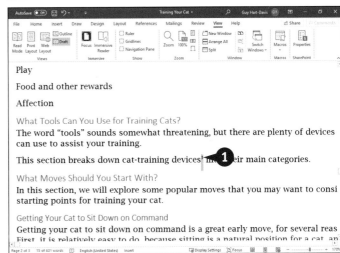

TIP

Can I print endnotes on a separate page?
Yes. Click in your document before the first endnote. Click **Insert** to display the Insert tab of the Ribbon, and then click **Page Break**. Word inserts a page break immediately before the endnotes, placing them on a separate page at the end of your document.

Convert Footnotes to Endnotes or Vice Versa

You can convert endnotes to footnotes or footnotes to endnotes without having to reenter them. Being able to convert each type of note to the other type enables you to try one type of note and then switch easily to the other type.

If your document contains both footnotes and endnotes, you can swap the two, switching footnotes to endnotes and endnotes to footnotes in a single move.

Convert Footnotes to Endnotes or Vice Versa

1 Click **References**.

The References tab appears.

2 Click the Footnotes group dialog box launcher (⌐⌐).

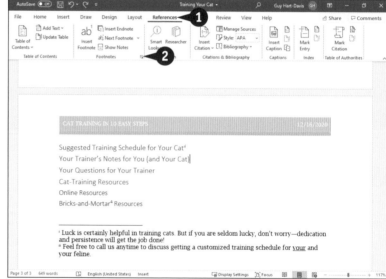

The Footnote and Endnote dialog box opens.

3 Click **Convert**.

The Convert Notes dialog box opens.

4 Click **Convert all footnotes to endnotes** (○ changes to ◉), **Convert all endnotes to footnotes** (○ changes to ◉), or **Swap footnotes and endnotes** (○ changes to ◉).

5 Click **OK**.

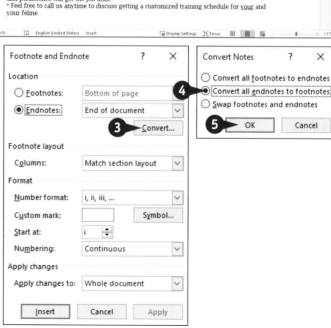

The Convert Notes dialog box closes, returning you to the Footnote and Endnote dialog box.

6 Click **Close**.

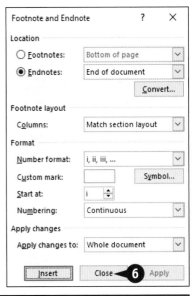

The Footnote and Endnote dialog box closes.

Ⓐ Word makes the conversion and renumbers footnotes and endnotes appropriately.

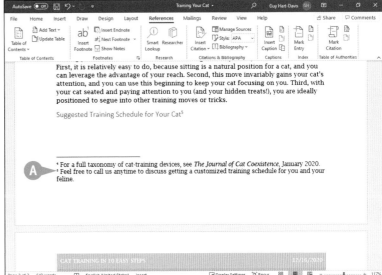

Generate a Table of Contents

You can use Word to generate a table of contents, or TOC, for your document that automatically updates as you change your document. You select from Word's gallery of TOC styles to establish the TOC's look and feel. You can most easily create a TOC if you apply heading styles—such as Heading 1, Heading 2, and Heading 3—to the paragraphs that should appear in the TOC, but you can include other styles if you want.

Once you have created a table of contents, you can update it whenever you need to.

Generate a Table of Contents

Insert a Table of Contents

1 Position the insertion point where you want the table of contents to appear.

2 Click **References**.

The References tab appears.

3 Click **Table of Contents**.

The Table of Contents gallery appears.

4 Click the table of contents layout you want.

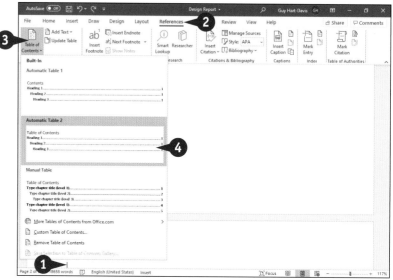

A Word inserts a table of contents at the location of the insertion point.

The information in the table of contents comes from text to which Heading styles 1, 2, and 3 are applied.

You can continue working in your document, adding new text styled with heading styles.

Note: Do not type directly in the table of contents; make corrections in the document.

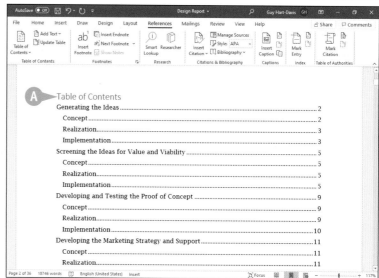

Update the Table of Contents

1 Click anywhere in the table of contents.

An outline appears around the table of contents, with two buttons on a panel at the top.

2 Click **Update Table**.

The Update Table of Contents dialog box opens.

3 Select **Update entire table** (○ changes to ◉).

4 Click **OK**.

Word updates the table of contents with the latest headings and page numbers.

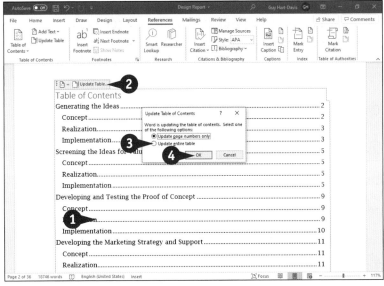

Create a Custom Table of Contents

1 On the References tab, click **Table of Contents**.

The Table of Contents gallery appears.

2 Click **Custom Table of Contents**.

The Table of Contents dialog box opens.

3 Click **Show levels** (⬍) to change the number of heading styles included in the table of contents.

B To include other styles, click **Options**.

4 Click **OK**.

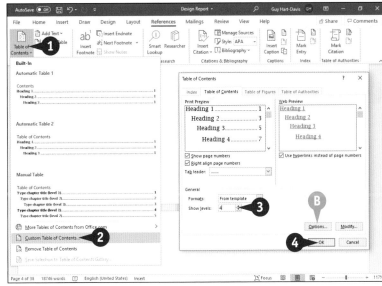

TIP

How do I remove a table of contents?
Click **References** to display the References tab of the Ribbon, go to the Table of Contents group, click **Table of Contents**, and then click **Remove Table of Contents** in the Table of Contents gallery.

Add a Watermark

You can add a watermark to your document to add interest or convey a message. A watermark is faint text or a picture that appears behind information in a document. For example, you can place a watermark on a document that marks it as a draft, as a copy, as confidential, or as urgent.

Watermarks are visible in Print Layout view, on printouts, and on PDF and XPS documents.

Add a Watermark

1 Click **Print Layout** (▤).

The document appears in Print Layout view.

2 Click **Design**.

The Design tab appears.

3 Click **Watermark**.

The Watermark gallery opens.

Ⓐ If you see a suitable watermark, click it and skip the remaining steps.

4 Click **Custom Watermark**.

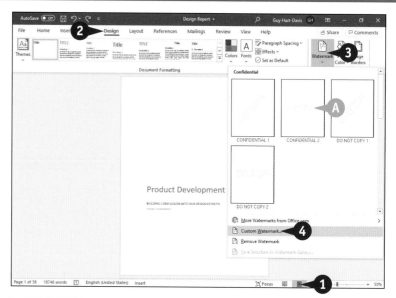

The Printed Watermark dialog box opens.

5 Select **Text watermark** (○ changes to ◉).

6 Click **Text** (⌄) and either select predefined text to use as a watermark or type your own text.

7 Click **Apply**.

Ⓑ The watermark appears in the document.

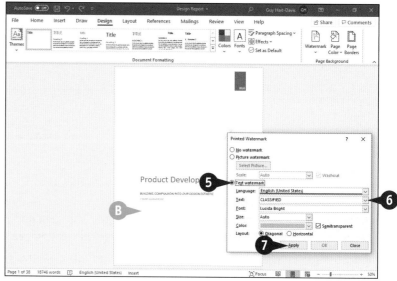

8 Make further changes as needed.

C For example, click **Color** (⌄), and then click the color to use for the watermark.

D Usually, it is best to select (☑) **Semitransparent**; if you deselect this check box, the watermark may overpower the document's contents.

9 Click **OK** if you have not yet clicked Apply to apply your changes; otherwise, click **Close**.

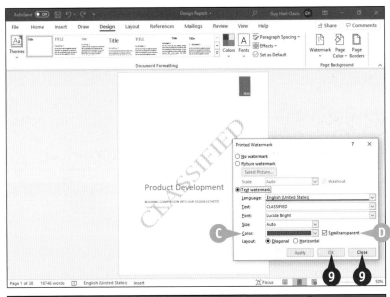

The Printed Watermark dialog box closes.

E The watermark appears on each page of your document.

TIP

How do I remove a watermark from a document?

Click **Design** to display the Design tab on the Ribbon, and then go to the Page Background group. Click **Watermark** to display the Watermark gallery, and then click **Remove Watermark**.

If you want to replace the existing watermark with another watermark, you do not need to remove the existing watermark first. Simply insert the new watermark, replacing the existing watermark.

Add a Page Border

You can add a border around each page of your document to add interest or make the document aesthetically appealing. You also can add borders around single or multiple paragraphs, as described in Chapter 6, but be aware that multiple borders can make your document hard to read. For example, do not use both paragraph and page borders.

You can apply one of Word's predesigned borders to your document, or you can create your own custom border—for example, bordering only the top and bottom of each page.

Add a Page Border

1 Click **Print Layout** (▤) to display your document in Print Layout view.

2 Click **Design**.

The Design tab appears.

3 Click **Page Borders**.

The Borders and Shading dialog box opens, displaying the Page Border tab.

4 Click the type of border you want to add to your document.

5 Click a style for the border line.

A The Preview area shows a preview of the border.

6 Click **Color** (⌄), and then click the color for the border.

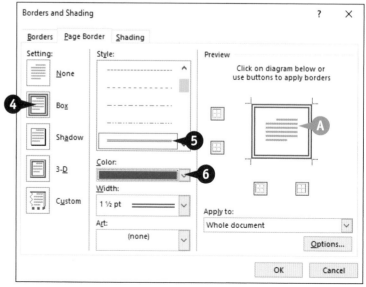

⑦ Click **Width** (⌄), and then click the width for the border.

⑧ Click **Apply to** (⌄), and then click an option to specify the pages on which the border should appear. For example, click **Whole document** to apply the border to every page.

⑨ Click **OK**.

Ⓑ Word applies the border you specified.

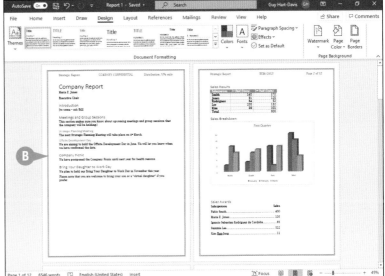

TIP

How do I add a border that does not surround the page?
Open the Borders and Shading dialog box, and then use the controls on the Page Border tab to specify the border type you want to apply. In the Preview area, click the border lines that you do not want to appear in your document. Click **OK** to close the Borders and Shading dialog box.

Apply Document Themes and Style Sets

You can give a professional look to a document using document formatting. You can apply a document *theme*, which consists of a set of theme colors that affect fonts, lines, and fill effects. Applying a theme to a document is a quick way to add polish to it. And once you apply a theme, you also can apply *style sets*, which vary the fonts.

The effect of applying a theme is more obvious if you have assigned styles such as headings to your document. The effects of themes are even more pronounced when you assign a background color to a page.

Apply Document Themes and Style Sets

Apply a Theme

1 Click **Design**.

The Design tab appears.

2 Click **Themes**.

The Themes gallery opens.

3 Move the pointer over a theme.

Live Preview shows you how the document would look using that theme.

4 Click a theme.

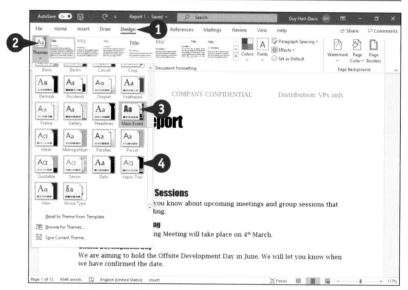

Ⓐ Your document appears using the theme you selected.

Apply a Style Set

1 Click **Design**.

The Design tab appears.

2 Move the pointer (⟈) over various style sets.

Live Preview shows you how the document would look using that style set.

3 Click a style set.

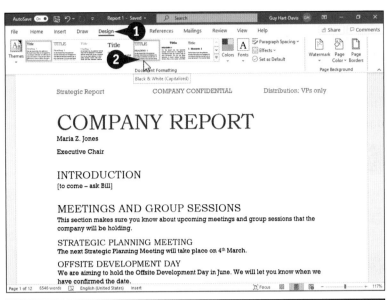

B Your document appears using the style set you selected.

How can I make the effects of my theme more obvious?

The effects of applying a theme become more obvious if you have applied heading styles and a background color to your document. To apply a background color, click **Design** to display the Design tab, click **Page Color**, and click a color in the palette. Word applies the color you selected to the background of the page. For help applying a style, see Chapter 6.

Create Newspaper-Style Columns

Word enables you to create columns like those used in newspapers or magazines, in which text runs from top to bottom of one column and then continues at the top of the next column to the right. Newspaper-style columns can be good for publications such as newsletters or brochures.

Word provides preset column formats that enable you to create a columnar document quickly. For greater control, you can create custom columns, choosing the number of columns you want to create in your document, indicating the width of each column, and more.

Create Newspaper-Style Columns

Create Quick Columns

1 Select the paragraphs you want to turn into multiple columns.

Note: If you want to apply columns to the whole document, click anywhere in it.

2 Click **Layout**.

The Layout tab appears.

3 Click **Columns**.

The Columns pop-up panel appears.

4 Click the number of columns that you want to assign.

Word displays the selected part of your document in that number of columns.

A When you apply multiple columns to part of a document, Word automatically inserts a Continuous section break before and after that part, isolating it in its own section.

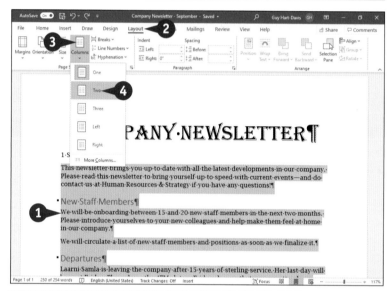

Create Custom Columns

1 Select the paragraphs you want to turn into multiple columns.

Note: If you want to apply columns to the whole document, click anywhere in it.

2 Click **Layout**.

The Layout tab appears.

3 Click **Columns**.

The Columns pop-up panel appears.

4 Click **More Columns**.

The Columns dialog box opens.

5 Click **Number of columns** and enter the number of columns.

B You can select **Line between** (☑) to include a vertical line separating the columns.

6 Deselect **Equal column width** (☐) to set exact widths for each column.

7 Set the exact column width and spacing for each column.

C You can click **Apply to** (⌄) to specify whether the columns apply to the selected text or the entire document.

8 Click **OK**.

Word applies the column format to the selected text.

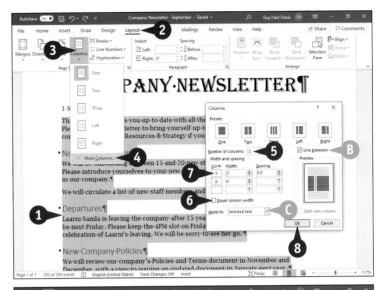

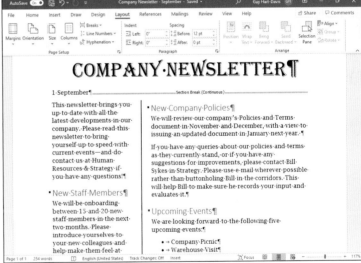

TIPS

How do I wrap column text around a picture or other object?

Click the picture or other object that you want to wrap, click **Format** to display the Format tab, click **Wrap Text**, and then click the type of wrapping that you want to apply.

How do I create a break within a column?

Click where you want the break to occur, and then press Ctrl + Shift + Enter. To remove a break, select it and press Delete. To return to a one-column format, click in the columns, and then click **Layout** to display the Layout tab. Click **Columns** to display the Columns pop-up panel, and then click **One**.

CHAPTER 8

Reviewing and Finalizing Documents

Word enables you to track the changes you and your colleagues make to documents. You can lock the tracking in place, quickly review and integrate tracked changes, and even collaborate in real time with colleagues on a document. Word provides tools for comparing different versions of a document and combining the changes they contain. You can also protect documents against changes, mark documents as final, and remove potentially sensitive information before sharing a document.

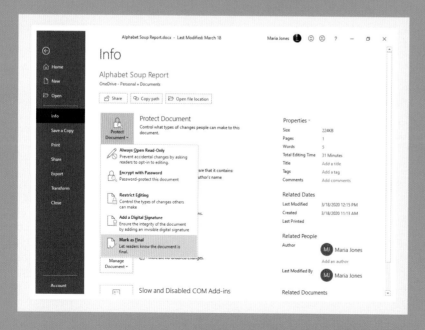

Track the Changes to a Document

ord's Track Changes feature enables you to track the editing and formatting changes made to a document. Track Changes is especially useful when you circulate documents to gather input from your colleagues. Track Changes uses a different color for each reviewer, so you can easily see who made which changes.

By default, Word displays changes in Simple Markup view, which displays indicators in the margins to mark areas that have changes. If you prefer to see changes as you make them, switch to All Markup view.

Track the Changes to a Document

1 Click **Review**.

The Review tab appears.

2 Click **Tracking**.

The Tracking pop-up panel opens.

3 Click **Track Changes**—the upper part of the button, not the pop-up button (⌄).

Word enables Track Changes.

4 Make changes to the document as needed.

A Red vertical bars called *changed bars* appear in the left margin beside lines containing changes.

5 Click **Tracking**.

The Tracking pop-up panel opens.

6 Click ⌄ to the right of **Display for Review** (📄).

The Display for Review pop-up menu opens.

7 Click **All Markup**.

Note: When you open a document containing tracked changes, Simple Markup is the default view.

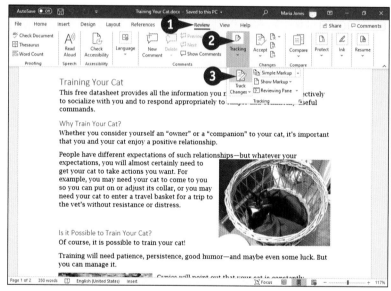

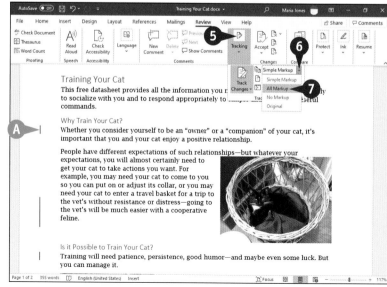

Word displays all the markup.

B Inserted text appears with an underline.

C Deleted text appears with strikethrough.

D The changed lines turn gray.

E You can position the pointer over a change to display a ScreenTip showing who made the change, the date and time of the change, and the type of change, such as "deleted" or "inserted."

8 To switch back to Simple Markup quickly, click a changed line.

F Word displays Simple Markup again.

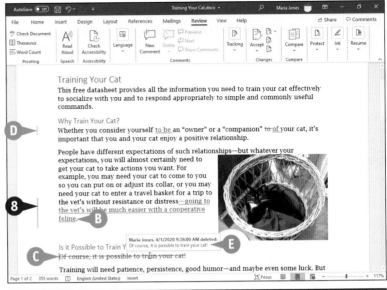

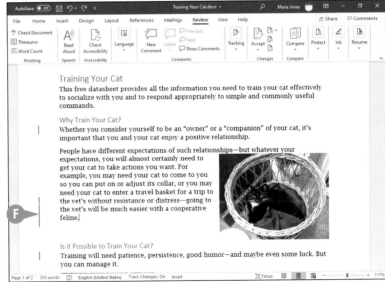

TIP

How can I easily tell if Track Changes is enabled?
For quick reference, add the Track Changes readout to the status bar. Right-click the status bar to display the Customize Status Bar menu, and then click **Track Changes**, placing a check mark next to it. The status bar then shows Track Changes: On or Track Changes: Off. You can click the readout to toggle Track Changes on or off.

Lock and Unlock Tracking

efore you send a document to your colleagues for review, you should not only turn on Track Changes in the document but also enable Lock Tracking, which requires a password to turn off Track Changes. Enabling Lock Tracking prevents your colleagues from turning off Track Changes and helps ensure that you can view your colleagues' changes easily when you receive the document back.

If you forget to enable Lock Tracking, you can use the Compare Documents feature to identify the changes in the reviewed document. See the section "Compare Two Versions of a Document," later in this chapter, for details.

Lock and Unlock Tracking

Lock Track Changes

1 In the document for which you want to lock tracked changes, click **Review**.

The Review tab appears.

2 Click **Tracking**.

The Tracking pop-up panel opens.

3 Click **Track Changes** to turn on tracking.

4 Click ⯆ on the lower part of the **Track Changes** button.

The Track Changes pop-up panel opens.

5 Click **Lock Tracking**.

The Lock Tracking dialog box appears.

6 Type the password in the Enter Password box.

7 Click **Reenter to confirm** and retype the password.

8 Click **OK**.

The Lock Tracking dialog box closes.

Note: Make sure you remember the password or you will not be able to turn off the Track Changes feature.

Word saves the password.

The Track Changes button appears dimmed and unavailable.

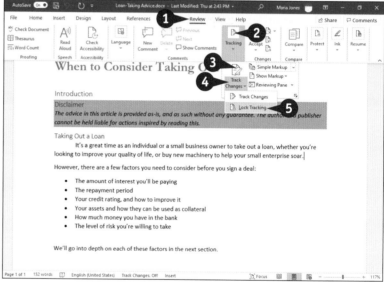

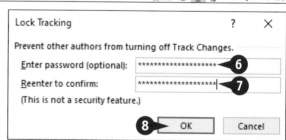

Unlock Track Changes

1 Open a document with Track Changes locked.

2 Click **Review**.

The Review tab appears.

3 Click **Tracking**.

The Tracking pop-up panel opens.

4 Click ⌄ at the bottom of the **Track Changes** button.

The Track Changes pop-up panel opens.

5 Click **Lock Tracking**.

The Unlock Tracking dialog box appears.

6 Type the password.

7 Click **OK**.

The Track Changes button becomes available again so that you can click it and turn off the Track Changes feature.

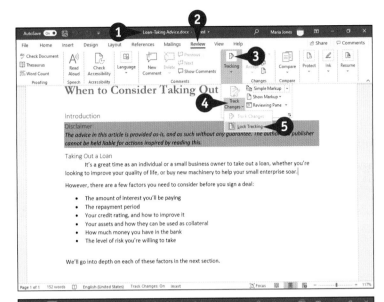

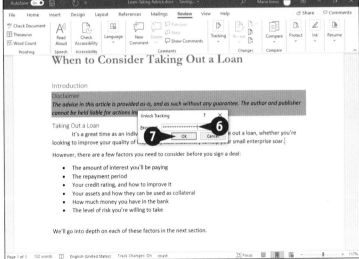

TIP

What happens if I supply the wrong password?
A message box opens saying "The password is incorrect." You can retry as many times as you want. If you cannot remember the password, you can create a new version that contains all revisions already accepted, which you can then compare to the original to identify changes. Press Ctrl+A to select the entire document. Then press Shift+← to unselect just the last paragraph mark in the document. Then press Ctrl+C to copy the selection. Start a new blank document and press Ctrl+V to paste the selection.

Review Tracked Changes

When you review a document containing tracked changes, you decide whether to accept or reject the changes. As you accept or reject changes, Word removes the revision marks from them.

When Word tracks revisions, it uses different colors to track the changes made and who made them so that you can easily identify who did what to a document. By default, Word displays changes in Simple Markup view, which displays changed bars in the margin to mark areas that have changes. You can use the Reviewing pane to identify who made each change, or you can hide the pane and work directly with the revisions.

Review Tracked Changes

Display the Reviewing Pane

1 Click **Review**.

The Review tab appears.

2 Click **Tracking**.

The Tracking pop-up panel opens.

3 Click **Reviewing Pane**.

The Revisions pane opens.

Ⓐ You can see the reviewer's name and brief details of the revision.

Ⓑ You can click ⌄ to hide the summary of revisions and view only the details of each revision.

Ⓒ You can click ✕ to close the pane.

Switch Markup from Balloons to Inline Display

Ⓓ The document may display markup in "balloons" in a pane on the right. For this example, you switch to displaying markup inline.

1 Click **Review**.

The Review tab appears.

2 Click **Tracking**.

The Tracking pop-up panel opens.

3 Click **Show Markup** (⌄).

The Show Markup pop-up panel opens.

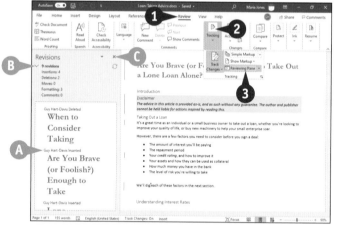

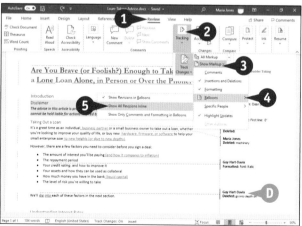

4 Click or highlight **Balloons**.

The Balloons submenu opens.

5 Click **Show All Revisions Inline**.

Note: Each reviewer's changes appear in a different color.

1 Press **Ctrl** + **Home** to place the insertion point at the beginning of the document.

2 Click **Next Change** (📄) to review the first change.

E Word highlights the change.

Note: You can click **Next** (📄) again to skip over the change without accepting or rejecting it.

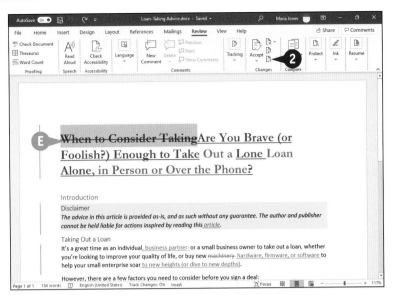

3 Click **Accept** to incorporate the change and select the next change.

F You can click **Reject** (📄 ▾) to reject the change and select the next change.

G For more options, click ▾ on the lower part of Accept to display the pop-up panel.

H If you need to move backward to a change you previously skipped, you can click **Previous Change** (📄).

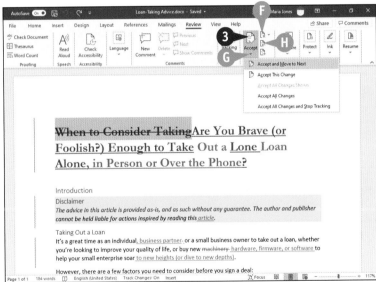

TIP

Can I print revisions?

You can print revisions in the document by simply printing the document. If you want to print a separate list of revisions, click **File** to display Backstage View, and then click **Print**. Click the button below **Settings**, and then click **List of Markup**. Click **Print** to print the list of markup.

Collaborate in Real Time on a Document

Word enables you to work with other people on the same document in real time. Editing a document collaboratively can help you to get input from various colleagues quickly without having to go through multiple rounds of revisions.

To begin editing a document collaboratively, you share it with your colleagues—or a colleague shares the document with you—on OneDrive or on SharePoint. Each participant opens the document from OneDrive or SharePoint. You can edit the document either in the Word Online app or in the desktop app.

Understand Collaborative Editing and the Alternatives

Long viewed by many as the ultimate goal of word processing, collaborative editing can be a great way of creating documents rapidly with your colleagues. However, it is certainly not suitable for all types of writing and editing, and you should use it only when appropriate in your documents.

Collaborative editing can be especially effective when you combine it with chat via text, voice, or both. Chat enables you to quickly establish who should be doing what next on the document and to avoid wasting time by getting in each other's way or working at cross purposes.

Collaborative editing is less effective for any knowledge work that requires time and consideration. If your work involves editing and reviewing documents, you will likely be better off using Word's other powerful revising and reviewing features, such as comments, Track Changes, Compare Documents, and Combine Documents.

If your work involves various people, each creating a different section of a document, it may be easier to create those sections in separate documents and then assemble them into a single document. Alternatively, you can use Word's master document feature, which builds a single document out of multiple subdocuments that can be opened and edited independently of the master document. See the sections "Create a Master Document" and "Work in a Master Document," both later in this chapter, for coverage of master documents.

Share a Document on OneDrive or SharePoint

To get started with collaborative editing, share the document on OneDrive or on SharePoint. For example, open the document in Word, and then click **Share** toward the right end of the Ribbon tab bar. In the Send Link dialog box that opens, verify that Anyone with the Link Can Edit appears below the document's name; if not, click **Anyone with the link can view** to display the Link Settings dialog box, click **Allow editing** (☐ changes to ☑), and then click **Apply**. In the Send Link dialog box, enter each recipient's name and an optional message, and then click **Send**.

Open a Document for Collaborative Editing

When you receive an email message informing you about a shared document, click **Open** to start the process of opening it. The document then opens in the Word Online app in your browser.

At first, the document opens for viewing, but you can open it for editing by clicking **Edit Document** on the toolbar at the top of the window to display the Edit Document drop-down menu, and then clicking **Edit in Desktop App** or **Edit in Browser**. Normally, editing in the desktop app is the better choice for full-on editing.

If the Please Confirm the Account You Want to Use to Access This Document dialog box opens, verify that it shows the account you want to use for editing, and then click **Continue**. If you need to use another account, click **Switch Accounts**, and then follow the prompts.

Windows then copies the document to your OneDrive account and opens the document from there in Word.

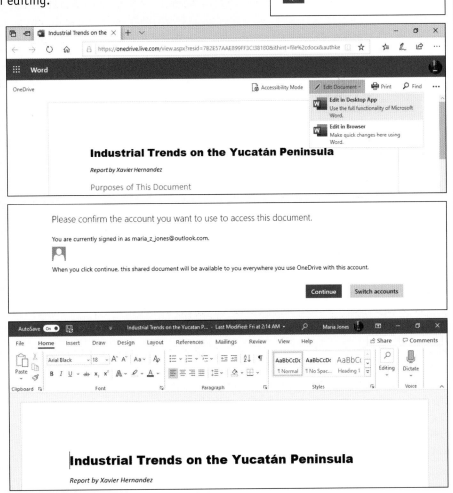

continued ►

Collaborate in Real Time on a Document (continued)

When you and your colleagues have a document open for collaborative editing, Word displays a separate insertion point for each participant, so you can see who is working on which part of the document. To avoid problems with conflicting changes, Word prevents two participants from editing the same part of a document simultaneously.

Normally, it is best to keep AutoSave enabled for documents on which you collaborate in real time. AutoSave not only saves your changes so your colleagues can see them but also updates your document with your colleagues' changes.

See Who Else Is Working on the Document

Word displays a round button at the right end of the Ribbon tab bar, to the left of the Share button, for each person other than you who has the document open. Each button has a different color and shows the person's initials. You can click the button to display a pop-up panel that shows the person's name; the person's current editing location, such as *On page 1*; and the following three commands:

- Click **Go to Location** to display the current location of the person's insertion point or selection.

- Click **Send Email** to start an email message in your default email app to that person at the email address they are using to edit the document.

- Click **Open Contact Card** to open the person's contact card—for example, so you can contact them via a different means, such as chat or phone, or a different email address.

View the Edits a Colleague Is Making

To view the edits a colleague is making, click that colleague's button on the right side of the Ribbon, and then click **Go to location** on the pop-up panel.

Word displays the location where the colleague is working, showing an insertion point that has the same color as the person's button. Move the pointer over the insertion point to display the colleague's name.

Be warned that Word may not always display the exact location of the colleague's insertion point. Instead, you may see a location where the colleague has worked recently, or you may see an insertion point when in fact the colleague has selected text or an object. To avoid data loss or synchronization problems, it is best to give each colleague's insertion point a wide berth. If you are chatting with the colleague while collaborating, ask which part of the document they are currently working on.

Work on the Document

Apart from avoiding the areas your colleagues are working in, you can work on a document much as you normally would. Word blocks you from taking any action that will interfere with changes your colleagues are currently making. That said, it is wise to avoid taking any actions likely to cause conflicts, even if Word fails to identify such actions as a problem. For example, if you select the entire document's content and then delete it, you will almost certainly cause problems for your colleagues.

Keep the AutoSave Feature Enabled

To keep your changes synchronized with those your colleagues make, keep the AutoSave feature set to On, as it is by default for documents stored on OneDrive and SharePoint. You can verify that AutoSave is on by looking at the AutoSave switch that appears at the left end of the Quick Access Toolbar.

Resolve Conflicts

When editing collaboratively, you may encounter conflicting changes, even if you keep AutoSave turned on. When Word detects conflicting changes, it displays the Upload Failed bar between the Ribbon and the document to warn you of the problem.

Click **Resolve** to display the Conflicting Changes pane, and then click the change you want to resolve first. On the Conflicts tab of the Ribbon, which appears automatically, go to the Conflicting Changes group, and then work through the conflicting changes by clicking **Accept My Change** or

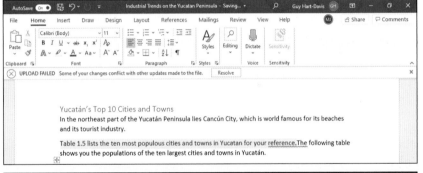

Reject My Change, as needed. To deal with all the changes at once, click the lower part of the Accept My Change button or the Reject My Change button, and then click **Accept All Conflicting Changes in Document** or **Reject All Conflicting Changes in Document**, as needed. After resolving all conflicts, go to the Close group and click **Close Conflict View**.

Compare Two Versions of a Document

ord's Compare feature enables you to compare two documents and create a document type called a *legal blackline* that shows what has changed between the documents. For example, if you send a document to a colleague for review, you can compare your colleague's reviewed document with your original document and create a document containing the changes.

The Compare feature works even if the changes in the reviewed document have been made without Track Changes enabled.

Compare Two Versions of a Document

1. Open the original document with which you want to compare your colleague's version.

2. Click **Review**.

   The Review tab appears.

3. Click **Compare**.

   The Compare pop-up panel opens.

4. Click **Compare**.

   The Compare Documents dialog box opens.

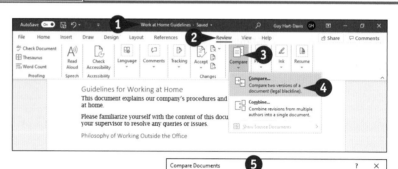

5. Click **Original document** (🔽), and then click the name of the open document on the drop-down list.

6. Click **Open** (📁) to the right of Revised Document.

   The Open dialog box appears.

7. Navigate to the folder that contains the other version of the document.

8. Click the document.

9. Click **Open**.

   The Open dialog box closes.

Ⓐ The document's name appears in the Revised Document box.

10. If necessary, edit the name in the Label Changes With box.

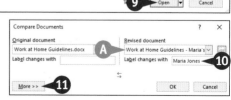

11. Click **More**.

The Compare Documents dialog box expands.

12 In the Comparison Settings area, select (☑) or deselect (☐) the options, as needed.

13 In the Show Changes At area, click **Character level** (○ changes to ◉) or **Word level** (○ changes to ◉), as needed.

14 In the Show Changes In area, click **New document** (○ changes to ◉).

15 Click **OK**.

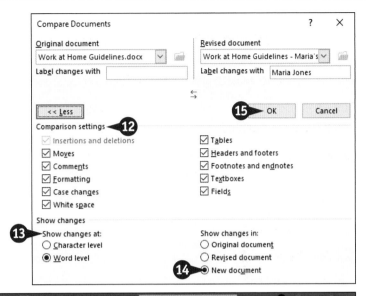

The Compare Documents dialog box closes.

Ⓑ The Compared Document pane shows the new document containing the differences between the two documents.

Ⓒ The Revisions pane appears.

Ⓓ The Original Document pane shows the original document.

Ⓔ The Revised Document pane shows the revised document.

You can now review the changes and accept or reject them.

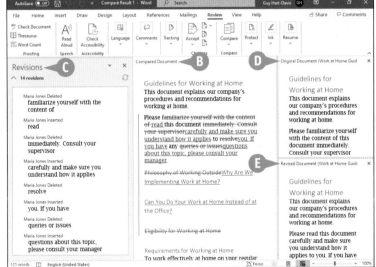

TIP

Which Comparison Settings items and Show Changes At items should I choose?

In the Comparison Settings area, deselect (☐) each item that you do not need to see. For example, deselect **Case changes** if you do not need to see changes of letters between uppercase and lowercase; deselect **White space** if you need not see changes to white space, such as insertions or deletions of tabs; or deselect **Fields** if you do not want to see changes in fields, many of which update automatically.

In the Show Changes At area, select **Word level** (◉) unless you need to see every single change—in which case, select **Character level** (◉).

Combine Changes into a Single Document

Word's Combine feature enables you to combine the changes contained in two different versions of the same document into one of the documents. The Combine feature can save you time and effort when you circulate a document to colleagues and receive multiple versions back. By combining changes from two documents at a time, you can quickly integrate all the changes in a single document and then review them.

Combine Changes into a Single Document

1 Open the original document with which you want to compare your colleague's version.

2 Click **Review**.

The Review tab appears.

3 Click **Compare**.

The Compare pop-up panel opens.

4 Click **Combine**.

The Combine Documents dialog box opens.

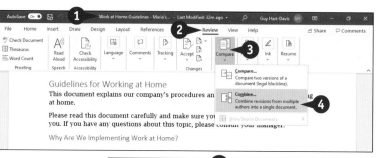

5 Click **Original document** (⌄), and then click the name of the open document.

6 If necessary, edit the name in the left Label Unmarked Changes With box.

7 Click **Open** (📁) to the right of Revised Document.

The Open dialog box appears.

8 Navigate to the folder that contains the other version of the document.

9 Click the document.

10 Click **Open** to close the Open dialog box.

A The document's name appears in the Revised Document box.

11 If necessary, edit the name in the right Label Changes With box.

12 Click **More**.

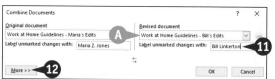

The Combine Documents dialog box expands.

13 In the Comparison Settings area, select (☑) or deselect (☐) the options, as needed.

14 In the Show Changes At area, click **Character level** (◯ changes to ◉) or **Word level** (◯ changes to ◉), as needed.

15 In the Show Changes In area, click **Original document** (◯ changes to ◉).

16 Click **OK**.

The Combine Documents dialog box closes.

B The Combined Document pane displays the original document with the differences shown using tracked changes.

C The Revisions pane appears.

D The Original Document pane shows the original document.

E The Revised Document pane shows the revised document.

F You can hide the source documents by clicking **Compare**, clicking **Show Source Documents**, and then clicking **Hide Source Documents**.

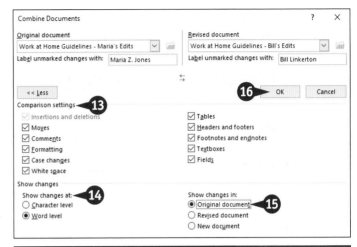

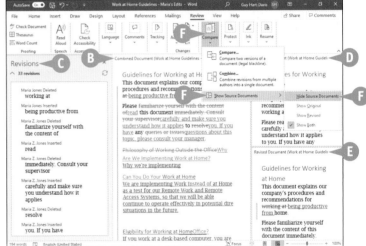

You can now review the changes and accept or reject them.

Work with Comments

You can add comments to your documents to provide extra information or feedback without directly changing the document content. For example, if you circulate a document so that your colleagues can add information, you can use comments to make clear what information is needed.

To indicate that a comment was added, Word displays a comment marker in the right margin. When you review comments, they appear in a window. Your name appears in comments you add, and you can easily review, reply to, or delete a comment. You can also indicate that you have addressed a comment.

Work with Comments

Add a Comment

1 Click or select the text about which you want to comment.

2 Click **Review**.

The Review tab appears.

3 Click **New Comment**.

A The markup area appears on the right side of the window.

B A comment balloon appears.

4 Type your comment.

5 Click in the document outside the selection to continue working.

Review a Comment

1 Click a comment marker.

C Word highlights the text associated with the comment.

D Word displays the Comments window and the text it contains.

2 Click in the document to hide the Comments window and its text.

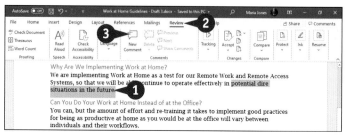

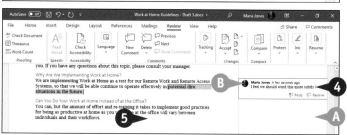

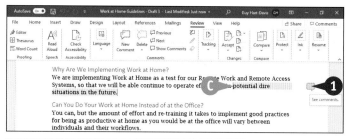

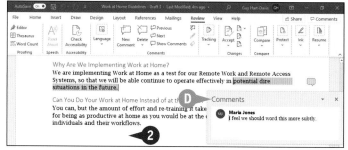

Reply to a Comment

1 Click a comment marker to open the Comments window.

2 Move the pointer over the text of the comment.

The Reply button and the Resolve button appear.

3 Click **Reply** (🗨).

E Word starts a reply under the comment.

4 Type your reply.

5 Click in the document to continue working.

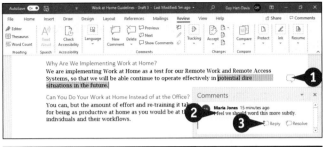

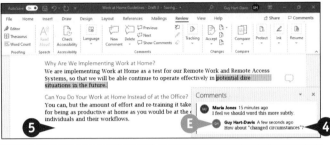

Delete a Comment

1 Click the comment you want to remove.

The Comments window appears.

2 Click **Review**.

The Review tab appears.

3 Click **Delete** (🗐).

Note: You can also right-click a comment, and then click **Delete Comment**. To delete all comments in the document, click ⌄ on the lower part of the **Delete** button, and then click **Delete All Comments in Document**.

Word deletes the comment.

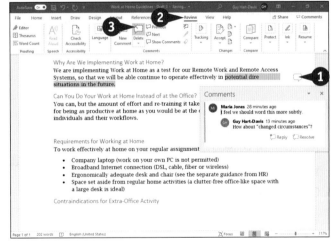

Can I indicate that I have addressed a comment without deleting it?
Yes, you can mark the comment as done. Right-click the text of the comment and choose **Resolve**. Word fades the comment text to light gray.

Work with Protected Documents

You can limit the changes others can make to a document by protecting it with a password. Word offers two kinds of protection: Password and User Authentication. User authentication, not shown in this section, relies on Windows authentication.

You can limit the styles available to format the document, the kinds of changes users can make, and the users who can make changes.

Work with Protected Documents

1 Click **Review**.

The Review tab appears.

2 Click **Protect**.

The Protect pop-up panel opens.

3 Click **Restrict Editing**.

Note: Depending on your screen resolution, you may or may not see **Protect**.

Ⓐ The Restrict Editing pane appears.

4 Click **Limit formatting to a selection of styles** (☐ changes to ☑) to limit document formatting to the styles you select.

5 Click **Settings**.

The Formatting Restrictions dialog box appears.

6 Deselect (☐) the styles you want to make unavailable.

7 Click **OK**.

8 Click **Allow only this type of editing in the document** (☐ changes to ☑) to specify editing restrictions.

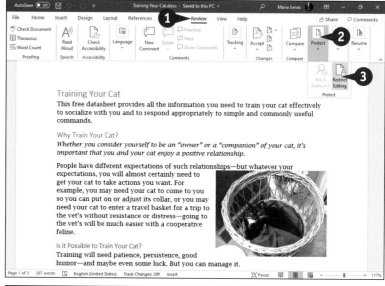

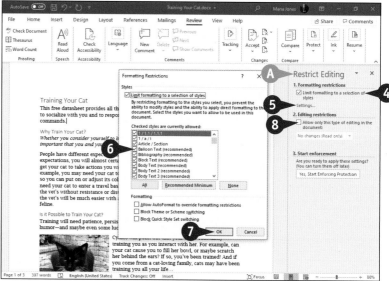

9 Click ⌄, and select the type of editing to permit.

You can select parts of the document to make them available for editing.

10 In the Groups box, select (☑) the check box for any group or user allowed to edit the selected parts of the document.

11 Click **Yes, Start Enforcing Protection**.

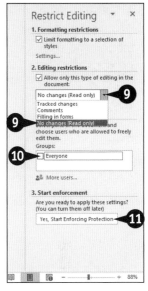

The Start Enforcing Protection dialog box opens.

12 Type a password, and then retype it.

Note: If your computer uses Information Rights Management (IRM), you can opt to use User Authentication, which also encrypts your document; only users you specify can remove document protection.

13 Click **OK**.

14 Click **Save** (💾).

Word protects the document and saves the protection.

15 Click ✕.

The Restrict Editing pane closes.

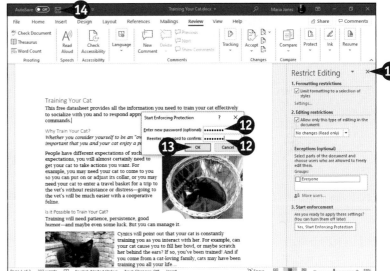

TIP

How do I work in a protected document?
When you open a protected document, Word highlights the areas you can edit. If you try to change an area that is not highlighted, a message appears in the status bar, explaining that you cannot make the modification because that area of the document is protected. To find the areas you can change, click **Review** to display the Review tab, click **Protect**, and then click **Restrict Editing** to display the Restrict Editing pane; then click **Show All Regions I Can Edit**. To turn off protection, you need the protection password.

Inspect a Document Before Sharing It

Before sharing a document, it is a good idea to use the Document Inspector feature to remove personal information from it.

The Document Inspector searches your document for comments, revision marks, versions, and ink annotations. It searches document properties for hidden metadata and personal information. It inspects for task pane apps saved in the document as well as text that has been collapsed under a heading. If your document contains custom XML data, headers, footers, watermarks, or invisible content, the Document Inspector alerts you.

Inspect a Document Before Sharing It

1 In the document you want to check for sensitive information, click **File**.

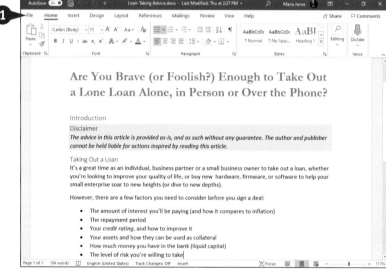

Backstage View appears.

2 Click **Info**.

The Info pane appears.

3 Click **Check for Issues**.

The Check for Issues pop-up panel opens.

4 Click **Inspect Document**.

Note: If the document contains unsaved changes, Word prompts you to save the document. Click **Yes**.

The Document Inspector window appears.

5 Deselect (☐) the check box for any element you do not want to inspect.

6 Click **Inspect**.

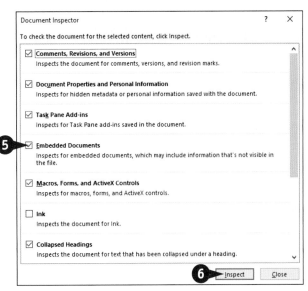

The Document Inspector looks for the information you specified and displays the results.

Ⓐ You can remove any identified information by clicking **Remove All** beside that element.

Ⓑ You can click **Reinspect** after removing identifying information.

7 Click **Close**.

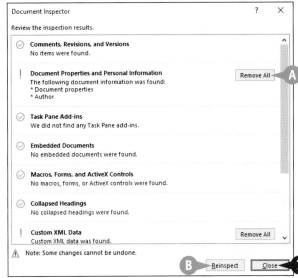

TIPS

Can I review the information that the Document Inspector displays before I remove it?

No. The only way to review the information before you remove it is to close the Document Inspector *without* removing information, use the appropriate Word features to review the information, and then rerun the Document Inspector as described in this section.

What happens if I remove information and then decide that I really want that information?

You cannot undo the effects of removing the information using the Document Inspector. However, to restore removed information, you can close the document *without* saving changes and then reopen it. If AutoSave is enabled for the document, you will need to close it before AutoSave runs.

215

Mark a Document as Final

When you have finalized a document, you can mark it as final. Doing so makes the document read-only, preventing you from making changes to it or inspecting it.

Marking a document as final is a convenience rather than a security feature. If you realize the document is actually not final and requires changes, you can quickly open the document for editing. Once you finish, you can mark it as final once more.

Mark a Document as Final

Mark the Document

1 Click **File**.

Backstage View appears.

2 Click **Info**.

The Info pane appears.

3 Click **Protect Document**.

The Protect Document pop-up panel opens.

4 Click **Mark as Final**.

A message box opens, explaining that Word will mark the document as final and then save it.

5 Click **OK**.

Word saves the document and displays another message box confirming that the document has been marked as final and telling you that editing commands are unavailable.

A If you do not want to see this message again, click **Don't show this message again** (☐ changes to ☑).

6 Click **OK**.

Backstage View highlights the Protect Document button in yellow to draw your attention.

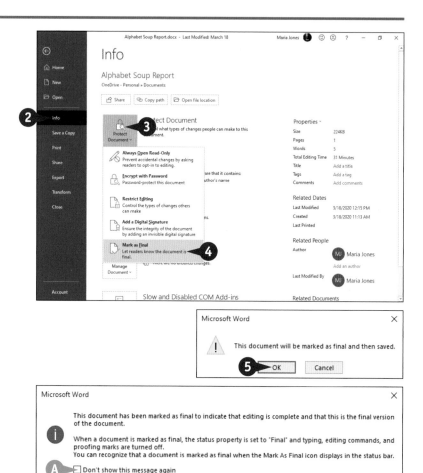

7 Click **Back** (⬅).

The document appears again.

Edit a Final Document

B The document is now read-only.

C Commands on the Quick Access Toolbar are unavailable.

D Word hides the Ribbon buttons because most editing commands are not available.

E The Marked as Final bar appears, indicating that the document has been marked as final.

8 Click **Edit Anyway**.

Word removes the document's Final status and opens the document for editing.

F Word no longer marks the document as read-only.

G Word redisplays and makes available all Ribbon buttons.

H Quick Access Toolbar buttons are available.

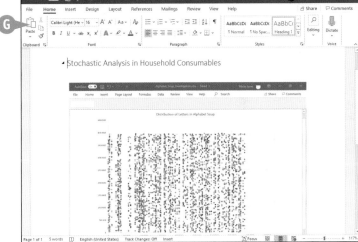

TIP

Can any user remove the "Marked as Final" status from a document?
Yes. If you absolutely do not want others to edit or change your document, consider other security options. For example, you can restrict editing with a password but, if you mark the document as final, you cannot require a password to open the document. You also can save your document as a PDF or XPS document, as described in the section "Save a Document in PDF or XPS Format" in Chapter 2, "Creating and Saving Documents."

Create a Master Document

Word's Master Document feature helps you to create and manipulate long documents. Instead of creating a single document containing, say, all the parts of a 100-page report, you create a separate document for each part of the report, and you create a master document to contain and organize these separate documents, which become subdocuments of the master document.

You can create a master document by converting an existing document that uses heading styles to a master document, as shown in the main text. Alternatively, you can create a master document from scratch, as explained in the tip.

Create a Master Document

1 Open the existing document you want to convert to a master document and subdocuments.

Note: If you want to create a master document from scratch, see the tip at the end of this section.

2 Format each paragraph that will start a subdocument with the Heading 1 style.

A For example, click the paragraph, and then click **Heading 1** in the Styles gallery or the Styles pane.

3 Click **View**.

The View tab appears.

4 Click **Outline**.

Word displays the document in Outline view.

The Outlining tab of the Ribbon appears.

5 Click **Show Level** (⌄), and then click the outline level you want to view.

In this example, you would click **Level 1** to display only the first-level headings, which include the Heading 1 paragraphs.

6 Click **Show Document**.

The Master Document group expands to show all its buttons.

7 Select the heading or headings you want to turn into subdocuments.

8 Click **Create**.

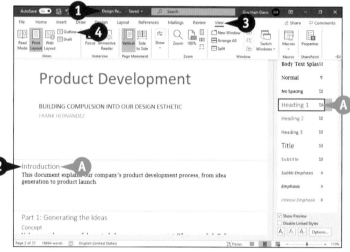

Word converts the open document to a master document.

Word creates a subdocument for each of the Heading 1 sections.

B The subdocument icon (▤) appears to the left of the subdocument's Heading 1 paragraph.

C An Expand/Collapse button (⊕) appears to the right of each subdocument icon. The plus (+) sign on this button indicates that the heading has content between it and the next heading shown.

9 Click **Expand/Collapse** (⊕) for a subdocument.

D The subdocument's content appears.

E The Outline button (⊖) indicates that there is no content between this heading and the next heading.

F You can click to place the insertion point, and then enter or edit text using standard techniques.

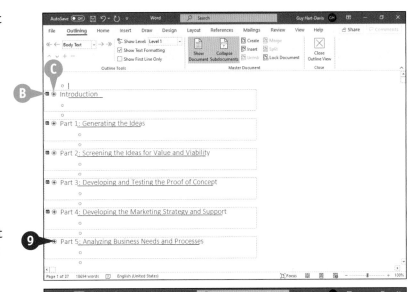

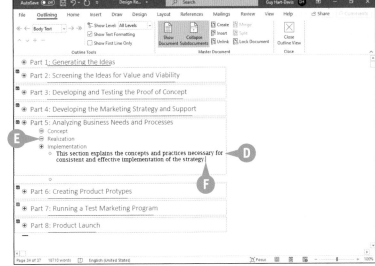

TIP

How do I create a master document from scratch?

Create a new document as usual. For example, press Ctrl + N to create a new blank document, or click **File** to open Backstage View, click **New** to display the New pane, and then click the appropriate template, such as a report template or book template. Save the document, ideally in its own folder. Click **View** to display the View tab, go to the Views group, and then click **Outline** to switch to Outline view. On the Outlining tab of the Ribbon, go to the Master Document group, and then click **Show Document**. You can now create new subdocuments or insert existing documents; see the next section, "Work in a Master Document," for details.

Work in a Master Document

After creating a master document, you can add documents to it as subdocuments. You need to add each document at the point where you want the subdocument to appear in the master document. For example, when adding documents to a new master document, add the first document first, the second document second, and so on. While you can drag a subdocument's contents up and down the master document, doing so removes the content from the subdocument, adding the content either to one of the other subdocuments or to the master document itself.

Work in a Master Document

Insert Subdocuments and Open a Subdocument for Editing

1. With the master document open and active, place the insertion point where you want to insert the subdocument.

2. Click **Insert**.

   The Insert Subdocument dialog box opens.

3. Navigate to the folder that contains the document you want to insert.

4. Click the document.

5. Click **Open**.

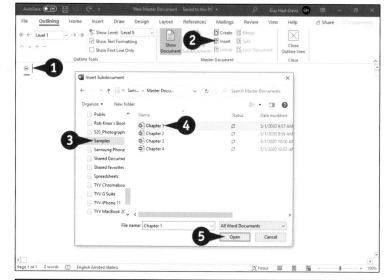

   The Insert Subdocument dialog box closes.

A. The document appears as a subdocument in the master document.

   You can now repeat steps **2** to **5** to insert other documents as subdocuments.

B. You can double-click **Subdocument** (▦) to open a subdocument in its own window.

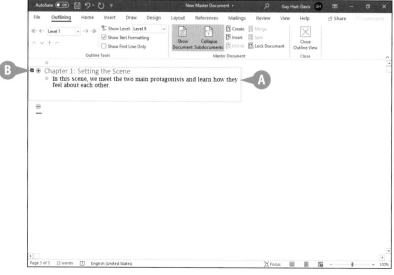

View and Edit the Whole Master Document

1 Click **Print Layout** (📄).

Note: If you prefer, you can use another view to work on the master document. For example, to use Draft view, click **View** to display the View tab of the Ribbon, go to the Views group, and then click **Draft**.

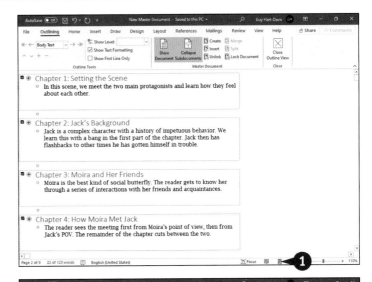

C Word displays the document in Print Layout view.

D The outdented divider bars indicate the divisions between the subdocuments.

You can now edit or format the master document as a whole. For example, you can click **Insert** to display the Insert tab of the Ribbon, go to the Header & Footer group, and then add headers and footers to the entire master document.

Note: When you are ready to return to Master Document view, click **View** to display the View tab of the Ribbon, go to the Views group, and then click **Outline**. The Outlining tab appears. Go to the Master Document group and click **Show Document**.

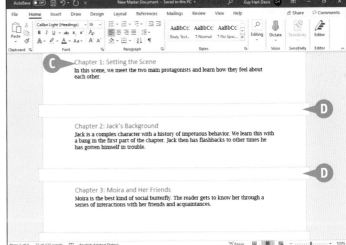

TIP

What do the Merge command and the Split command do?

If you need to merge two or more subdocuments into a single subdocument, select those subdocuments, and then click **Merge** in the Master Document group on the Outlining tab of the Ribbon. Word moves the content of those subdocuments into a single subdocument.

When you need to split one subdocument into two subdocuments, create a top-level heading—such as a Heading 1 paragraph—at the point where the second subdocument should begin. Click in this paragraph, and then click **Split** in the Master Document group on the Outlining tab. Word moves the heading and its following paragraphs into a new subdocument.

CHAPTER 9

Working with Tables and Charts

Tables can be a great way to present complex information in an easy-to-read format. Word enables you to insert tables quickly and format them to look the way you want. You can also insert charts in your documents to present information visually.

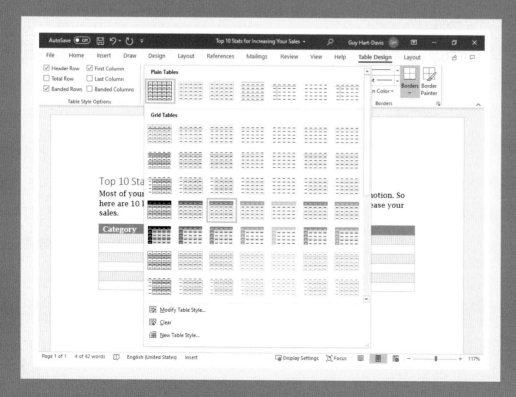

Create a Table

Word enables you to create tables for presenting data in an organized fashion. For example, you might add a table to your document to display a list of items or a roster of classes. Tables contain vertical columns and horizontal rows, which intersect to form *cells*.

You can insert all types of data in cells, including text and graphics. To enter text in a cell, click in the cell and then type your data. As you type, Word wraps the text to fit in the cell, as needed.

Create a Table

Insert a Table

1 Click in the document where you want to insert a table.

2 Click **Insert**.

The Insert tab appears.

3 Click **Table**.

A The Table pop-up panel appears.

4 Move the pointer (↳) to select the number of rows and columns you want to preview.

B Word previews the table as you drag over cells.

5 Click the square representing the number of rows and columns you want.

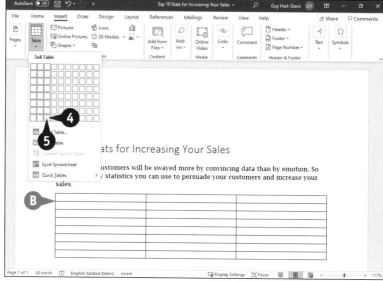

The table appears in your document.

C The Table Design tab and the Layout tab appear on the Ribbon.

6 Click in a table cell and type information.

D If necessary, Word expands the row height to accommodate the text.

You can press **Tab** to move the insertion point to the next cell.

Note: Press **Shift** + **Tab** to move to the previous cell.

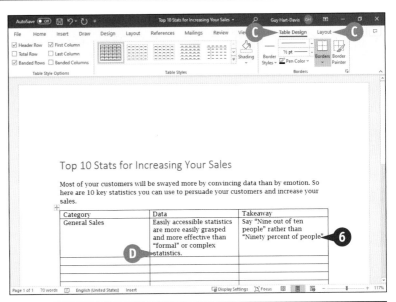

Delete a Table

1 Click anywhere in the table you want to delete.

2 Click **Layout**.

The Layout tab appears.

3 Click **Delete**.

The Delete pop-up panel opens.

4 Click **Delete Table**.

Word removes the table and its contents from your document.

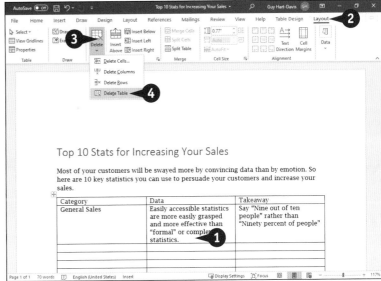

TIPS

How do I add rows to a table?

To add a row to the bottom of the table, place the insertion point in the last cell and press **Tab**. To add a row anywhere else, use the buttons in the Rows & Columns group on the Layout tab.

What exactly is a table cell?

A *cell* is the rectangular space created by the intersection of a row and a column. In spreadsheet programs, columns are named with letters, rows are named with numbers, and cells are named using the column letter and row number. For example, the cell at the intersection of Column A and Row 2 is called A2.

Change the Row Height or Column Width

Word automatically changes the row height to accommodate the tallest cell in the row. You can also change row height manually, as needed. Similarly, you can change column width manually—for example, to improve the layout of the table.

The Word window must be in either Print Layout view or Web Layout view for you to be able to change row height or column width, so you may need to switch to one of these views before making changes.

Change the Row Height or Column Width

Change the Row Height

1 Click **Print Layout** (▤) or **Web Layout** (▥) if neither button is currently active.

Word switches to the view you chose.

2 Position the pointer over the bottom of the row you want to change (I changes to ⬍).

3 Drag the row border up to reduce the row height or down to increase it.

A A dotted line marks the current position of the border you drag.

4 When the row height suits you, release the mouse button.

B Word adjusts the row height.

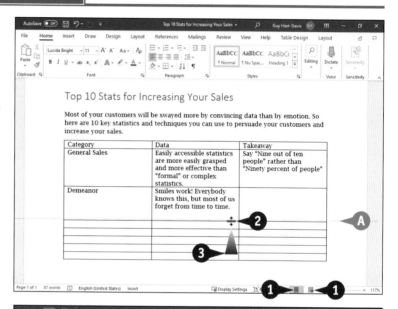

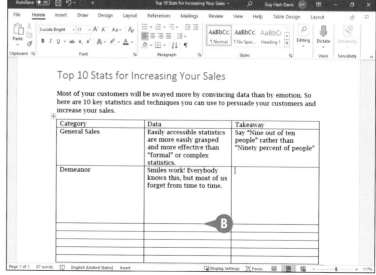

Change the Column Width

1 Position the pointer over the right side of the column you want to change (I changes to +‖+).

2 Drag the column edge right to increase the column width or left to reduce it.

C A dotted line marks the current position of the column border.

3 Release the mouse button.

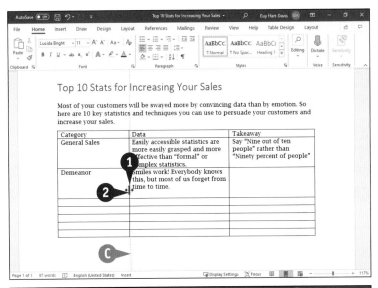

D Word adjusts the column width.

Note: For any column except the rightmost column, changing the column's width also changes the width of the column to its right, but the overall table size remains constant. When you change the width of the rightmost column, you change the width of the entire table.

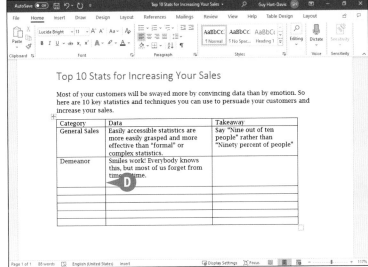

I tried to change the row height, but the pointer did not change, and I could not drag the row. What did I do wrong?

You can change row height only when displaying your document in either Print Layout view or Web Layout view. Make sure the window is in one of those views by clicking **Print Layout** (▤) or **Web Layout** (▥) on the status bar. See Chapter 3, "Entering Text in Documents," for more on understanding document views and switching between them.

How can I change a column width so that it accommodates the longest item in the column?

Double-click the right edge of the column. Word widens or narrows the column based on the widest entry in the column and adjusts the overall table size.

Move a Table

Y ou can move a table to a different location in your document. You might discover, for example, that you inserted a table prematurely in your document and, as you continue to work, you decide that the table would better help you make your point if you move it to a location farther down in your document. You do not need to reinsert the table and reenter its information; instead, move it.

Make sure that you are working from Print Layout or Web Layout view; you can use the buttons on the status bar or on the View tab to switch views, if necessary.

Move a Table

1 Click **Print Layout** (▤) or **Web Layout** (▣) if neither button is currently active.

Word switches to the view you chose.

2 Move the pointer (I) over the table.

Note: Alternatively, click in the table.

A A table selection handle (✛) appears in the upper-left corner of the table.

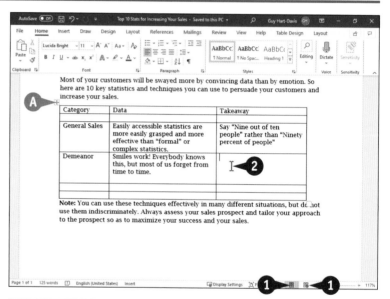

3 Move the pointer over the table selection handle (✛); I changes to ✛.

4 Drag the table to a new location (✛ changes to ⟊).

B A dashed line shows where the table will land when you drop it.

5 Release the mouse button.

The table appears in the new location.

Note: To copy the table, perform these steps but press and hold Ctrl in step **3**.

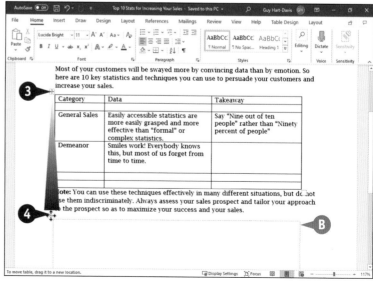

Resize a Table

If your table dimensions do not suit your purpose, you can resize the table from Print Layout view or Web Layout view. For example, you may want to resize a table to make it longer and narrower, especially if your table is small; in that case, you could reduce the space occupied by the table and wrap text in your document around it using the Table Properties box.

Resize a Table

1 Click **Print Layout** (▤) or **Web Layout** (▥) if neither button is currently active.

Word switches to the view you chose.

2 Move the pointer (I) over the table.

Ⓐ A handle (▢) appears in the lower-right corner of the table.

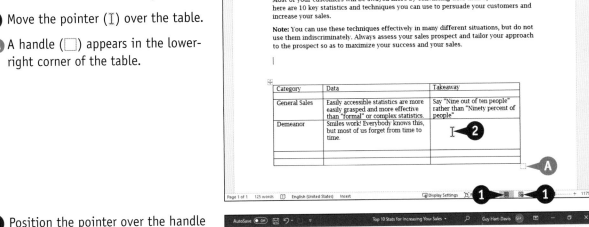

3 Position the pointer over the handle (I changes to ↘).

4 Drag up, down, left, right, or diagonally to adjust the table's size (↘ changes to +).

Note: Dragging diagonally simultaneously changes the table width and height.

Ⓑ The table outline displays the proposed table size.

5 Release the mouse button to change the table's size.

Note: On the Layout tab, you can click **Properties** to control how text wraps around the outside of your table.

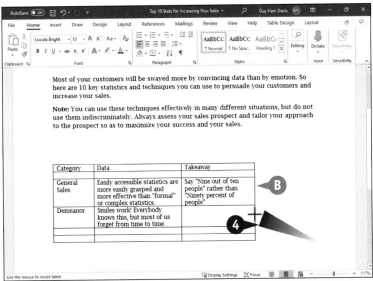

Add or Delete a Row

You can easily add rows to make room for more information or remove rows you do not need. Word automatically adds a row to the bottom of a table if you place the insertion point in the last table cell and press `Tab`. If you need additional rows in the middle of your table, you can insert extra rows.

To add a new first row to your table, see the first tip at the end of this section.

Add or Delete a Row

Add a Row

1 Move the pointer (I) outside the left edge of the row below which you want to add a new row.

Ⓐ I changes to ⬩, and a plus sign (⊕) attached to a pair of horizontal lines that span the width of the table appears.

2 Click ⊕.

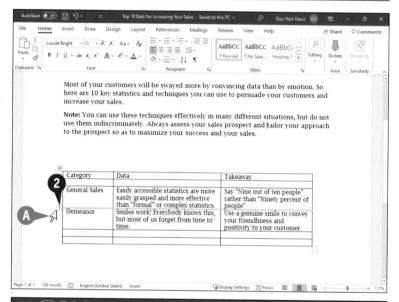

Ⓑ Word inserts a row above the row you identified in step **1** and selects it.

When you move the pointer away from the row, ⊕ disappears. You can click in the row to add information to the table.

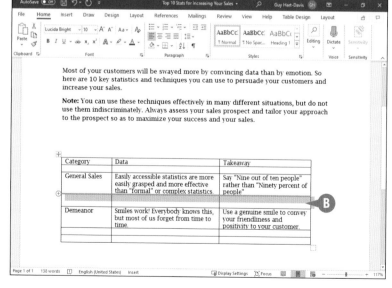

230

Delete a Row

1 Click anywhere in the row you want to delete.

2 Click **Layout**.

The Layout tab appears.

3 Click **Delete**.

4 Click **Delete Rows**.

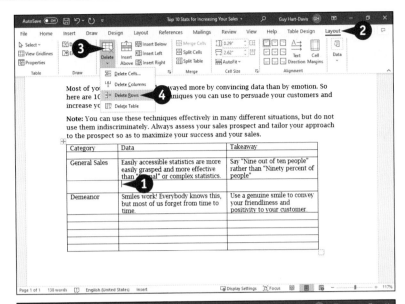

C Word removes the row and any text it contained from the table.

Note: To delete a row or a column using the keyboard, select the row or column, and then press Backspace.

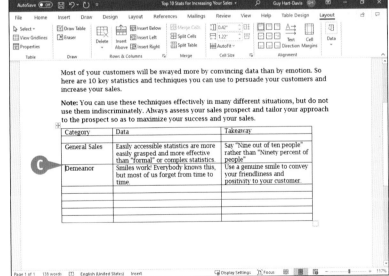

How can I insert a new first row in my table?

Place the insertion point anywhere in the first table row. Click **Layout** to display the Layout tab, go to the Rows & Columns group, and then click **Insert Above**.

How do I delete more than one row at a time?

Select the rows you want to delete and perform steps **2** to **4** in the subsection "Delete a Row." To select the rows, position the pointer (⌐) outside the left side of the table. Drag to select the rows you want to delete. The same approach works for inserting rows; select the number of rows you want to insert before you begin.

Add or Delete a Column

You can add or delete columns to change the structure of a table to accommodate more or less information. If you need additional columns in the middle of your table, you can insert extra columns; if the table has columns you do not need, you can delete those columns.

When you add a column, Word decreases the width of the other columns to make space for the new column but retains the overall width of the table.

Add or Delete a Column

Add a Column

Note: If you need to add a column to the left side of your table, click anywhere in the first column and, on the Layout tab, click **Insert Left**.

1 Move the pointer (I) to just above the top edge of the column to the right of which you want to add a column.

A I changes to ⌖ and a plus sign (⊕) attached to a pair of vertical lines that span the height of the table appears.

2 Click ⊕.

B Word inserts a new column in the table to the right of the column you identified in step **1** and selects the new column.

Note: Word maintains the table's overall width.

You can click in the column to add text to it.

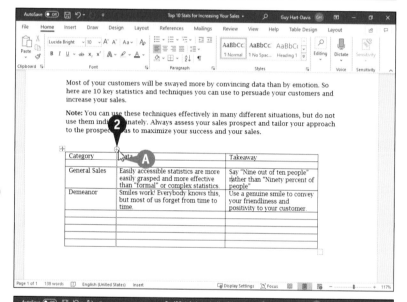

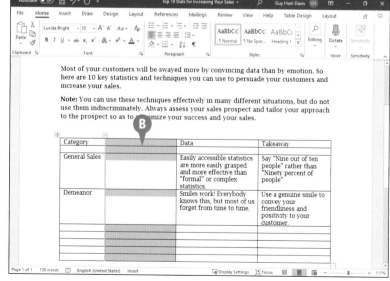

Delete a Column

1 Click anywhere in the column you want to delete.

2 Click **Layout**.

The Layout tab appears.

3 Click **Delete**.

4 Click **Delete Columns**.

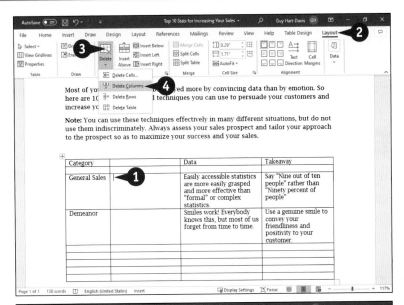

C Word removes the column and any text it contained from the table.

D The insertion point appears in the column to the right of the one you deleted.

Word does not resize existing columns to use the space previously occupied by the deleted column.

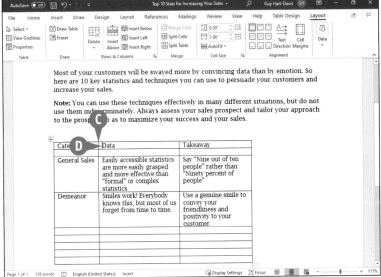

TIP

Is there a way I can easily enlarge a table to fill up the space between the left and right margins after deleting a column?

Yes. Click anywhere in the table. Then click **Layout** to display the Layout tab, go to the Cell Size group, click **AutoFit**, and then click **AutoFit Window**. Word adjusts the table content and columns to fill the space.

Set Cell Margins

You can set the top, bottom, left, and right margins in table cells to control the amount of space that appears between the cell contents and the cell borders. For example, you may want to increase the cell margins to provide plenty of space around the cell contents, making the text easier to read.

Normally, you would first set the default margins for all the table's cells. After that, you would set different margins for specific cells or groups of cells.

Set Cell Margins

Set Default Cell Margins for the Whole Table

1 Click anywhere in the table.

2 Click **Layout**.

The Layout tab appears.

3 Click **Cell Margins**.

The Table Options dialog box opens.

4 Click **Top**, **Bottom**, **Left**, or **Right**, and adjust the setting, as needed.

5 Click **OK**.

The Table Options dialog box closes.

Word applies the cell margin settings you chose.

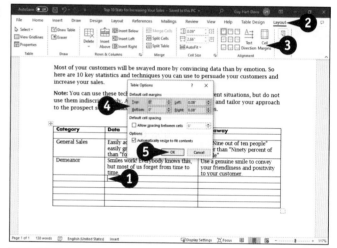

Set Cell Margins for Specific Cells

1 Select the cell or cells.

2 Click **Properties**.

The Table Properties dialog box opens.

3 Click **Cell**.

The Cell tab appears.

4 Click **Options**.

The Cell Options dialog box opens.

5 Click **Same as the whole table** (☑ changes to ☐).

6 Click **Top**, **Bottom**, **Left**, or **Right**, and adjust the setting, as needed.

7 Click **OK**.

The Options dialog box closes.

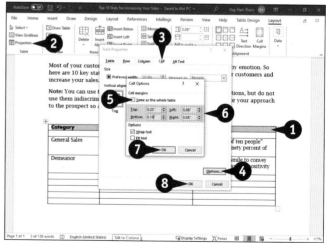

8 Click **OK**.

The Table Properties dialog box closes.

Word applies the cell margin settings you chose.

Add Space Between Cells

You can set spacing between table cells. When you allow additional spacing between cells, Word applies the spacing both horizontally and vertically; you cannot allow additional space in only one direction.

To adjust space in only one direction, adjust cell margins as described in the previous section, "Set Cell Margins." When you adjust cell margins, you can have Word automatically adjust the cell contents within the margins.

Add Space Between Cells

1 Click anywhere in the table.

2 Click **Layout**.

The Layout tab appears.

3 Click **Cell Margins**.

The Table Options dialog box opens.

4 Click **Allow spacing between cells** (□ changes to ✓).

5 Enter the setting for space between cells.

6 Click **OK**.

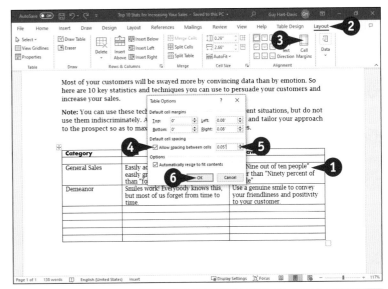

Ⓐ Word adds space between cells.

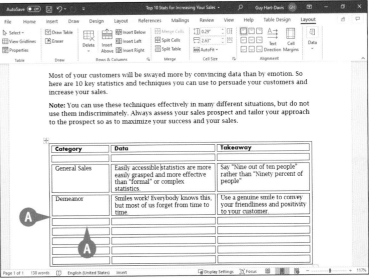

Merge Two or More Cells into a Single Cell

You can combine two or more cells to create one larger cell. Word uses the term *merge* for combining cells like this.

Merging cells is useful for creating table titles or subtitles that span an entire row. You can merge cells either before or after adding contents to them. When you merge cells that have contents, Word puts all the contents into a single cell, separated into different paragraphs.

Merge Two or More Cells into a Single Cell

1 Position the pointer inside and at the left edge of the first cell you want to merge (I changes to ➤).

2 Drag the pointer (➤) across the cells you want to merge to select them.

3 Click **Layout**.

The Layout tab appears.

4 Click **Merge Cells**.

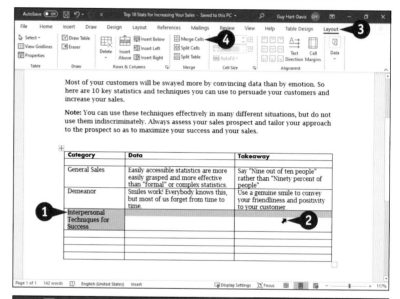

A Word combines the cells into one cell and selects that cell.

To center a table title, see the section "Align Text in Cells," later in this chapter.

You can click anywhere to cancel the selection.

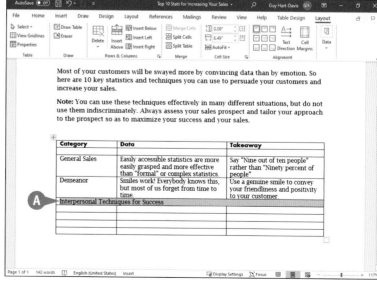

Split One Cell into Two or More Cells

Y ou can split one cell into two or more cells. Splitting a cell can be helpful if you find that you have more information in one cell than you want. By splitting the cell, you can make room for additional information.

You can split any cell; you are not limited to splitting a cell that you previously merged. When you split a cell, the new cells that you create can span one row, one column, or multiple rows and columns.

Split One Cell into Two or More Cells

1 Click anywhere in the cell you want to split.

Note: If you want Word to divide the cell's contents among the cells into which you split it, create a separate paragraph for each new cell.

2 Click **Layout**.

The Layout tab appears.

3 Click **Split Cells**.

The Split Cells dialog box opens.

4 Click **Number of columns** and enter the number of columns into which you want to split the cell.

5 Click **Number of rows** and enter the number of rows.

6 Click **OK**.

Ⓐ Word splits the cell and selects the resulting cells.

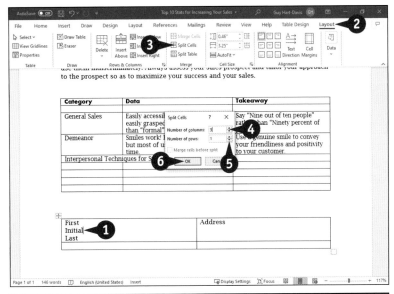

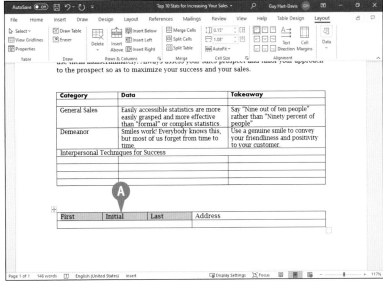

Split a Table into Two

You can split one table into two. This feature is useful if you discover, after entering information in a table, that you should have created separate tables. Splitting provides an easy way of dividing one table into two.

If you need to divide one table into two tables, but you need each of the resulting tables to retain some common content, you may do better to copy the table via Copy and Paste or drag and drop, and then edit down each of the resulting two tables.

Split a Table into Two

1 Position the insertion point anywhere in the row that should appear as the first row of the new table.

2 Click **Layout**.

The Layout tab appears.

3 Click **Split Table**.

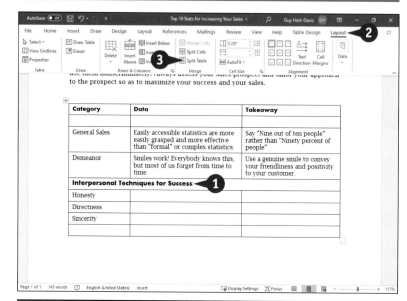

Ⓐ Word separates the table into two tables.

Ⓑ The insertion point appears between the tables.

Ⓒ Because the insertion point is not in a table cell, the Table Design tab and the Layout tab no longer appear on the Ribbon.

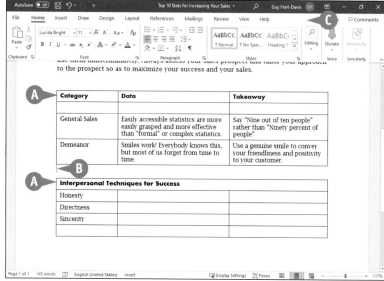

Add a Formula to a Table

You can place a formula in a cell to calculate a value. Word analyzes the values in the neighboring cells and tries to suggest the right formula for the situation. For example, if the cells above the formula cell contain numbers, Word may suggest a SUM() formula.

As of this writing, Word provides 18 functions—many fewer than Excel, but enough to add automation to your tables. The functions include SUM() for adding numbers, AVERAGE() for calculating an average, MIN() for identifying the smallest value, MAX() for identifying the largest value, and COUNT() for counting the number of values.

Add a Formula to a Table

1 In a table containing numbers, click in a cell that should contain a formula.

2 Click **Layout**.

The Layout tab appears.

3 Click **Data**.

The Data pop-up panel appears.

4 Click **Formula**.

The Formula dialog box opens, suggesting a formula.

5 If you need to change the formula, click ⌄ to the right of **Paste function**, and then click the function to use.

A You can click ⌄ to select a number format. For example, click **#,##0** to show the number with a comma separator for thousands.

6 Click **OK**.

Word enters the formula.

B The cell displays the result of the formula.

Note: Unlike Excel, Word does not update formula results automatically. So after changing any value in the cells the formula uses, click in the formula cell and press `F9` to update the result.

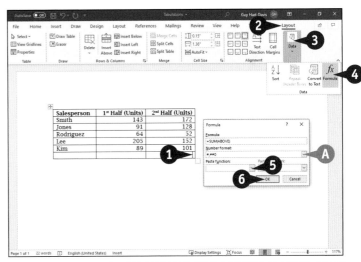

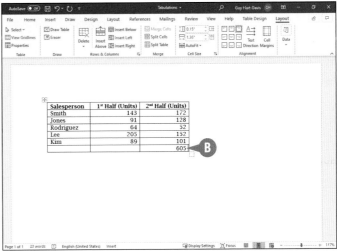

Align Text in Cells

By default, Word aligns table entries at the top left edge of each cell. This alignment works well for many cells, but for others, you will likely want to set alignment manually. For example, you may want to center a title in its cell or align values with the right side of their cells.

You can set horizontal alignment and vertical alignment by using the buttons in the Alignment group on the Layout tab of the Ribbon. You can also set horizontal alignment quickly using standard keyboard shortcuts.

Align Text in Cells

1 Select the cells you want to align.

Note: To align a single cell, simply click in the cell.

2 Click **Layout**.

The Layout tab appears.

3 Click the appropriate alignment button.

Following this example, you would click **Align Top Right** (▤) to align a title with the top edge and the right edge of its cell.

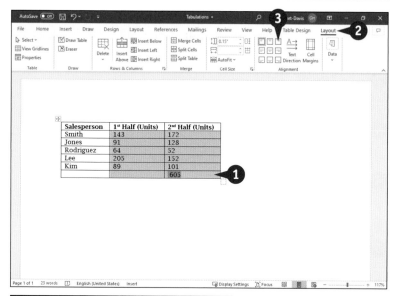

A Word aligns the text accordingly in the cells.

You can click anywhere to cancel the selection.

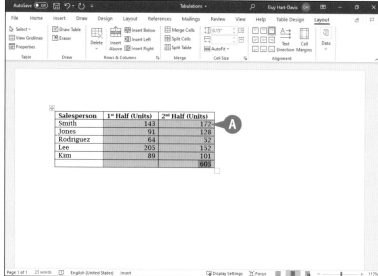

Add Shading to Cells

You can add shading to cells to call attention to them. Shading adds depth to drawings and can improve the appearance of a table if you apply it properly. For example, you might want to shade a table title or table column or row headings, or both title and headings to help ensure that the reader will notice them and better understand the table content.

Be careful not to apply too much shading or too dark a shade, which can make text unreadable, especially on printouts.

Add Shading to Cells

1 Select the cells you want to format.

Note: To add shading to a single cell, simply click in the cell.

2 Click **Table Design**.

The Table Design tab appears.

3 Click ☞ on **Shading**.

Ⓐ The Shading gallery appears.

Ⓑ You can position the pointer (I) over a color, and Live Preview displays a sample of the selected cells shaded in the proposed color.

4 Click the color you want to apply.

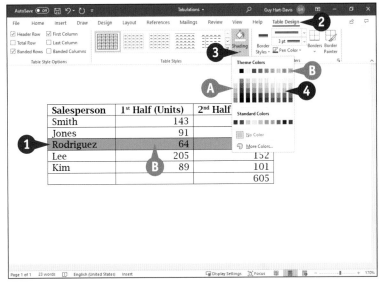

Ⓒ Word applies the shading to the selected cells.

5 You can click anywhere outside the cells to continue working.

Ⓓ The Shading button takes on the color you chose. You can apply that color quickly to a selection by clicking the main part of the Shading button, without opening the Shading gallery.

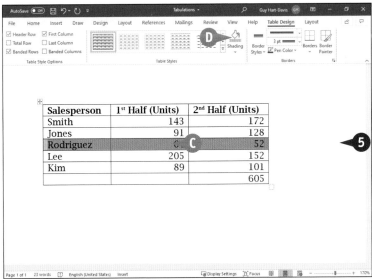

Change Cell Borders

By default, Word displays the borders that separate each cell, to help you enter information into a table and to help your reader read the table's information. You can change the appearance of the borders surrounding selected cells to call attention to them.

You can select a border style, which applies a predetermined line style, weight, and color, or you can manually choose the style, weight, and color. You can apply your selection to individual borders by using the Border Painter tool or to an entire cell by using the Borders tool.

Change Cell Borders

Paint a Border Style

1 Click anywhere in the table.

The Table Design tab and the Layout tab appear on the Ribbon.

2 Click **Table Design**.

The Table Design tab appears.

3 Click ⌄ on the **Border Styles** button.

Ⓐ The Theme Borders gallery appears.

4 Click a color and style.

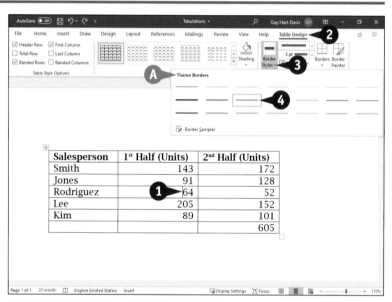

Ⓑ 𝖑 changes to 🖊.

5 Move the pointer (🖊) over the table border to which you want to apply the border style you chose in step **4**, and click the border.

Word applies the selected border style.

6 Repeat step **5** for each border you want to change.

Ⓒ You can click **Border Painter** (🖋) or press Esc to stop applying the border.

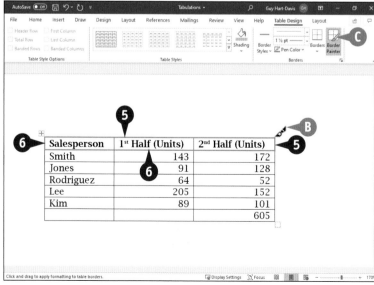

Change Cell Borders Manually

1 Click in the cell whose borders you want to change.

2 Click **Table Design**.

The Table Design tab appears.

3 Click ⌄ to the right of **Line Style** to display the Line Style gallery, and then click the line style.

4 Click ⌄ to the right of **Line Weight** to display the Line Weight gallery, and then click the line weight.

5 Click ⌄ to the right of **Pen Color** to display the Pen Color gallery, and then click the color.

D Word selects the Border Painter button (🖊).

6 Click ⌄ on **Borders**.

The Borders gallery appears.

7 Click the type of border to apply. This example uses **Outside Borders**.

E Word applies the border using the selected line style, weight, and pen color to the selected cell.

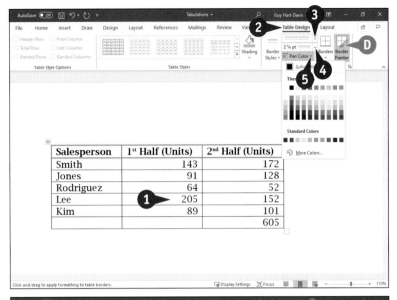

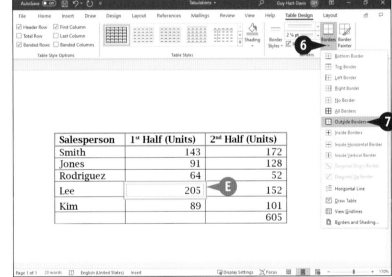

How can I remove borders from table cells?

Click in the cell whose borders you want to remove. Click **Table Design** on the Ribbon to display the Table Design tab. Click ⌄ on **Borders**, and then click **No Border**. Word removes the borders from the table cells and replaces them with dotted gridlines, which do not print.

Format a Table Using a Table Style

Y{ou can easily apply formatting to your tables by using the table styles found in the Table Styles gallery on the Table Design tab. Earlier sections in this chapter show you how to apply shading and borders to your table. Each table style in the Table Styles gallery contains its own unique set of formatting characteristics, and when you apply a table style you simultaneously apply shading, color, borders, and fonts to your table. You also can set table style options that add a header row or a total row, emphasize the table's first column, and more.

Format a Table Using a Table Style

1 Click anywhere in the table.

The Table Design tab and the Layout tab appear on the Ribbon.

2 Click **Table Design**.

The Table Design tab appears.

3 Click **More** (⤓) in the Table Styles group.

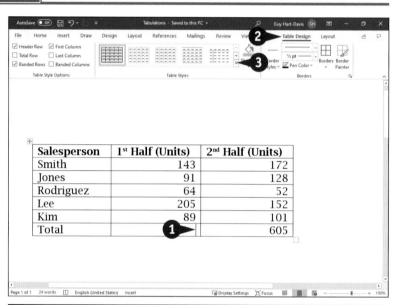

Ⓐ The Table Styles gallery appears.

4 Position the pointer (⏷) over the table style you want to preview.

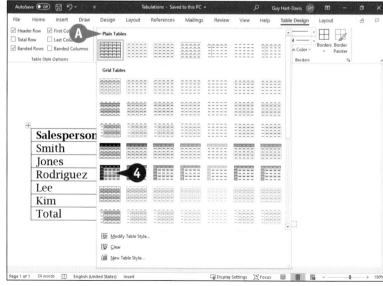

B Live Preview displays the table in the proposed table style, using the style's fonts, colors, and shading.

5 Click the table style you want to use.

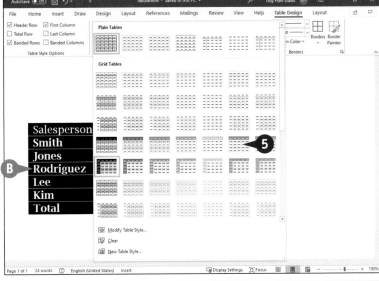

C Word displays the table in the style you selected.

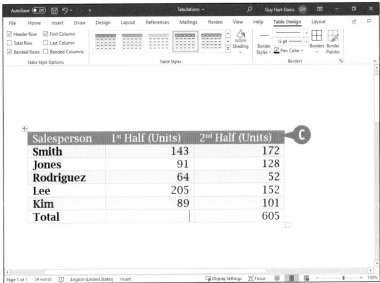

Salesperson	1st Half (Units)	2nd Half (Units)
Smith	143	172
Jones	91	128
Rodriguez	64	52
Lee	205	152
Kim	89	101
Total		605

TIP

How can I remove a table formatting design?
If you just applied the formatting, you can click **Undo** (⤺). If you have performed other actions since applying the table formatting design, click the table, click **Table Design** to display the Table Design tab, click **More** (⤓), and then click **Clear**.

Add a Chart

You can add a chart to a Word document by borrowing Excel's charting functionality and in effect creating a miniature Excel workbook in the Word document. This approach works well for charts that use little enough data to type into the Excel workbook.

However, if you already have the chart data in an Excel workbook, it is usually better to create the chart in Excel and then paste it into your Word document. This approach lets you take full advantage of Excel's powerful charting features.

Add a Chart

1 Click in the document where you want a chart to appear.

2 Click **Insert**.

The Insert tab appears.

3 Click **Chart** (◫).

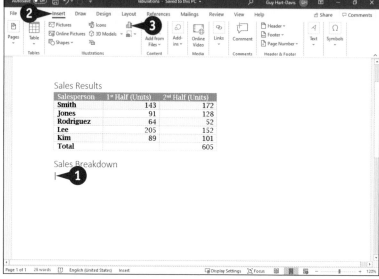

The Insert Chart dialog box opens.

Ⓐ Chart types appear here.

4 Click a chart type.

Ⓑ You can click a subtype of the selected chart type.

5 Click **OK**.

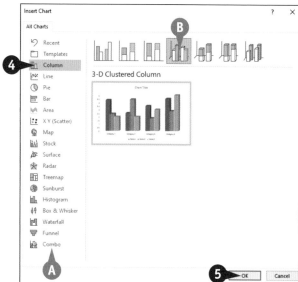

C Microsoft Excel opens. The Chart in Microsoft Word window displays sample data.

D The chart for the sample data appears in Word.

E You can click the **Chart Title** placeholder and type the chart title.

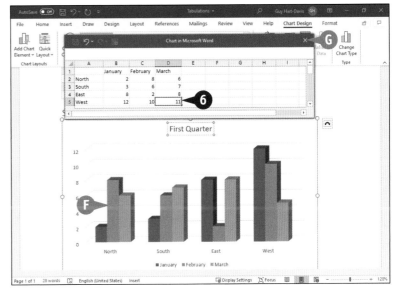

6 Change the data in Excel.

F The chart in Word updates to reflect the changes in Excel.

G You can close Excel without saving by clicking the **Close** button (✕). The chart retains the changes you made in the Excel window.

TIP

Can I format the chart in Word?

Yes. When you select the chart, Word displays the Chart Design tab on the Ribbon and, next to the chart, formatting buttons: **Layout Options** (⌐), **Chart Elements** (+), **Chart Styles** (✎), and **Chart Filters** (▽). Using either the Ribbon tools or the formatting buttons, you can select a layout and style, add and format shape styles and WordArt styles, set up chart and axis titles, add data labels and a data table, and modify the legend. You also can control how text wraps around your chart, change the color and style of your chart, and filter data from your chart to highlight specific values.

Understanding Word's Chart Types

Wh_en creating a chart, you have a wide variety of choices to communicate information in different ways. In addition to the commonly used charts listed below, you can create treemap, sunburst, box and whisker, waterfall charts, and combo charts. A *treemap* chart presents data in a hierarchical fashion. A *sunburst* chart is a variation of a pie chart. A *box and whisker* chart focuses on the middle half of your data points. A *waterfall* chart is a variation of a stock chart. A *combo chart* combines two chart types—for example, combining a line chart with a clustered column chart.

Column Charts

A column chart shows data changes over a period of time and can compare different sets of data. A column chart contains vertical bars.

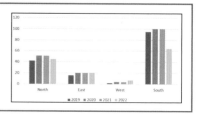

Line Charts

Line charts help you see trends. A line chart connects many related data points; by connecting the points with a line, you see a general trend.

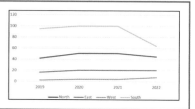

Pie Charts

Pie charts demonstrate the relationship of a part to the whole. Pie charts are effective when you are trying to show, for example, the percentage of total sales for which the Midwest region is responsible.

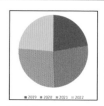

Bar Charts

Bar charts typically compare different sets of data and can also show data changes over time. A bar chart closely resembles a column chart, but the bars are horizontal rather than vertical.

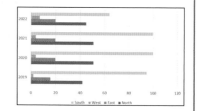

Area Charts

Area charts show data over time, but an area chart helps you see data as broad trends, rather than individual data points.

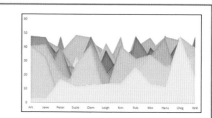

XY (Scatter) Charts

Statisticians often use an XY chart, also called a scatter chart, to determine whether a correlation exists between two variables. Both axes on a scatter chart are numeric, and the axes can be linear or logarithmic.

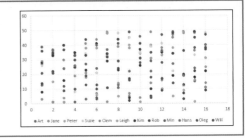

Stock Charts

Also called High-Low, Open-Close charts, stock charts are used for stock market reports. This chart type is very effective for displaying data that fluctuates over time. Waterfall charts are similar to stock charts and focus on showing increases and decreases in sequentially introduced positive or negative values.

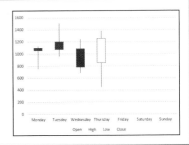

Surface Charts

Topographic maps are surface charts, using colors and patterns to identify areas in the same range of values. A surface chart is useful when you want to find the best-possible combination between two sets of data.

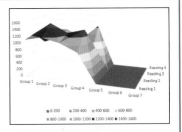

Radar Charts

You can use a radar chart to compare data series that consist of several variables. Each data series on a radar chart has its own axis that "radiates" from the center of the chart—hence the name radar chart. A line connects each point in the series.

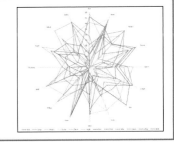

Histogram Charts

A histogram chart groups numeric data into bins; these charts are often used by teachers to depict the distribution of grades in a grading curve.

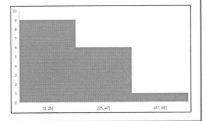

CHAPTER 10

Working with Graphics

Word provides a variety of graphics that you can insert to spruce up your documents. After inserting a graphic, you can edit it to give it the appearance you want. In this chapter, you learn how to insert and edit pictures, clipart images, screenshots, WordArt decorations, shapes, and text boxes.

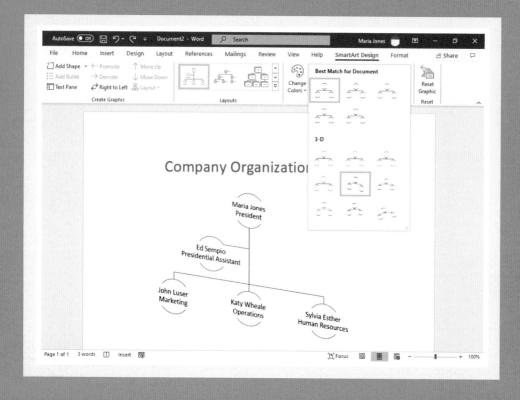

Add Decorative Text Using WordArt

WordArt is decorative text that you can add to a document as an eye-catching visual effect. You can create text graphics that bend and twist or display a subtle shading of color. You find the various WordArt options on the Insert tab of the Ribbon.

You can create WordArt text at the same time that you create a WordArt graphic, or you can apply a WordArt style to existing text. After you convert text into a WordArt object, you can resize, move, or modify the graphic in the ways described in the section "Understanding Graphics Modification Techniques," later in this chapter.

Add Decorative Text Using WordArt

1 Click in the document where you want to add WordArt.

Note: Alternatively, you can select existing text, and then apply WordArt to it.

2 Click **Insert**.

The Insert tab appears.

3 Click **WordArt** (◢▾).

Ⓐ The WordArt gallery appears.

4 Click the WordArt style you want to use.

Ⓑ If you selected text in step **1**, your text appears selected in the WordArt style you applied; otherwise, the words "Your Text Here" appear selected at the location you selected in step **1**.

Ⓒ Handles (○) surround the WordArt graphic.

Ⓓ Drag the rotate handle (⟳) to rotate the graphic.

Ⓔ The Layout Options button (⌂) controls text flow as described in the section "Wrap Text Around a Graphic."

Ⓕ The Shape Format tab appears on the Ribbon. You can use tools on this tab to format WordArt.

5 If necessary, type text.

G Word converts the text to a WordArt graphic.

6 If you want to rotate the WordArt object, drag the rotate handle (⟳).

7 Click **Layout Options** (⌂) if you want to change the text wrapping.

8 Click anywhere outside the WordArt to continue working.

Note: You can move, resize, or rotate the WordArt; see the section "Move or Resize a Graphic," later in this chapter.

Note: You can change the size of the WordArt font by selecting the WordArt text and, on the Home tab, selecting a different font size from the Font list in the Font group.

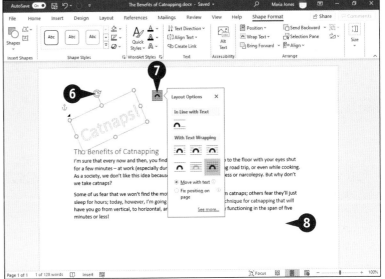

TIPS

How do I edit a WordArt object?
Click inside the WordArt drawing. Handles (○) appear around the WordArt object. Edit the text as needed.

How do I delete a WordArt object?
Click insert the WordArt object to select it, click any handle or any border, and then press Delete.

253

Add a Picture

You can include a picture stored on your computer to add punch to your Word document. After you insert a picture, you can resize, move, or modify the graphic in a variety of ways. The section "Understanding Graphics Modification Techniques," later in this chapter, describes the many ways you can edit an image or add effects to an image.

Add a Picture

1 Click in your document where you want to add a picture.

2 Click **Insert**.

The Insert tab appears.

3 Click **Pictures**.

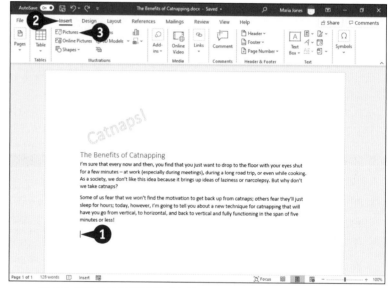

The Insert Picture dialog box opens.

Ⓐ The folder you are viewing appears here.

Ⓑ You can click in the folder list to navigate to commonly used locations where pictures may be stored.

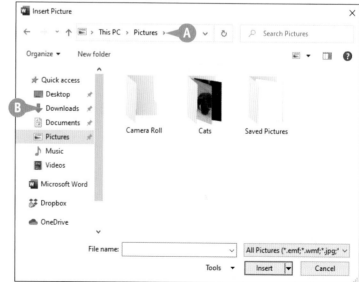

4 Navigate to the folder containing the picture you want to add.

5 Click the picture you want to add to your document.

6 Click **Insert**.

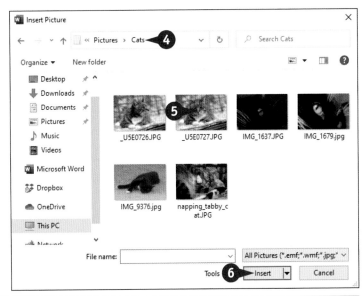

C The picture appears in your document, selected and surrounded by handles (○).

D You can drag the rotate handle (↻) to rotate the picture.

E You can click the Layout Options button (▣) to control text flow around the picture. See the section "Wrap Text Around a Graphic," later in this chapter.

F The Picture Format tab appears on the Ribbon; you can use tools on this tab to format pictures.

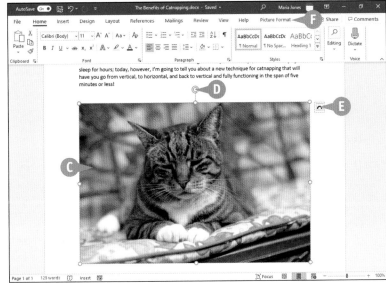

TIP

How can I delete a picture?
Move the pointer over the picture so that ▷ changes to ✛. Click the picture to select it, and then press Delete.

Insert an Online Picture

In addition to pictures stored on your computer's hard drive, you can insert a picture from an online source into a Word document.

The online picture search uses Bing Image Search by default; all images you find are licensed under Creative Commons. To avoid violating copyright laws, exercise care in choosing online pictures. Make sure that they fall into the public domain or that you have written permission to use the picture.

Insert an Online Picture

1 Click in your document where you want to add a picture.

2 Click **Insert**.

The Insert tab appears.

3 Click **Online Pictures**.

The Online Pictures window appears.

4 Click here and type a description of the type of image you want.

5 Press Enter.

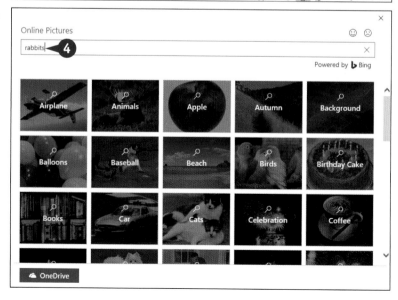

The results of your search appear.

A You can click the arrows (▲ and ▼) to navigate through the search results.

B You can click **Back** (←) to return to the Insert Picture window and search for a different image.

6 Click the picture you want to add to your document.

7 Click **Insert**.

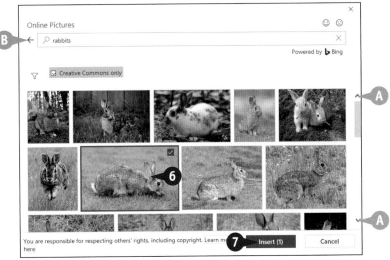

C The picture appears in your document, selected and surrounded by handles (○).

D You can drag the rotate handle (⟳) to rotate the picture.

E The Layout Options button (⌐) controls text flow around the picture, as described in the section "Wrap Text Around a Graphic," later in this chapter.

F The Picture Format tab appears on the Ribbon. You can use tools on this tab to format the picture.

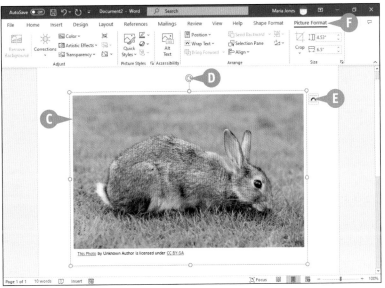

TIP

Why must I make sure that the image I choose falls into the public domain?

Images that are privately owned are often available for use only if you agree to pay a fee, give credit to the owner of the image, or both. To use a public domain image, you do not need to pay a royalty or get permission from an image owner to use the image.

You should also check the license for any restrictions. For example, the license may allow free personal use but not commercial use.

Insert a Video

You can insert a video available on the Internet into a Word document. After you have inserted the video, you can play it directly from the Word document.

You can insert videos you find using Bing Search or videos available on YouTube, or you can insert a video embed code—an HTML code that uses the src attribute—to define the video file you want to embed. Many videos posted on the Internet are public domain, but if you are unsure, do some research to determine if you can use the video freely.

Insert a Video

1 In a browser, navigate to the video you want to include in the Word document.

Note: This example uses YouTube. The specific steps may vary on other video sites.

2 Click **Share**.

The Share dialog opens, showing a shortened version of the URL for the video.

Ⓐ You can click **Start at** (☐ changes to ☑) to make the video start at the current playback point.

3 Click **Copy**.

The browser copies the URL to the Windows Clipboard.

4 Click **Word** (🔲) on the Taskbar, and then click the thumbnail for the appropriate document.

5 Click where you want to add a video.

6 Click **Insert**.

The Insert tab appears.

7 Click **Online Video**.

The Insert a Video dialog box opens.

8 Paste in the copied URL. For example, right-click, and then click **Paste** on the context menu.

9 Click **Insert**.

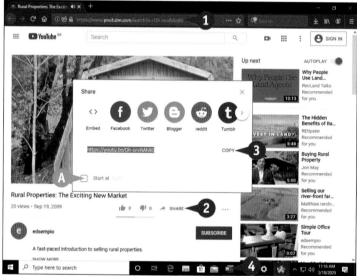

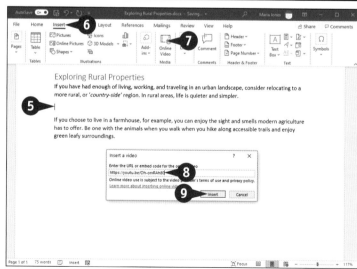

The Insert a Video dialog box closes.

Ⓑ The video appears in your document, selected and surrounded by handles (○).

Ⓒ You can drag the rotate handle (⟳) to rotate the video.

Note: Rotating, moving, or resizing the video affects only the preview frame. When playing, the video appears centered and at a fixed size.

Ⓓ The Picture Format tab appears on the Ribbon; you can use tools on this tab to format the appearance of the video preview in your document.

⑩ To change the layout, click Layout Options (⌐), and then click the icon for the wrapping you want.

Ⓔ The video appears with the wrapping you chose.

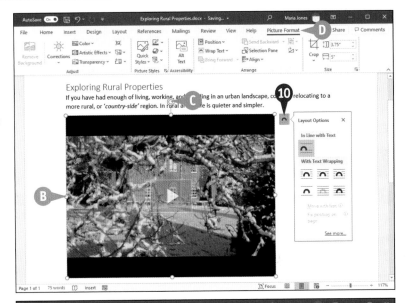

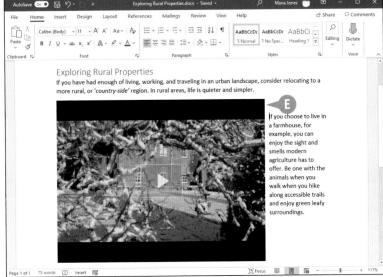

TIP

How do I play an inserted video?
From Print Layout view or Read Mode view, click **Play** (▶). The video player appears as a layer in front of the document. Click **Play** (▶) in the video player to set the video playing.

To stop the video and return to the document, click anywhere outside the video player or press Esc.

Add a Screenshot

Y ou can insert an image called a *screenshot* into a Word document. You can capture a screenshot of another document open in Word or of a document open in another program.

Screenshots are exact pictures of the open document at the moment you take the screenshot. In addition to including a screenshot in a Word document, if you are having a problem on your computer, you can use a screenshot to help capture the problem so that you can provide accurate and detailed information to the technical support person who helps you.

Add a Screenshot

1 Open the document you want to capture.

A This example shows a chart in Excel.

2 Switch to the Word document in which you want to insert the screenshot. For example, click the document's button on the Taskbar.

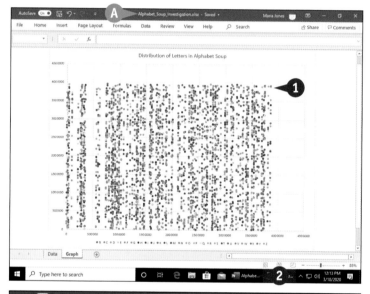

The Word document appears.

3 Position the insertion point where you want the screenshot to appear.

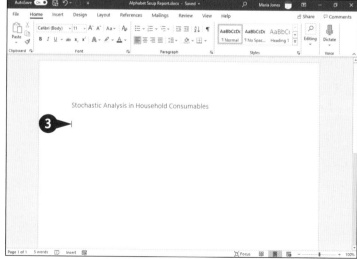

④ Click **Insert**.

The Insert tab appears.

⑤ Click **Screenshot** (📷▾).

Ⓑ The Screenshot gallery shows open programs and available screenshots of those programs.

⑥ Click the screenshot you want to insert in your Word document.

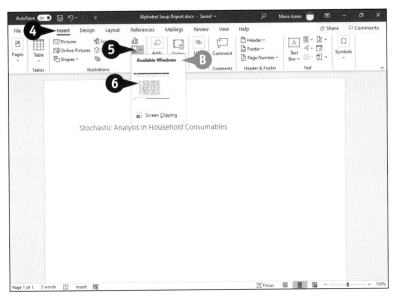

Ⓒ The screenshot appears in your Word document, selected and surrounded by handles (○).

Ⓓ You can drag the rotate handle (⟳) to rotate the screenshot.

Ⓔ The Layout Options button (⌃) controls text flow around the screenshot, as described in the section "Wrap Text Around a Graphic," later in this chapter.

Ⓕ The Picture Format tab appears on the Ribbon. You can use tools on this tab to format the screenshot.

⑦ Click anywhere outside the screenshot to continue working.

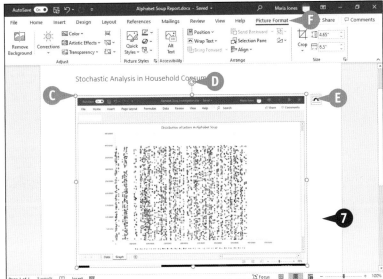

TIP

Can I take a picture of my desktop?
You cannot use the Screenshot feature to take a picture of your desktop. But here is a workaround: While viewing your desktop, press [Print scrn]. Then switch to Word and position the insertion point where the screenshot should appear. Press [Ctrl]+[V] to paste the image into your Word document.

Add a Shape

To give your Word document pizzazz, you can add graphic shapes such as lines, arrows, stars, and banners. Word provides a wide variety of shapes, which you can resize and format to suit the needs of your documents.

Shapes are visible in Print Layout, Web Layout, and Read Mode views.

Add a Shape

1 In the document where you want to include a shape, click **Insert**.

The Insert tab appears.

2 Click **Shapes**.

The Shapes gallery appears.

3 Click the shape you want to add.

The Shapes gallery closes and the pointer (I) changes to +.

4 Position the pointer at the upper-left corner of the place where you want the shape to appear.

5 Drag the pointer (+) down and to the right until the shape is the size you want.

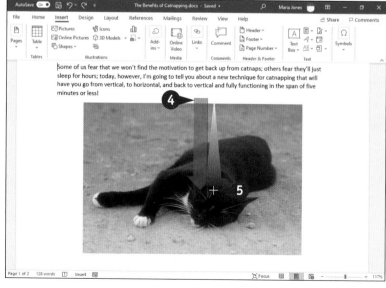

Ⓐ When you release the mouse button, the shape appears in your document, selected and surrounded by handles (Ⓞ).

Ⓑ You can drag the rotate handle (⟳) to rotate the shape.

Ⓒ The Layout Options button (⌂) controls text flow around the shape, as described in the section "Wrap Text Around a Graphic," later in this chapter.

Ⓓ The Shape Format tab appears on the Ribbon.

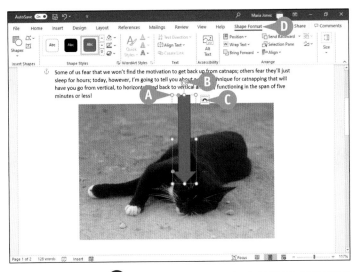

6️⃣ To change the color of the shape, click **Shape Format** if the Shape Format tab is not currently displayed.

The Shape Format tab appears.

7️⃣ Click **Shape Fill** (🖌▾).

The Shape Fill gallery appears.

8️⃣ Move the pointer over the color you want.

Ⓔ Word previews the color.

9️⃣ Click the color you want.

Word applies the color to the shape.

🔟 Press Esc or click outside the shape to continue working in your document.

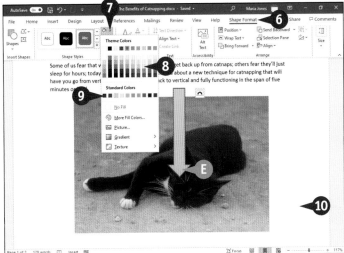

TIP

How can I work with several shapes at once?

If you need to work with several shapes together just one time, click the first shape, and then press Shift while you click each of the others. You can then work with all the shapes at once.

If you need to work with several shapes together frequently, group them. Select the shapes as just described, then right-click in the selection to display the context menu. Click or highlight **Group** to display the Group submenu, and then click **Group** on the submenu to group the shapes. You can then work with the group as a single object. To ungroup the shapes, click **Ungroup** on the Group submenu.

Add a Text Box

Y ou can add a text box graphic to your document to control the placement and appearance of the text that appears in the box. Use text boxes to draw attention to specific text, to easily move text around within a document, or to display text vertically instead of horizontally.

Word inserts your text box near the insertion point, but you can move the text box the same way you move any graphic element; see the next section, "Move or Resize a Graphic," for details. Text boxes are visible only in Print Layout, Web Layout, and Read Mode views.

Add a Text Box

1 Click near the location where you want the text box to appear.

2 Click **Insert**.

The Insert tab appears.

3 Click **Text Box**.

The Text Box gallery appears.

4 Click a text box style.

A You can scroll down to view many more styles.

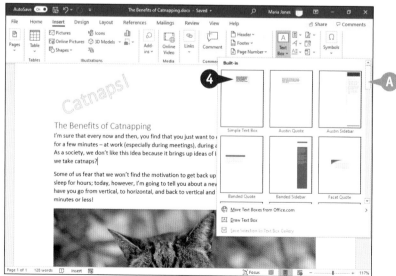

B The Text Box gallery closes and Word places a text box in your document.

Sample text appears inside a text box, and Word selects the sample text.

C Existing text flows around the box.

D You can drag the rotate handle (⟳) to rotate the text box.

E The Shape Format tab appears on the Ribbon. You can use tools on this tab to format the text box.

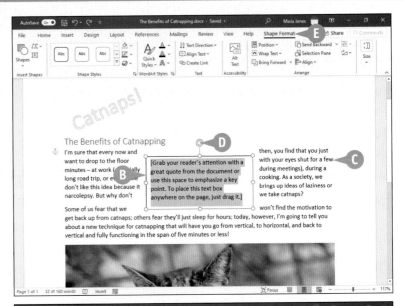

5 To replace the sample text, start typing.

F The Layout Options button (⌷) appears; use it to control text flow around the shape, as described in the section "Wrap Text Around a Graphic," later in this chapter.

6 Click outside the text box when you want to continue work in the document.

Note: You can format the text using the techniques described in Chapter 5, "Formatting Text."

TIP

What should I do if I do not like any of the predefined text box formats?

You can examine additional styles available from Office.com, or you can draw your own text box and format it. Complete steps **1** to **3** in this section. Click **More Text Boxes from Office.com** to view some additional text box styles. Alternatively, click **Draw Text Box** (I changes to +). Drag the pointer (+) from the upper-left to the lower right-corner of where you want the text box. The text box then appears.

Move or Resize a Graphic

Word enables you to easily move a graphic to a different location in a document and to resize it as needed. When you move a graphic, Word displays alignment guides to help you position the graphic where it is needed.

Word automatically reflows text around a graphic when you move it or resize it. You can also control the wrapping manually, as explained in the section "Wrap Text Around a Graphic," later in this chapter.

Move or Resize a Graphic

Move a Graphic

1 Click the graphic.

A Handles (○) appear around the graphic.

2 Position the pointer over the graphic (I changes to ✥).

Note: When moving a text box, position the pointer over one of the text box's edges (I changes to ✥) rather than over the inside of the text box.

3 Drag the graphic to a new location.

B Green alignment guides help you position the graphic.

Note: If, when you drag the graphic, green alignment guides do not appear but the move pointer (⯭) appears, the graphic is in the text layer of the document. To move it to a different layer, right-click the graphic, click or highlight **Wrap Text** on the context menu, and then click a different wrap type, such as **Behind Text**.

4 Release the mouse button.

The graphic appears in the new location, and the alignment guides disappear.

5 Click outside the graphic to deselect it.

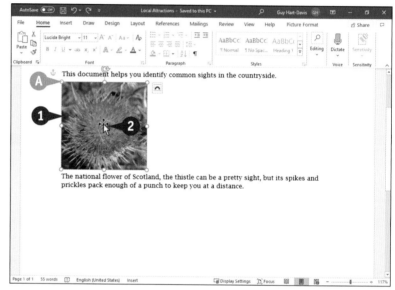

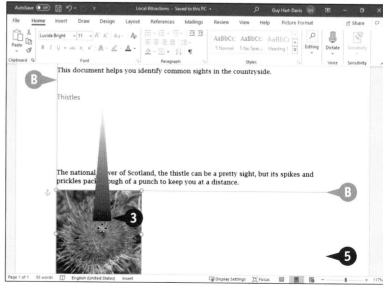

Resize a Graphic

1 Click the graphic.

C Handles (○) surround the graphic.

2 Position the pointer over one of the handles (I changes to ⬉, ↕, ⬈, or ↔).

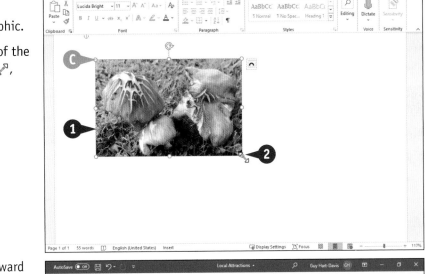

3 Drag the handle inward or outward until the graphic is the appropriate size (⬉, ↕, ⬈, or ↔ changes to +).

4 Release the mouse button.

The graphic appears at the new size.

5 Click outside the graphic to deselect it.

TIP

Does it matter which handle I use to resize a graphic?

If you click and drag any of the corner handles, you maintain the proportion of the graphic as you resize it. The handles on the sides, top, or bottom of the graphic resize the width or the height only of the graphic, so using one of them can make your graphic look distorted, especially if you resize a picture, video, or screenshot using any handle except a corner handle.

Understanding Graphics Modification Techniques

In addition to moving or resizing graphics, you can modify their appearance using commands that appear on the Ribbon. When you select a graphic, the Ribbon displays context tabs that contain commands for that type of graphic.

You can adjust the size, brightness or contrast, and color of a picture. You can rotate a graphic or make it three-dimensional. You also can add a shadow or apply a color outline or style to a graphic.

Crop a Picture

The Crop tool enables you to crop the image down to only the part you want to show. You can crop to a particular aspect ratio, such as Square, or to a shape, such as a circle or a star. Cropping an object hides the parts of the object you specify but does not actually remove them, so you can adjust the cropping later, if needed. The Crop tool appears in the Size group on the Picture Format contextual tab of the Ribbon.

Rotate or Flip a Graphic

You can rotate or flip an object, such as a picture or a shape, either to correct a problem or to create dramatic effect. To do so, use the Rotate tool in the Arrange group on the Picture Format context tab of the Ribbon. You cannot rotate text boxes.

Correct Images

You can change the brightness and contrast of an image to improve its appearance, and you can sharpen or soften an image. The image-correction tools appear on the Picture Format context tab of the Ribbon.

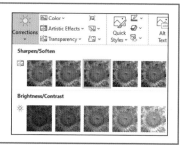

Make Color Adjustments

You can adjust the color of a picture, screenshot, or clipart image by increasing or decreasing color saturation or color tone. You also can recolor a picture, screenshot, or clipart image to create an interesting effect.

Color saturation controls the intensity of a color, expressed as the degree to which it differs from white in a photo. Color tone controls the appearance of a photo as the result of mixing a pure color with any grayscale color.

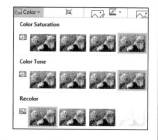

Remove the Background of an Image

You can remove the background of a picture, screenshot, or clipart image. To do so, click Remove Background on the Picture Format context tab, and then use the controls on the Background Removal context tab that appears.

Add a Picture Effect or a Shape Effect

Word provides picture effects for enhancing pictures and shape effects for enhancing shapes. For example, you can apply a shadow effect, create a mirrored reflection, apply a glow effect, soften the object's edges, make a bevel effect, or generate a 3-D rotation effect. You can find these tools on the Format tab of the Ribbon.

Apply a Style to a Graphic

You can apply a predefined style to a shape, text box, WordArt graphic, picture, or clipart image. Styles contain predefined colors and effects and help you give your graphics a standard look.

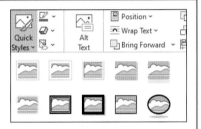

Add a Picture Border or a Drawing Outline

You can add a border to a picture, shape, text box, WordArt graphic, clipart image, or screenshot by using the Picture Border tool or the Shape Outline tool, which you can find on the Picture Format tab or the Shape Format tab. You can format the border color, weight, and style.

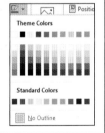

Apply Artistic Effects

Word's Artistic Effects tool helps you liven up your pictures, screenshots, and clipart images. For example, you can make an image appear as though it was rendered in marker, pencil, chalk, or paint. You find the Artistic Effects button on the Picture Format tab of the Ribbon.

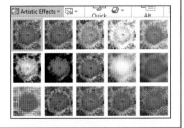

Understanding Text Wrapping and Graphics

Word enables you to control the way text wraps around graphics you insert in a document. For example, you can wrap text around a graphic, force text to skip a graphic and leave its left and right sides blank, or place a graphic on top of text or underneath text. By default, most graphics have a relatively square boundary, even if the graphic is not a square, and most text-wrapping options relate to that relatively square boundary.

By editing a graphic's wrap points, you can change the square boundary to more closely match the graphic's shape and wrap text more closely around the shape.

Button	Function
In Line with Text	Text does not wrap around the graphic. Word positions the graphic exactly where you placed it. The graphic moves to accommodate added or deleted text, but no text appears on the graphic's right or left.
Square	This option wraps text in a square around your graphic regardless of its shape. You can control the amount of space between text and all your graphic's sides.
Tight	This option wraps text around the graphic's outside edge. The difference between this option and Square becomes apparent with a nonsquare shape; with Tight, you can control the space between the text and the graphic's right and left sides. Word leaves no space between text and the graphic's top and bottom sides.
Through	With this option, if you edit a graphic's wrap points by dragging them to match the shape of the graphic, you can wrap text to follow the graphic's shape.
Top and Bottom	Wraps text around the graphic's top and bottom but leaves the space on either side of a graphic blank.
Behind Text	With this option, the text runs over the graphic, as if the graphic were not there.
In Front of Text	With this option, the graphic appears to block the text underneath the graphic's location.
Edit Wrap Points	Displays handles that represent an image's wrap points. You can drag the handles to change the position of the wrap points. Changing a wrap point does not change the image's appearance but affects the way text wraps around the image.
✓ Move with Text Fix Position on Page	Choose one of these options to determine the way Word positions an image. Choose **Move with Text** to have the image move as you add text; choose **Fix Position on Page** to keep the image exactly where you placed it on the page.

Wrap Text Around a Graphic

You can control the way that Word wraps text around a graphic image in your document. Controlling the way text wraps around a graphic becomes very important when you want to place graphics in a document where space is at a premium, such as a two-column newsletter. See the previous section for details on text wrapping methods. The information in this section shows text wrapping for a picture but applies to text wrapping for any kind of graphic.

Wrap Text Around a Graphic

1 Click a graphic.

A Handles (○) appear around the image.

2 Click **Picture Format**.

The Picture Format tab appears.

3 Click **Wrap Text**.

The Wrap Text pop-up panel opens.

4 Move the pointer (↖) over a wrapping style to see how it affects the text and the image.

5 Click the wrapping style you want to apply.

B Word wraps text around the graphic using the text wrapping option you selected.

Work with Diagrams

You can use the SmartArt feature to create all kinds of diagrams to illustrate concepts and processes. For example, you might insert a diagram in a document to show the hierarchy in your company or to show the workflow in your department.

SmartArt offers predefined diagram types, including list, process, cycle, hierarchy, relationship, matrix, pyramid, and picture. In addition, you can choose from several diagram styles within each type. For example, if you choose to create a hierarchy diagram, you can choose from several different styles of hierarchy diagrams.

Work with Diagrams

Add a Diagram

1 Click in your document where you want the diagram to appear.

2 Click **Insert**.

The Insert tab appears.

3 Click **SmartArt** (🖼).

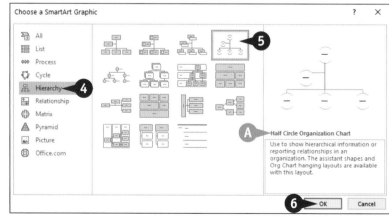

The Choose a SmartArt Graphic dialog box appears.

4 Click the diagram category.

5 Click the type of diagram you want to add.

A A description of the selected diagram appears here.

6 Click **OK**.

Word adds the diagram.

Note: Each object within the diagram is called a *shape*.

Ⓑ The handles (○) surrounding the diagram indicate that the diagram is selected; the border will not print.

Ⓒ The SmartArt Design tab and the Format tab appear on the Ribbon.

Ⓓ The Text pane appears. Each bullet in the Text pane matches a text block in the diagram.

Note: If you do not see the Text pane, click **Text Pane** in the Create Graphic group on the SmartArt Design tab.

Add Text to the Diagram

① If the Text pane is not visible, on the SmartArt Tools Design tab, click **Text Pane**.

② Click a bullet in the Text pane and type the text you want to add.

Ⓔ Text you add appears both in the Text pane and on the diagram.

Note: You do not need to use the Text pane; you can click and type directly in a shape.

③ Repeat step **2** for each shape in the diagram. When you finish, click ✕ to close the Text pane and click a blank spot on the diagram.

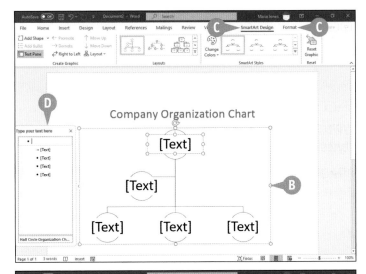

TIPS

How can I add two lines of text to a shape?
After you type the first line of the text in the Text pane, press Shift + Enter. Then type the second line. Word adjusts the font size of the text to fit the shape, and for consistency, Word adjusts the font size of all text in the diagram to match.

How can I control the size and position of the diagram on the page?
You can size the diagram using its handles. Word sets the default position on the diagram in line with your text. You can position the diagram by dragging it.

continued ▶

You can customize a SmartArt diagram by adding or removing shapes as needed. For example, you may need to add extra positions to an organization chart after hiring staff or delete them after firing staff.

To give your diagrams a professional look that helps them convey your meaning clearly, you can apply Word's predefined styles to the diagrams.

Work with Diagrams (continued)

Add or Delete Shapes

1 With the diagram selected, click **SmartArt Design**.

The SmartArt Design tab appears.

2 Click the shape above or beside which you want to add a shape.

F Handles (○) surround the shape.

3 Click ✔ beside **Add Shape**.

4 Click the appropriate button to specify where the new shape should appear relative to the selected shape.

This example adds a shape after the selected shape.

G The new shape appears.

You can add text to the new shape by following the steps in the previous subsection, "Add Text to the Diagram."

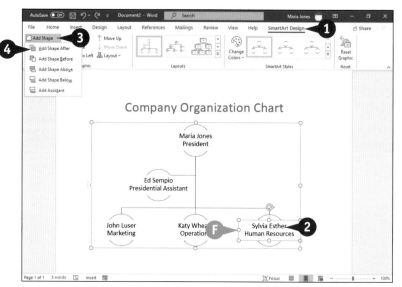

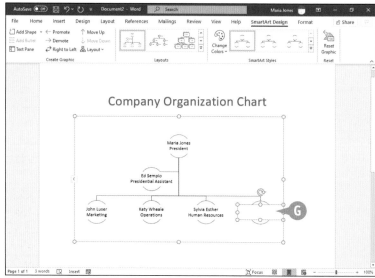

274

Apply a Diagram Style

1 Click the diagram to select it.

2 Click **SmartArt Design**.

The SmartArt Design tab appears.

3 Click **More** (▽) in the SmartArt Styles group.

Ⓗ The SmartArt Styles gallery appears.

Ⓘ The current style appears highlighted.

4 Move the pointer (▷) over the style you want to preview.

Note: The selection box for the current style and the selection box for the Live Preview look the same, which can be confusing.

Ⓙ The Live Preview shows how the diagram will look using that style.

5 Click the style you want to apply.

Word applies the selected style to the diagram.

6 Click anywhere outside the diagram to continue working.

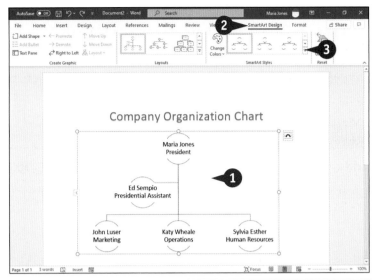

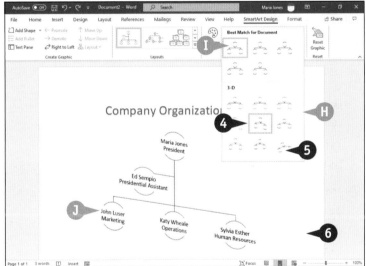

TIPS

How do I delete a shape?
Click the outside border of the shape; handles (○) appear around the shape. Then press Delete. If the shape has an element outside its text box, you must select the text box—but not the text inside it—before pressing Delete.

How do I change the layout of an organization chart diagram after I insert it?
Click the diagram to select it. Then click **SmartArt Design**, go to the Layouts group, click the **More** button (▽) to display the Layouts gallery, and then click a different organization chart structure. To select a different type of diagram, click **More Layouts** at the bottom of the Layouts gallery to reopen the Choose a SmartArt Graphic dialog box.

CHAPTER 11

Customizing Word

Word's default settings are designed to work for as many people as possible, but you will likely want to customize Word to make it work the way you prefer. For example, you can customize the Quick Access Toolbar, the status bar, and the Ribbon; create custom keyboard shortcuts; and even create custom commands by recording macros.

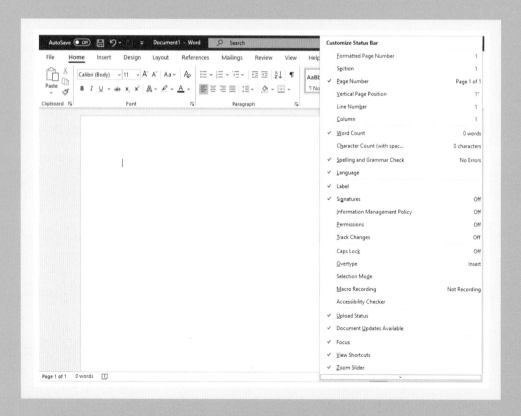

Control the Display of Formatting Marks

As explained in detail in Chapter 6, "Formatting Paragraphs," you can display formatting marks—such as spaces, tabs, and paragraph marks—by clicking **Show/Hide** (¶) in the Paragraph group on the Home tab of the Ribbon. Displaying formatting marks is often helpful for resolving layout peculiarities, such as blank space where you do not want it.

By default, clicking **Show/Hide** (¶) toggles the display of all formatting marks. For greater control, you can open the Word Options dialog box and specify what formatting marks you want to see.

Control the Display of Formatting Marks

1 Click **File**.

Backstage view appears.

2 Click **Options**.

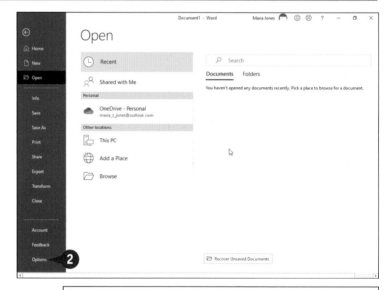

The Word Options dialog box opens.

3 Click **Display**.

Ⓐ You can click **Show all formatting marks** (☐ changes to ☑) to display all formatting marks.

4 Click the formatting marks you want to display (☐ changes to ☑).

5 Click **OK**.

Word displays only the selected formatting marks in your document.

Customize the Status Bar

You can customize the status bar to display the information you want visible while you work. By default, Word displays some information on the status bar, such as the page number and number of pages and words in your document. You can add a wide variety of information, such as the position of the insertion point by line and column number or by vertical page position. You also can display indicators of spelling and grammar errors and typing mode—insert or overtype.

Customize the Status Bar

1 Right-click the status bar.

The Customize Status Bar pop-up menu appears.

2 Click the option you want to display on the status bar.

A check appears next to the option.

3 Repeat step 2 for each option you want to display.

4 Click outside the Customize Status Bar menu.

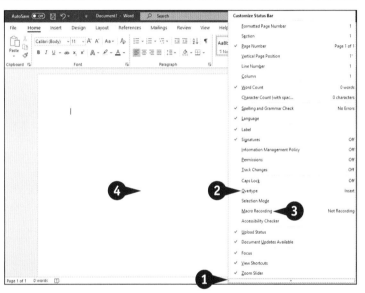

The Customize Status Bar menu closes.

A Word displays the option or options you selected on the status bar.

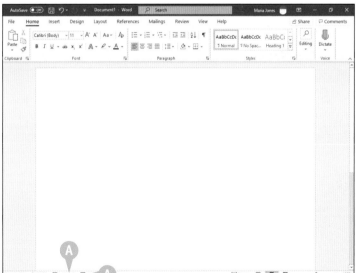

Hide or Display Ribbon Buttons

By default, Word "pins" the Ribbon, keeping it on the screen all the time. When you need more space, you can unpin the Ribbon to hide it, and then redisplay it when you need it.

When you unpin and hide the Ribbon, the tab names still appear on screen. When you click a tab name, the Ribbon reappears; after you click a control to give a command, it disappears again. Hiding the Ribbon has no effect on the Quick Access Toolbar.

Hide or Display Ribbon Buttons

Ⓐ By default, Word displays the Ribbon.

① Click **Unpin the Ribbon** (⌃).

Ⓑ Word unpins the Ribbon, hiding the buttons but continuing to display the tabs.

② Work in your document as usual.

③ When you need a Ribbon button, click that Ribbon tab.

Note: You can click any Ribbon tab, but it is quickest to click the tab that contains the button you need.

C Word redisplays the Ribbon buttons.

4 Click the button you need.

D Word performs the button's action.

5 Click anywhere outside the Ribbon.

E Word hides the Ribbon buttons again.

How can I redisplay the Ribbon buttons permanently?
Click any Ribbon tab to display the Ribbon. Then click **Pin the Ribbon** (⇥) in the lower-right corner of the Ribbon.

Is there another way to hide the Ribbon buttons?
Yes. Click **Ribbon Display Options** (▭) to display a pop-up menu. The Auto-Hide Ribbon option hides Ribbon buttons, tabs, and the controls to minimize, maximize, and restore the window. The Show Tabs option hides Ribbon buttons but displays the other controls. The Show Tabs and Commands option displays everything: the Ribbon tabs and buttons and the window-control buttons.

Add a Predefined Group to a Ribbon Tab

You can customize the Ribbon to suit your working style. You can work more efficiently if you customize the Ribbon to place the groups of buttons that you use most often on a single Ribbon tab.

For example, suppose that most of the buttons you need appear on the Home tab, but you often use the Page Setup group on the Page Layout tab to change document margins and set up columns. You can add the Page Setup group to the Home tab. That way, you do not need to switch tabs to get to the commands you use most often.

Add a Predefined Group to a Ribbon Tab

1 Click **File**.

Backstage view appears.

2 Click **Options**.

The Word Options dialog box opens.

3 Click **Customize Ribbon**.

The Customize Ribbon category appears.

4 Click **Choose Commands from** (⌄) and select **Main Tabs**.

5 Click ⊞ beside the tab containing the group you want to add (⊞ changes to ⊟).

6 Click the group you want to add.

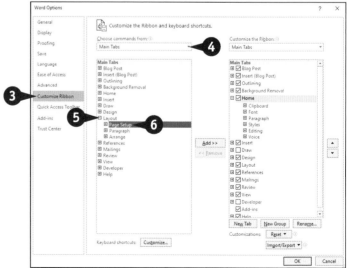

7 Click ⊞ beside the tab where you want to place the group you selected in step **6** (⊞ changes to ⊟).

8 Click the group you want to appear on the Ribbon to the left of the new group.

9 Click **Add**.

Ⓐ Word adds the group you selected in step **6** below the group you selected in step **8**.

10 Repeat steps **5** to **9**, as needed.

11 Click **OK**.

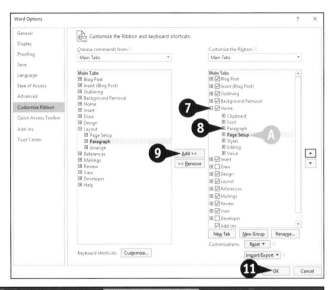

Ⓑ Word adds the group you selected to the appropriate Ribbon tab.

Ⓒ Word might collapse other groups to fit the new group on the tab. In this example, Word has collapsed the Styles group.

How do I add a single button—rather than a group—to one of the existing groups on the Ribbon?

Create your own group that contains only those buttons you want to use, and then hide the default group that Word displays. See the next section, "Create Your Own Ribbon Group."

If I change my mind, how can I eliminate the changes I made to the Ribbon?

Complete steps **1** to **3**. In the column on the right, select the Ribbon tab and group you added. Just above the OK button, click **Reset**, and from the menu that appears, click **Reset only selected Ribbon tab**. Then click **OK**.

Create Your Own Ribbon Group

Y ou cannot add or remove buttons from predefined groups on a Ribbon tab, but you can create your own group and place the buttons you want in the group. Creating your own groups of Ribbon buttons can help you work more efficiently because you can place all the buttons you use regularly together and save yourself the time of switching groups and even Ribbon tabs.

To create your own Ribbon group, you first make a group, placing it on the tab and in the position where you want it to appear. Then you name it, and finally you add buttons to it.

Create Your Own Ribbon Group

Make a Group

1 Click **File**.

Backstage view appears.

2 Click **Options**.

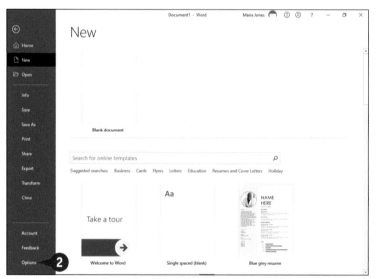

The Word Options dialog box opens.

3 Click **Customize Ribbon**.

The Customize Ribbon category appears.

4 Click ⊞ beside the tab to which you want to add a group (⊞ changes to ⊟).

5 Click the group you want to appear on the Ribbon to the left of the new group.

6 Click **New Group**.

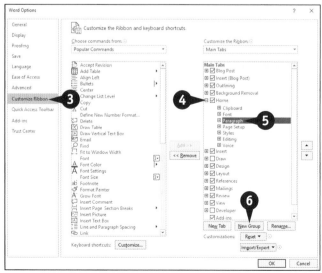

Ⓐ Word adds a new group to the tab below the group you selected in step **5** and selects the new group.

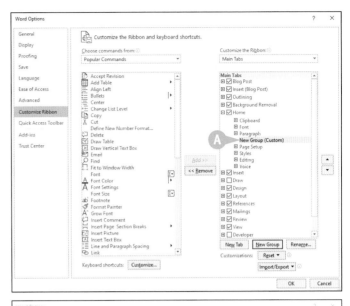

Assign a Name to the Group

① Click the group you created in the previous subsection, "Make a Group."

② Click **Rename**.

The Rename dialog box opens.

③ Type a name for your group.

④ Click **OK**.

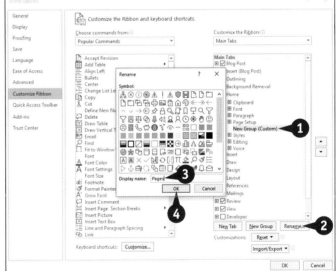

TIP

How can I move my group to another tab?
In the Customize Ribbon category of the Word Options dialog box, click ⊞ to the left of the tab that contains the group you want to move, expanding the tab's groups. Click ⊞ to the left of the destination tab, expanding that tab's groups too. Click the group you want to move, and then click **Up** (⬆) or **Down** (⬇) as needed to reposition the group. When you finish, click **OK** to save your changes.

continued ▶

After you add a group to a tab, you can assign a name to it that you find meaningful—for example, something that describes the buttons you intend to include in the group or something that differentiates the group you created from the standard groups on the default Ribbon.

After you name your group, you can then add whatever buttons you need to the group. You are not limited to selecting buttons that appear together on one of the default Ribbon tabs; you can include buttons from any Ribbon tabs and buttons that do not ordinarily appear on the Ribbon.

Create Your Own Ribbon Group (continued)

Ⓑ Word assigns the name to your group.

Add Buttons to Your Group

❶ Click the group you created.

❷ Click a command.

Ⓒ If the command you want does not appear in the list, click ⌄ and select **All Commands**.

❸ Click **Add**.

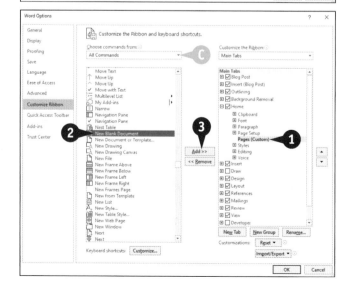

D The command appears below the group you created.

4 Repeat steps **2** and **3** for each button you want to add to your group.

5 Click **OK**.

The Word Options dialog box closes.

Use Your Own Ribbon Group

1 Click the tab on which you placed the group. For example, click **Home**.

The tab appears.

2 If the group is collapsed, click its button.

The panel for the group appears.

3 Click the button you want to use.

Are there any restrictions for the names I assign to groups I create?

You can freely create names up to 512 characters long; much shorter names are much more practical. Word even lets you use a name that already appears on the Ribbon, such as Font, and you can place that custom group on the Home tab, where the predefined Font group already exists.

Can I assign keyboard shortcuts to the buttons I add to my group?

Word assigns keyboard shortcuts for you, based on the keys already assigned to commands appearing on the tab where you place your group. If you place the same button on two different tabs, Word assigns different keyboard shortcuts to that button on each tab.

Create Your Own Ribbon Tab

In addition to creating groups on the Ribbon in which you can place buttons of your choosing, you can create your own tab on the Ribbon.

Creating your own tab can help you work efficiently; you can store the buttons you use most frequently in groups on your tab. Then you can position your tab on the Ribbon so that it appears by default when you open Word. With all the buttons you use most frequently automatically visible, you save the time of locating the buttons you need on the various Ribbon tabs.

Create Your Own Ribbon Tab

Create a New Tab

1 Click **File**.

Backstage view appears.

2 Click **Options**.

The Word Options dialog box opens.

3 Click **Customize Ribbon**.

The Customize Ribbon category appears.

4 Click the existing tab to the right of which you want to position the new tab.

5 Click **New Tab**.

Ⓐ Word creates a new tab below the tab you selected in step **4**, along with a new group on that tab.

Note: If you remove a tab, Word removes all the groups and commands the tab contains without confirmation.

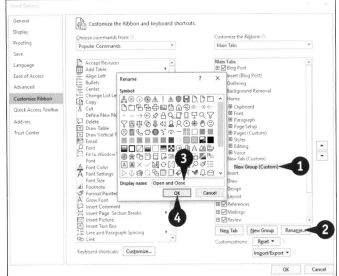

Name the New Tab and New Group

① Click the group you created, labeled as **New Group (Custom)**.

② Click **Rename**.

The Rename dialog box opens.

③ Type a name for your group.

④ Click **OK**.

The Rename dialog box closes, and the group takes on the name.

continued ▶

TIPS

How do I reposition my tab?
Click the tab you want to move, and then click **Up** (▲) or **Down** (▼) as needed to reposition the tab.

How can I make a Ribbon tab visible when Word opens?
You can make your tab visible immediately every time you open Word by placing it above the Home tab.

Wen you create a custom tab, Word automatically creates one group for you so that you can quickly and easily add buttons to the new tab. You can add other groups to the tab and place buttons in them; see the section "Create Your Own Ribbon Group," earlier in this chapter.

You can assign a name of your choice to each custom tab or custom group you create. Normally, you will do best to assign each item a descriptive name based on its contents and the functionality those contents provide.

Create Your Own Ribbon Tab (continued)

5 Click the new tab you created, which is labeled **New Tab (Custom)**.

6 Click **Rename**.

The Rename dialog box opens.

7 In the Display Name box, type the name you want to give the tab.

8 Click **OK**.

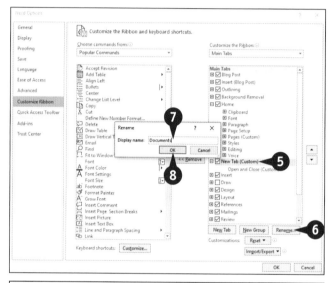

The Rename dialog box closes.

B The tab takes on the name you assigned.

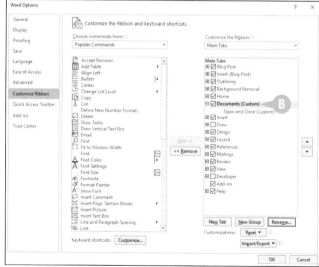

Add Buttons to Your Group

1 Click the group on the tab you created.

2 Click a command.

C If the command you want does not appear in the list, click **Choose commands from** (⌄), and then click **All Commands**.

3 Click **Add**.

D The command appears below the group you created.

4 Repeat steps **2** and **3** for each button you want to add to the group.

5 Click **OK**.

The Word Options dialog box closes.

E The new tab appears on the Ribbon, along with the group containing the buttons you added.

Note: Some third-party apps may add a group to the Ribbon in Word. For example, installing Adobe Acrobat adds the Acrobat group to the Ribbon in Word.

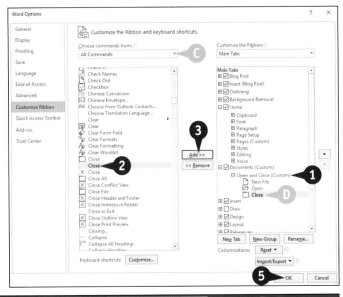

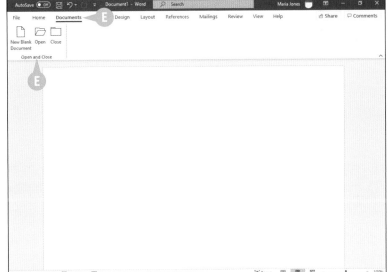

How can I not display my tab without deleting it?
You can hide the tab. Complete steps **1** to **3** in the subsection "Create a New Tab." Click the tab you want to hide (☑ changes to ☐), and then click **OK**. Word redisplays the Ribbon without your custom tab, but your custom tab remains available. When you want to display the tab again, open the Word Options dialog box, click the tab (☐ changes to ☑), and then click **OK**.

Customize the Quick Access Toolbar

Y ou can customize the Quick Access Toolbar by putting on it the commands you use most frequently. The Quick Access Toolbar is always visible as you work in Word, so by adding controls to it, you can reduce your reliance on the Ribbon.

By default, the Quick Access Toolbar contains only four controls—the AutoSave switch, the Save button, the Undo button, and the Redo/Repeat button—and appears in the Word title bar. You can display the Quick Access Toolbar below the Ribbon instead, which gives you space to add many more controls to the Quick Access Toolbar.

Customize the Quick Access Toolbar

Change Where the Quick Access Toolbar Appears

1 Click **Customize Quick Access Toolbar** (▾).

The Customize Quick Access Toolbar menu appears.

2 Click **Show Below the Ribbon**.

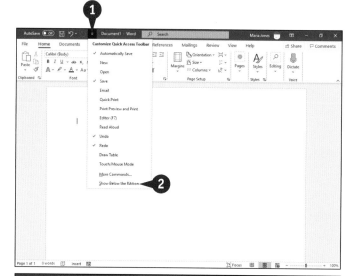

Ⓐ The Quick Access Toolbar appears below the Ribbon instead of above it.

You can repeat these steps to move the Quick Access Toolbar back above the Ribbon.

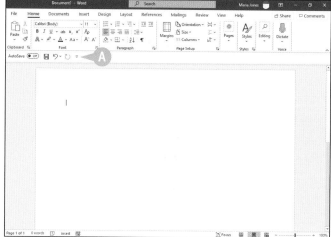

Add Buttons to the Quick Access Toolbar

1 Click **Customize Quick Access Toolbar** (▼).

The Customize Quick Access Toolbar menu appears.

B A check mark (✔) appears beside commands already on the Quick Access Toolbar.

C You can click any listed command to add it to the Quick Access Toolbar and skip the rest of these steps.

2 If you do not see the command you want to add, click **More Commands**.

The Word Options dialog box opens, showing the Quick Access Toolbar category.

D You can add any of these commands to the Quick Access Toolbar.

E At first, the Choose Commands from list shows the Popular Commands category. If the command you want to add does not appear in this list, click **Choose commands from** (▼), and then click **All Commands**.

F Commands already on the Quick Access Toolbar appear here.

G You can click **Customize Quick Access Toolbar** (▼), and then click **For all documents (default)** or **For [this document]**.

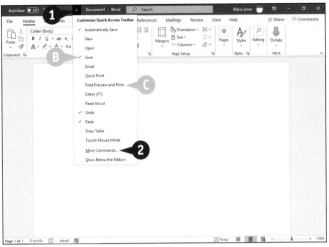

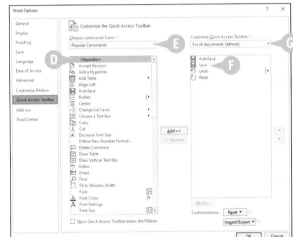

TIP

Is there an easy way to get rid of changes I made to the Quick Access Toolbar?
Yes. You can remove an individual button by right-clicking it on the Quick Access Toolbar, and then clicking **Remove from Quick Access Toolbar**. You can reset the Quick Access Toolbar by opening the Word Options dialog box, clicking the Quick Access Toolbar category in the left pane, clicking **Reset**, and then clicking **Reset only Quick Access Toolbar**. The Reset Customizations dialog box opens, asking if you are sure of your action. Click **Yes**, and Word resets the Quick Access Toolbar. Click **OK** to close the Word Options dialog box.

continued ▶

Customize the Quick Access Toolbar (continued)

In addition to repositioning the Quick Access Toolbar either below or above the Ribbon and adding buttons to or removing buttons from the Quick Access Toolbar, you can reorganize the order in which buttons appear on the Quick Access Toolbar. You also can quickly add a button on the Ribbon to the Quick Access Toolbar, as described in the tip at the end of this section.

Customize the Quick Access Toolbar (continued)

3 Click ☰ to display the various categories of commands.

H You can select **All Commands** to view all commands in alphabetical order regardless of category.

4 Click a category of commands.

This example uses the **Commands Not in the Ribbon** category.

5 Click the command you want to add to the Toolbar.

6 Click **Add**.

I Word moves the command from the list on the left to the list on the right.

7 Repeat steps **3** to **6** for each command you want to add to the Quick Access Toolbar.

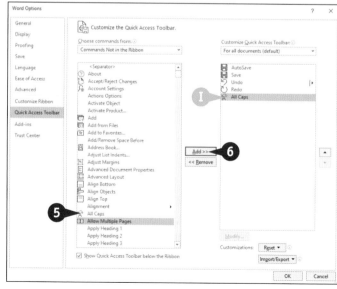

Rearrange the Buttons on the Quick Access Toolbar

1 While viewing the Quick Access Toolbar category in the Word Options dialog box, click a command in the right column.

2 Click ▲ or ▼ to move the selected command left or right along the Quick Access Toolbar.

3 Repeat steps **1** and **2** to reorder other commands.

4 Click **OK**.

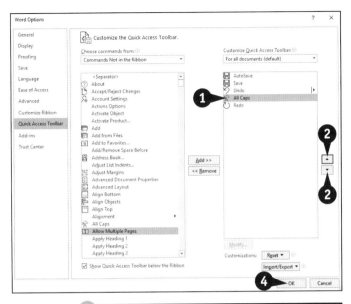

J The updated Quick Access Toolbar appears.

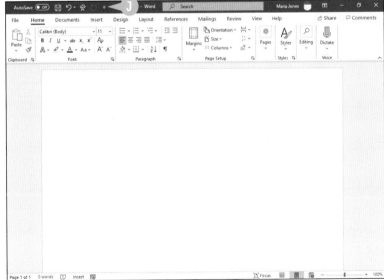

TIP

How do I add a button from the Ribbon to the Quick Access Toolbar?
To add a button from the Ribbon to the Quick Access Toolbar, right-click the button, and then click **Add to Quick Access Toolbar**. Word adds the button to the Quick Access Toolbar.

Create Custom Keyboard Shortcuts

Y ou can add keyboard shortcuts for commands you use frequently. Using a keyboard shortcut can be faster and more efficient than clicking a button on the Ribbon or the Quick Access Toolbar because you can keep your hands on your keyboard, increasing typing speed and efficiency.

You can create keyboard shortcuts for any command, including macros you create, as explained in the section "Create a Macro," later in this chapter. You can even create keyboard shortcuts to apply styles or insert building blocks in your documents.

Create Custom Keyboard Shortcuts

1 Click **File**.

Backstage view appears.

2 Click **Options**.

The Word Options dialog box opens.

3 Click **Customize Ribbon**.

The Customize Ribbon category appears.

4 Click **Customize**.

The Customize Keyboard dialog box opens.

Ⓐ The Categories box shows different categories of commands, such as Home Tab, Styles, and Macros.

Ⓑ The Commands box shows the commands within the selected category.

5 Click the category containing the command to which you want to assign a keyboard shortcut.

6 Click the command.

Ⓒ The Current Keys box shows any existing keyboard shortcuts for the selected command.

7 Click in the Press New Shortcut Key box, and then press a keyboard combination.

Ⓓ The keys you press appear here.

Ⓔ Any command to which the shortcut is currently assigned appears here.

Note: To try a different combination, press `Backspace` to delete the existing combination, and then repeat step **7**.

8 Click **Assign**.

9 Click **Close**.

The Customize Keyboard dialog box closes.

10 Click **OK**.

The Word Options dialog box closes.

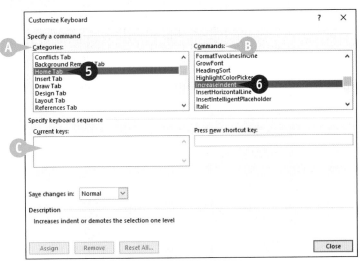

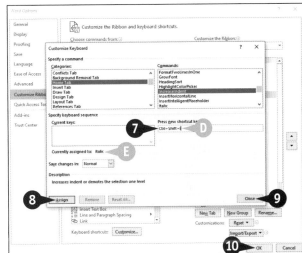

TIP

How can I test my shortcut to make sure it works?
The easiest way to test the shortcut is to press the keys you assigned. If the command needs you to make a particular type of selection first, do so before pressing the keys.

Create a Macro

You can create a macro to save time and repetitive keystrokes. A macro combines a series of actions into a single command. For example, if you often need to change the page orientation, you can create a macro to do so for you.

To create a macro, you turn on the Macro Recorder and assign a name for the macro. You then perform the actions you want the macro to take. After that, you turn off the Macro Recorder.

Create a Macro

Ⓐ Display the Macro Recording indicator (🖥) on the status bar by right-clicking the status bar and choosing **Macro Recording** from the Customize Status Bar menu.

① Click **View**.

The View tab appears.

② Click ⌄ on the lower part of the **Macros** button.

The Macros panel opens.

③ Click **Record Macro**.

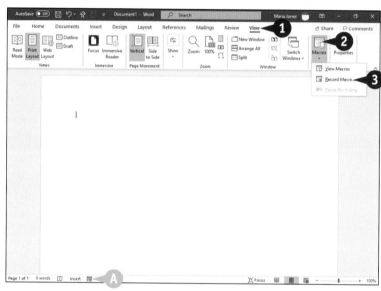

The Record Macro dialog box opens.

④ Type a name for the macro.

Note: Macro names must begin with a letter and contain no spaces. You can use underscores to separate words.

⑤ Type a description for the macro here.

⑥ Click **OK**.

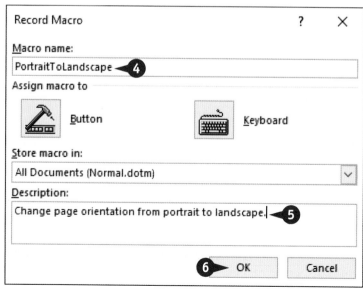

The Record Macro dialog box closes.

B The Macro Recording indicator (📠) changes to a Stop Recording indicator (☐).

7 Perform the actions you want included in the macro.

Note: Macros can include typing, formatting, and commands. You cannot use the mouse (↳) to position the insertion point.

The mouse (↳) changes to ↳.

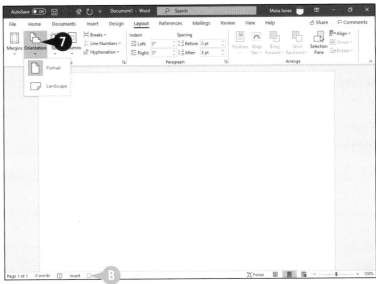

8 When you have taken all the actions you want to include in the macro, click **View**, click ∨ on the lower part of the **Macros** button, and then click **Stop Recording**.

C You can click **Pause Recording** (⊙II) if you want to pause recording the macro. Click **Resume Recorder** (⊙II), which replaces Pause Recording, when you want to resume.

D You can also stop recording by clicking **Stop Recording** (☐) on the status bar.

Word saves the macro.

In the Record Macro dialog box, what do the Button and Keyboard buttons do?

They enable you to assign a macro to a button on the Quick Access Toolbar or to a keyboard shortcut at the same time that you create the macro. You can always assign a macro to a Quick Access Toolbar button or a keyboard shortcut after you create it. See the next section, "Run a Macro."

Do I need to re-create my macros from an earlier version of Word?

No. If you upgrade from an earlier version, Word converts the Normal template you used in that version, which typically contains all your macros.

Run a Macro

You can save time by running a macro you created because Word performs whatever actions you stored in the macro. The method you choose to run a macro depends primarily on how often you need to run it. If you use the macro only occasionally, you can run it from the Macros window. If you use it often, you can assign a macro to a keyboard shortcut or a Quick Access Toolbar button.

To record a macro, see the previous section, "Create a Macro."

Run a Macro

Use the Macros Dialog Box

Note: If your macro is dependent on the position of the insertion point, click in your document where you want the results of the macro to appear.

1 Click **View**.

The View tab appears.

2 Click **Macros**.

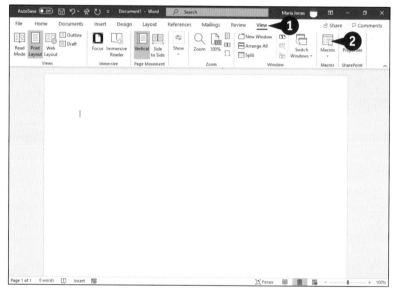

The Macros dialog box opens.

Ⓐ Available macros appear here.

3 Click the macro you want to run.

Ⓑ The selected macro's description appears here.

4 Click **Run**.

Word performs the actions stored in the macro.

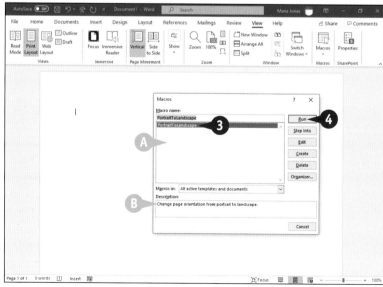

Assign and Use a Quick Access Toolbar Button

1 Click **File**.

Backstage view appears.

2 Click **Options**.

The Word Options dialog box opens.

3 Click **Quick Access Toolbar**.

The Quick Access Toolbar category appears.

4 Click **Choose commands from** (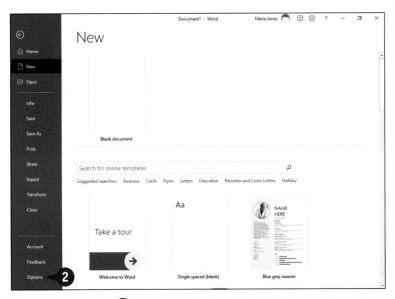),
and then click **Macros**.

5 Click the macro to add to the Quick Access Toolbar.

6 Click **Add**.

C Word adds the macro to the Quick Access Toolbar.

7 Click **OK**.

The Word Options dialog box closes.

8 Click the macro's button on the Quick Access Toolbar to perform the actions stored in the macro.

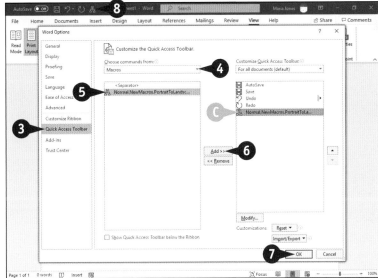

How do I assign a keyboard shortcut to a macro?

Follow the steps in the section "Create Custom Keyboard Shortcuts," earlier in this chapter. In step **5**, scroll to the bottom of the list and select **Macros**. In step **6**, select the macro.

Can I create a ScreenTip for my Quick Access Toolbar button that contains a name I recognize?

Yes. Complete steps **1** to **6** in the subsection "Assign and Use a Quick Access Toolbar Button." In the list on the right, click the macro, and below the list, click **Modify**. In the Modify Button dialog box, type a name for your macro in the Display Name text box below the button symbols.

CHAPTER 12

Printing, Sharing, and Mail Merge

Once you have finalized the content of a document, you can distribute it. In this chapter, you learn how to preview and print documents, how to print envelopes and labels, and how to share a document from Word. You also learn how to create letters and labels for mass mailings.

Preview and Print a Document

When you need a paper copy of a document, you can print it out. Word makes it easy both to print a document and to preview the document on screen for layout errors before you print it.

When the document is ready to print, you can either print it quickly using default print settings or customize those settings. For example, you may want to print only some pages from the document rather than print every page.

Preview and Print a Document

1 Open the document you want to print.

Note: To print only selected text, select that text.

2 Click **File**.

Backstage view appears.

3 Click **Print**.

A A preview of your document appears here.

4 Click **Next Page** (▶) or **Previous Page** (◀) to page through your document.

5 To magnify the page, drag the **Zoom** slider.

6 To print more than one copy, type the number of copies to print here or click ▲▼.

7 To change the printer, click **Printer** (▾), and then click the printer you want to use.

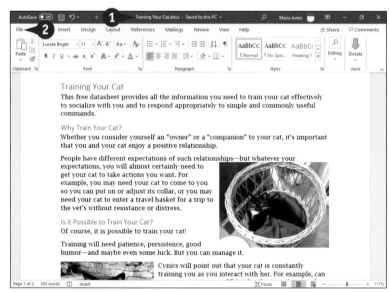

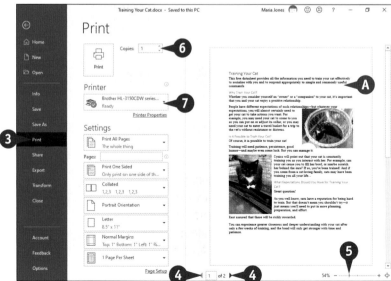

8 Click ▾ to select what to print.

B You can print the entire document, text you selected, or only the current page.

C You can click **Up** (▲) and **Down** (▾) to select document elements to print, such as document properties or a list of styles used in the document.

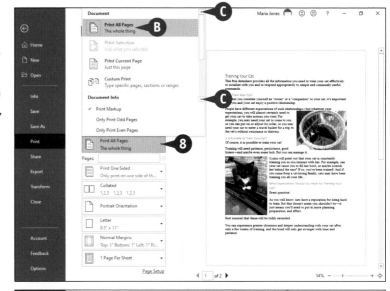

9 To print the document, click **Print**.

D If you change your mind and do not want to print, click **Back** (◐) to return to the document window.

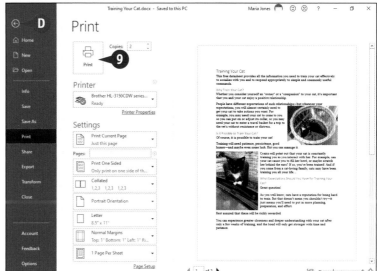

TIP

How can I print only some pages from my document?
Click in the **Pages** box, and then type the pages you want to print. Use a hyphen to indicate a range—for example, type **1-3** to print the first three pages of a document that is not divided into sections. Use a comma to separate individual page numbers or ranges—for example, type **1, 3, 5** or **1, 4-6, 10**. If your document uses sections, type **p** for *page* and **s** for *section*; for example, type **p1s2-p4s2** to print pages 1–4 of the second section.

Print on Different Paper Sizes

You can print one part of your document on one size of paper and another part on a different size of paper. For example, you may want to print one portion of your document on legal-sized paper to accommodate a particularly long table, and then print the rest of the document on letter-sized paper.

You must insert section breaks to create a separate section for each part of the document that you want to print on different paper sizes. To learn how to insert section breaks, see Chapter 7, "Formatting Pages."

Print on Different Paper Sizes

1 After dividing your document into sections, place the insertion point in the section that you want to print on a different paper size.

2 Click **Layout**.

The Layout tab appears.

3 Click the Page Setup group dialog box launcher (⌐⌐).

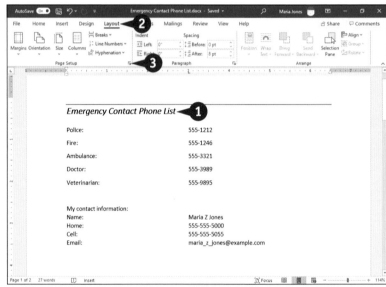

The Page Setup dialog box opens, displaying the Margins tab.

4 Click **Paper**.

The Paper tab appears.

5 Click ⌄, and then click the paper size you want to use.

A The width and height of the paper size you select appear here.

B A preview of your selection appears here.

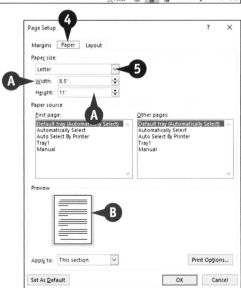

6 In the First Page box, click the paper tray for the first page in the section.

7 In the Other Pages box, click the paper tray for the rest of the section.

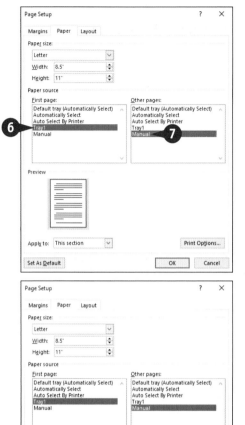

8 Click **Apply to** (⌄).

The Apply To drop-down list opens.

9 Click **This section**.

10 Click **OK**.

The Page Setup dialog box closes.

11 Repeat steps **1** to **10** for other sections of the document, as needed.

What happens when I click Print Options in the Page Setup dialog box?
The Word Options dialog box opens, showing the Display category. In the Printing Options section, choose settings to control which elements print. Select **Print drawings created in Word** (☑) to include drawings when printing. Select **Print background colors and images** (☑) to include background colors and images. Select **Print document properties** (☑) to print a list of document properties, such as Title and Subject. Select **Print hidden text** (☑) to include hidden text. Select **Update fields before printing** (☑) to force all fields to update before printing. Select **Update linked data before printing** (☑) to force an update of data linked from other files.

Print an Envelope

I f your printer supports printing envelopes, Word can print a delivery and return address on an envelope for you. You can also have Word automatically fill in the recipient's name and address. Word checks the currently open document for information that appears to be an address; if it finds an address, Word fills in the address automatically. To save yourself time and typing, open the letter you intend to mail before you follow the steps in this section to print the envelope.

Consult your printer manual to determine whether your printer supports printing envelopes.

Print an Envelope

1 Click **Mailings**.

The Mailings tab appears.

2 Click **Envelopes**.

The Envelopes and Labels dialog box opens.

3 Click **Envelopes**.

The Envelopes tab appears.

Note: If Word finds an address near the top of your document, it displays and selects that address in the Delivery Address box.

4 You can type a delivery address.

You can remove an existing address by pressing `Delete`.

By default, Word displays no return address in the Return Address box.

5 Click here to type a return address.

6 Click **Options**.

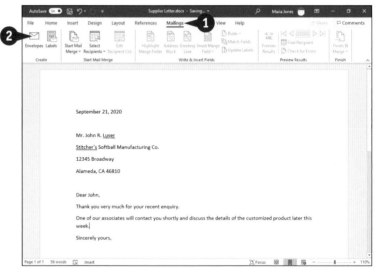

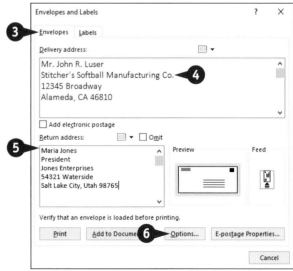

The Envelope Options dialog box opens, with the Envelope Options tab displayed.

Ⓐ You can set the envelope size.

Ⓑ You can format and position the delivery address.

Ⓒ You can format and position the return address.

⑦ Click **Printing Options**.

The Printing Options tab appears.

Ⓓ You can configure the feed method for the printer.

Ⓔ You can choose which tray to feed from.

⑧ Click **OK**.

The Envelope Options dialog box closes.

⑨ In the Envelopes and Labels dialog box, click **Print**.

A dialog box opens if you supplied a return address.

Note: If you save the return address, Word displays it each time you print an envelope and does not display this dialog box.

⑩ Click **Yes**.

Word saves the return address as the default return address and prints the envelope.

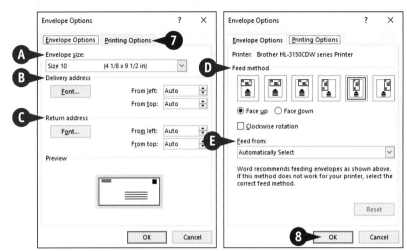

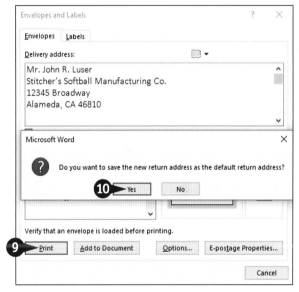

TIP

What happens if I click E-Postage Properties in the Envelopes and Labels dialog box?
If you have installed electronic postage software, Word displays the E-Postage Properties dialog box, in which you can set up electronic postage for the envelope you are printing. If you have not installed electronic postage software, Word displays a dialog box telling you that you need to do so; click **Yes** in this dialog box to display a page on the Microsoft Office website that provides information about electronic postage add-in software.

Word enables you to print labels using many types of standard labels from various vendors, including Avery, 3M, Microsoft, Office Depot, and Staples. You can print whatever information you need on the labels, from address labels to name tags or file folder labels.

This section shows you how to create a blank page of address labels onto which you can type address label information. After creating labels, you can print them as discussed in the section "Preview and Print a Document," earlier in this chapter.

Set Up Labels to Print

1 Click **Mailings**.

The Mailings tab appears.

2 Click **Labels**.

The Envelopes and Labels dialog box opens.

3 Click **Labels**.

The Labels tab appears.

A The Label box shows the label currently selected.

4 Click **Options**.

Note: You can click the label preview in the Label box instead of clicking Options.

The Label Options dialog box opens.

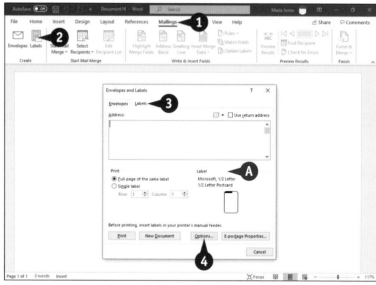

5 In the Printer Information area, click **Continuous-feed printers** (○ changes to ●) or **Page printers** (○ changes to ●), as needed.

6 For Page Printers, click **Tray** (⌄), and then click the tray.

7 Click **Label vendors** (⌄), and then click the appropriate vendor.

8 In the Product Number list, click the product number of your labels.

9 Click **OK**.

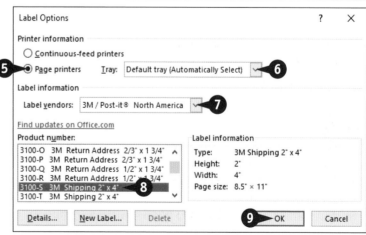

The Label Options dialog box closes, returning you to the Envelopes and Labels dialog box.

Ⓑ The Label area shows the label type you selected.

❿ Select **Full page of the same label** (⦿).

⓫ Click **New Document**.

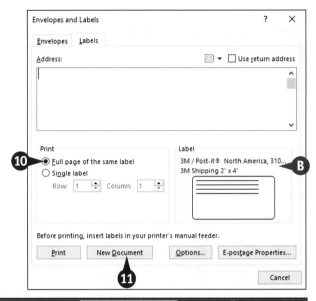

The Envelopes and Labels dialog box closes.

Word displays a new document, set up for label information.

⓬ If you do not see gridlines separating labels, click **Layout** at the right end of the Ribbon, go to the Table group, and then click **View Gridlines**.

⓭ Type the first label.

⓮ Press [Tab] to move to the next table cell.

⓯ Type the next label.

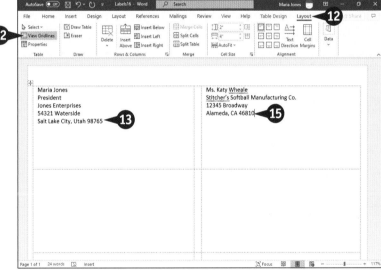

TIP

How do I print a single label?

On the Labels tab of the Envelopes and Labels dialog box, click **Single label** (○ changes to ⦿). Click **Row** and type the row number of the label on the page, then click **Column** and type the column number—for example, Row 1 Column 1 for the first label. Click **Options** to open the Label Options dialog box, select the label to use, and then click **OK**. Back in the Envelopes and Labels dialog box, type the address in the Address box, and then click **Print**. Word closes the Envelopes and Labels dialog box and prints the label.

Share a Word Document on OneDrive

Word enables you to share a document quickly in two ways. First, if you have stored the document on OneDrive, you can send the recipient a link to the document, enabling them to access the same copy of the document and, optionally, edit it. Second, if you have stored the document on your computer, or if you do not want to share the same copy on OneDrive, you can send a copy of the document via email.

This section shows you how to share a OneDrive document. The next section shows you how to email a document.

Share a Word Document on OneDrive

Share a Document

Note: You must be signed in to Microsoft 365, and the document you want to share must be stored on OneDrive. See the tip at the end of this section for details.

1 Open the document you want to share.

2 Click **Share**.

The Send Link pane opens.

3 Click **Anyone with the link can edit**.

The Link Settings dialog box opens.

4 Select (☑) or deselect (☐) **Allow editing**, as needed.

5 Optionally, click **Set expiration date**, and then click the expiration date on the date picker panel that opens.

6 Optionally, click **Set password** and type a password to protect the document.

7 Click **Apply**.

The Link Settings dialog box closes, returning you to the Send Link dialog box.

8 Click **Enter a name or email address**, and then type the recipient's name or address.

A button appears for each match the OneDrive lookup process returns for the name or address.

9 Click the button for the appropriate address.

A An address button appears for the recipient.

B You can click here and enter another recipient's name or address.

10 Click **Add a message (optional)**.

11 Type a message to the recipient.

C You can click **Copy Link** to copy the document link so that you can use it elsewhere.

12 Click **Send**.

The Send Link dialog box closes.

Word sends the recipient an email message containing a link to the document.

A dialog box opens confirming that Word sent the link.

13 Click **Close** (✕).

The dialog box closes.

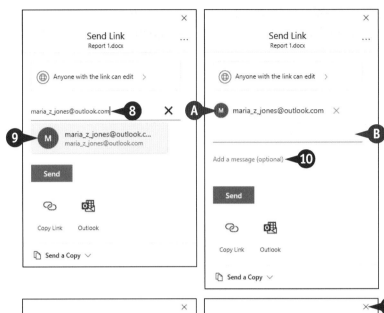

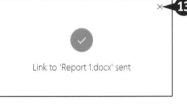

TIP

Why do I see a screen indicating I must upload my document before sharing it?
If you have not previously saved your document to OneDrive, Word prompts you to do so before starting the Share process. Click your OneDrive account to upload the document.

In the previous section, you learned how to share a document stored on OneDrive by emailing a recipient a link to that document. Word also enables you to share a document by attaching it to an email message. This method works both for documents stored on your computer and documents stored on OneDrive.

When you share a document this way, the recipient gets a copy of the document and can change it without affecting your original document.

Email a Document as an Attachment

Email a Document Stored on Your Computer

1 Open the document you want to send as an attachment.

2 Click **Share**.

The Share panel opens.

Note: If the file is stored on OneDrive, the Send Link panel opens instead of the Share panel. See the next subsection.

3 Click **Word Document**.

A new message window opens in Outlook.

A Outlook enters the document's filename, minus the file extension, in the Subject field. You can edit the Subject field if you want.

B Outlook inserts the document as an attached file.

4 Type the recipient's name or email address, or click **To** and choose a contact in the Select Names dialog box that opens.

5 Type any message body needed.

6 Click **Send**.

Outlook sends the message.

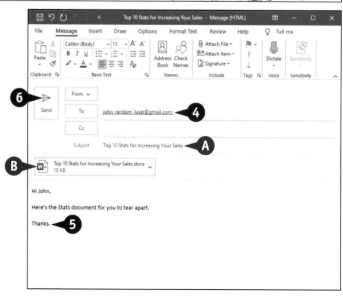

Email a Document Stored on OneDrive

1 Open the document you want to share.

2 Click **Share**.

The Send Link panel opens.

3 Click **Send a Copy**.

The Send a Copy pop-up menu opens.

4 Click **Word Document**.

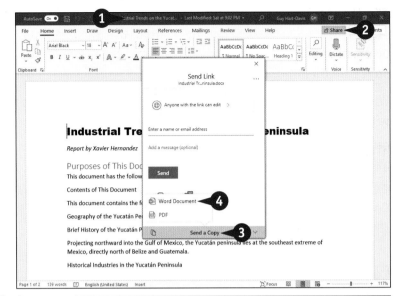

A new message window opens in Outlook.

C Outlook enters the document's filename in the Subject field. You can edit the Subject field if you want.

D Outlook inserts the document as an attached file.

5 Type the recipient's name or email address, or click **To** and choose a contact in the Select Names dialog box that opens.

6 Type any message body needed.

7 Click **Send**.

Outlook sends the message.

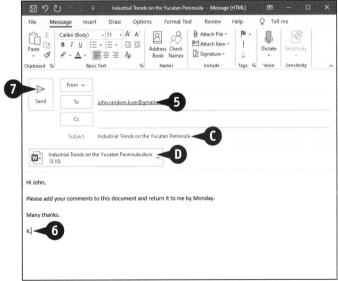

TIP

What happens if I click PDF in the Send a Copy pop-up menu?
Word creates a PDF version of the document and attaches the PDF version to the email message instead of attaching the Word document.

sing a form letter and a mailing list, you can quickly and easily create a mass mailing that merges the addresses from the mailing list into the form letter. Typically, the only information that changes in the form letter is the addressee information. Wherever changing information appears, you insert a placeholder that Word replaces when you merge.

You can create the mailing list as you create the mass mailing, you can use a mailing list that exists in another Word document or an Excel file, or you can use your Outlook Contact List. This example uses a Word document.

Create Letters to Mass Mail

Set Up for a Mail Merge

1 Open the Word document that you want to use as the form letter.

Note: The letter should not contain any information that will change from letter to letter, such as the inside address.

2 Click **Mailings**.

The Mailings tab appears.

3 Click **Start Mail Merge**.

The Start Mail Merge pop-up panel opens.

4 Click **Letters**.

The screen flashes, indicating that Word has set up the document as the main document for a mail merge.

Select or Create a Data Source

1 Click **Select Recipients**.

The Select Recipients pop-up panel opens.

2 Click **Type a New List**, **Use an Existing List**, or **Choose from Outlook Contacts**.

This example uses **Type a New List**.

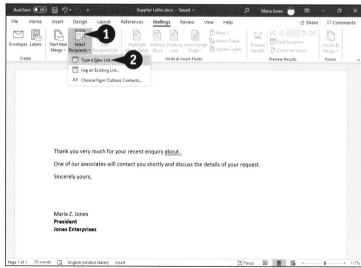

The New Address List dialog box opens.

Ⓐ The address list contains standard fields for name, address, and contact information. Each field appears as a column.

③ To customize the columns, click **Customize Columns**.

The Customize Address List dialog box opens.

④ Click the field before which you want the new field to appear.

⑤ Click **Add**.

The Add Field dialog box opens.

⑥ Type the name for the field.

⑦ Click **OK**.

The Add Field dialog box closes.

Ⓑ The field appears in the Customize Address List dialog box.

⑧ Select the field you want to change.

Ⓒ You can click **Delete** to delete the field.

Ⓓ You can click **Rename** to rename the field.

Ⓔ You can click **Move Up** or **Move Down** to reposition the field.

⑨ Click **OK**.

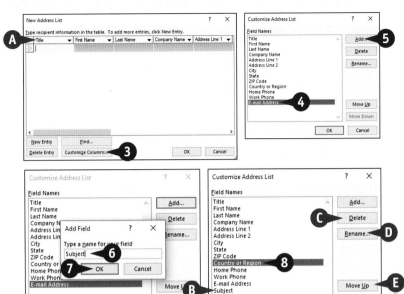

TIP

How do I use an Excel workbook as a data source?
Click **Mailings** to display the Mailings tab of the Ribbon, go to the Start Mail Merge group, and then click **Select Recipients**. On the pop-up panel, click **Use an Existing List** to open the Select Data Source dialog box. Navigate to the appropriate folder, click the Excel workbook, and then click **Open**. In the Select Table dialog box that opens, click the appropriate table, and then click **OK**.

continued ▶

Once you have specified the data source from the mail merge, you can choose between merging just some record in the data source and merging all the records.

You insert merge fields in your main document to tell Word where to insert data from the data source. For many mail merges, you will insert an address block containing the merge fields for the recipient's name and address, and a greeting line that greets the recipient with a suitable degree of formality or informality.

Create Letters to Mass Mail (continued)

The Customize Address List dialog box closes, returning you to the New Address List dialog box.

10 With the first row selected, type the data for the first record, pressing `Tab` to move from one column to the next.

Note: You can press `Shift`+`Tab` to move to the previous column.

11 For each additional record, click **New Entry** to add another row, and then type the data for that record.

F You can click **Find** to search for particular text in the address list—for example, to find records that contain that text.

G You can click **Delete Entry** to delete the selected record.

12 Click **OK**.

The New Address List dialog box closes.

The Save Address List dialog box opens.

H The default location for saving data sources is the My Data Sources folder in your Documents folder.

13 Type a filename.

14 Click **OK**.

The Save Address dialog box closes.

318

Select the Recipients for the Mail Merge

1 Click **Edit Recipient List**.

The Mail Merge Recipients dialog box opens.

I A check box (☑) appears beside each person's name, identifying the recipients of the form letter.

2 Click any addressee for whom you do not want to prepare a form letter (☑ changes to ☐).

3 Click **OK**.

The Mail Merge Recipients dialog box closes.

Create the Address Block

1 Click the location where you want the inside address to appear in the form letter.

2 Click **Address Block**.

The Insert Address Block dialog box opens.

3 Click a format for each recipient's name.

J You can preview the format here.

4 Click **OK**.

K The <<Address Block>> merge field appears in the letter.

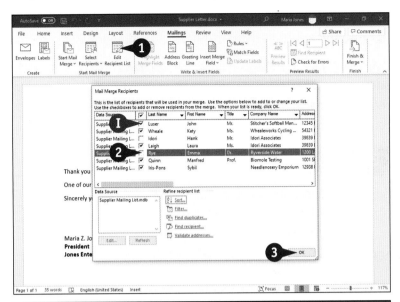

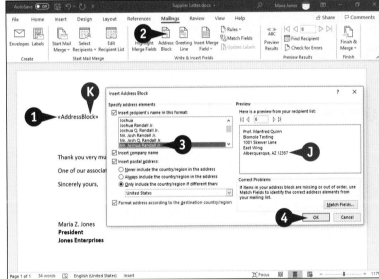

TIP

What should I do if the preview in the Insert Address Block dialog box is blank or incorrect?

Perform the steps that follow: After you complete step **3** in the subsection "Create the Address Block," click **Match Fields**. The Match Fields dialog box opens. Beside each field you use in your merge, click and select the corresponding field name in your mailing list file. Click **OK** and continue with step **4** in the subsection "Create the Address Block." Word matches your fields.

continued ►

Before printing merged documents, you should preview the documents to make sure that the information from the data source fits neatly into the main document.

After you review the documents, you can print them. Or, if your mailing list contains email addresses, you can send the letters as email messages; Word prompts you for a subject line and a format—HTML, plain text, or an attachment—and then places the message in the Outlook outbox. You then open Outlook and send the messages.

Create Letters to Mass Mail (continued)

Create a Greeting

1 Click where you want the greeting to appear.

2 Click **Greeting Line**.

The Insert Greeting Line dialog box opens.

3 Use the three Greeting Line Format drop-down lists to specify the greeting format.

L A preview of the greeting appears here.

4 Click **OK**.

M The <<Greeting Line>> merge field appears in the letter.

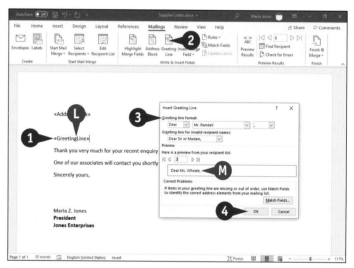

Insert Merge Fields in the Body of the Document

1 Click where you want the merge field to appear.

2 Click the lower part of **Insert Merge Field** (⌄).

The Insert Merge Fields pop-up panel opens.

3 Click the field you want to insert.

Word inserts the field at the position of the insertion point.

4 After inserting all the merge fields the document needs, click **Preview Results**.

The preview of the merge results appears.

Preview and Merge the Documents

1 Click **Finish & Merge**.

The Finish & Merge pop-up panel opens.

2 Click **Edit Individual Documents**.

The Merge to New Document dialog box opens.

3 Click **All** (○ changes to ◉); or click **Current record** (○ changes to ◉); or click **From** (○ changes to ◉), and then enter the appropriate numbers in the From box and the To box.

4 Click **OK**.

N Word merges the form letter information with the mailing list information, placing the results in a new document named Letters1.

O The new document contains individual letters for each mailing list recipient.

You can now save and print the letters using standard techniques. For example, press Ctrl+S to save the Letters document, and then press Ctrl+P to open the Print screen in Backstage.

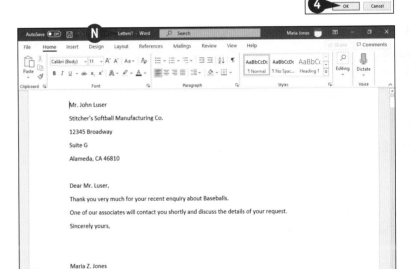

TIP

Can I create envelopes to go with my form letter?

Yes. Open the form letter containing merge fields. Click **Mailings** to display the Mailings tab, go to the Create group, and then click **Envelopes** to display the Envelopes and Labels dialog box. Click **Add to Document** to place an envelope in your document. You can type a return address in the upper-left corner of the envelope. Click in the lower center of the envelope to locate the address box; dotted lines surround it. Complete the steps in the subsections "Create the Address Block" and "Preview and Merge the Documents."

Create Labels for a Mass Mailing

Word's Merge feature enables you to create mailing labels for mass mailings. Mailing labels can save you time and effort if your printer cannot print envelopes or if you need to mail items in large envelopes or in packages.

Word's Merge feature enables you to select from a wide variety of commonly used labels from various vendors, including Avery, 3M, Microsoft, Office Depot, and Staples. You can also create a custom label size, if necessary.

Create Labels for a Mass Mailing

Select a Label Format

1 Start a new blank document.

2 Click **Mailings**.

The Mailings tab appears.

3 Click **Start Mail Merge**.

The Start Mail Merge pop-up panel opens.

4 Click **Labels**.

The Label Options dialog box opens.

5 In the Printer Information area, click **Continuous-feed printers** (○ changes to ◉) or **Page printers** (○ changes to ◉), as needed.

6 For Page Printers, click **Tray** (⌄), and then click the tray.

7 Click **Label vendors** (⌄), and then click the appropriate vendor.

That vendor's labels appear in the Product Number box.

8 Click the product number of your labels.

9 Click **OK**.

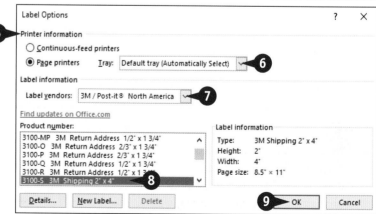

Word sets up the document for the labels you selected.

Note: If you do not see gridlines separating labels, click **Layout** at the right end of the Ribbon, go to the Table group, and then click **View Gridlines**.

Connect the Data Source to the Main Document

1. Click **Select Recipients**.

2. Click to identify the type of recipient list you plan to use.

   In this example, an existing list in an Excel file is used.

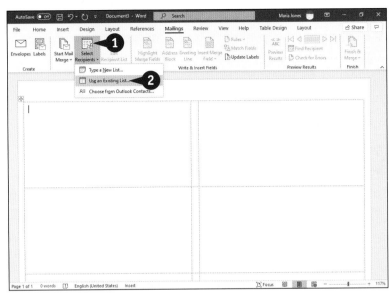

The Select Data Source dialog box opens.

3. Navigate to the folder containing the mailing list file.

4. Click the file containing the mailing list.

5. Click **Open**.

The Select Data Source dialog box closes.

Word connects the data source with the label document.

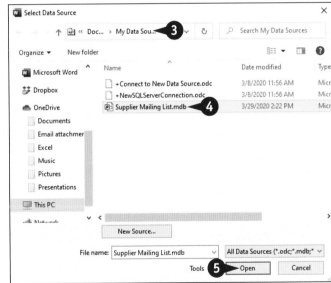

TIP

What happens if I click Details in the Label Options dialog box?
A dialog box opens, displaying the margins and dimensions of each label, the number of labels per row, and the number of rows of labels, along with the page size. Although you can change these dimensions, you run the risk of having label information print incorrectly if you do.

continued ▶

Using the label type you specify, Word sets up a document of labels to which you attach your data source, the file containing recipient information. You can use an existing file or your Outlook contacts, or you can create a new recipient list. You also can select specific recipients from the mailing list for whom to create labels.

You insert a merge field in the label document to mark where the recipient's address should appear. You can modify the appearance of the recipient's address to, for example, include or exclude titles such as "Mr."

Create Labels for a Mass Mailing (continued)

Ⓐ Word inserts a <<Next Record>> field in each label except the first one.

Select the Recipients for the Mail Merge

1 Click **Edit Recipient List**.

The Mail Merge Recipients dialog box opens.

Ⓑ A check box (☑) appears beside each person's name, including that record in the merge.

2 Click any addressee for whom you do not want to create a label (☑ changes to ☐).

3 Click **OK**.

The Mail Merge Recipients dialog box closes.

Create the Address Block

1 Click the location where you want the inside address to appear in the form letter.

2 Click **Address Block**.

The Insert Address Block dialog box opens.

3 Click the format for each recipient's name.

Ⓒ You can preview the format here.

4 Click **OK**.

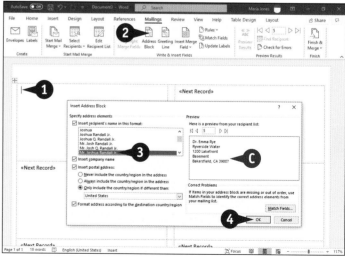

D Word adds the <<Address Block>> merge field to the first label.

Note: When you merge the information, Word replaces the merge field with information from the data source.

5 Click **Update Labels**.

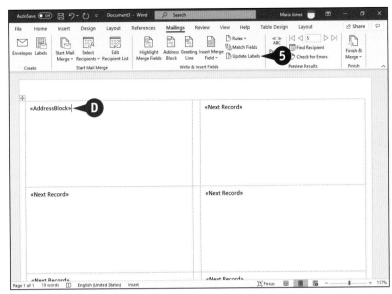

E Word adds the <<Address Block>> merge field to every label.

Preview and Print

1 Click **Preview Results** to preview your merged results.

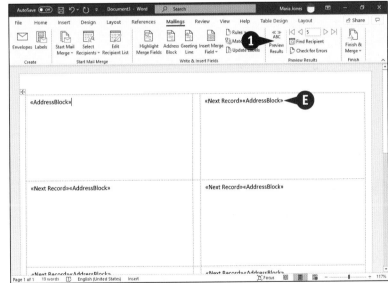

TIP

What happens if I click New Label in the Label Options dialog box?
The Label Details dialog box opens, showing the details for the current label. You can then change any of the settings—such as the label height and width, the label margins, and the page size—to create your own custom label. Type a descriptive name for the label, and then click **OK** to save the details and start using the label.

continued ▶

Create Labels for a Mass Mailing (continued)

Before printing your merged labels, be sure to preview the labels to verify that the address records from the data source have slotted neatly into the label document. Address records often contain enough variation to create some layout surprises.

After you review the labels and make any changes necessary, you can print the labels from Backstage view using standard printing commands.

Create Labels for a Mass Mailing (continued)

Word displays a preview of your labels, replacing the merge field with information from the data source.

F You can click **Next Record** (▷) to preview the next label and **Previous Record** (◁) to preview the previous label.

② When you finish reviewing the labels, click **Preview Results**.

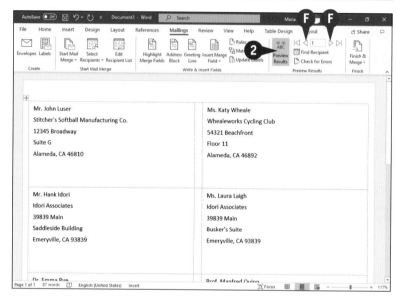

The merge fields reappear.

③ Click **Finish & Merge**.

The Finish & Merge pop-up panel appears.

④ Click **Edit Individual Documents**.

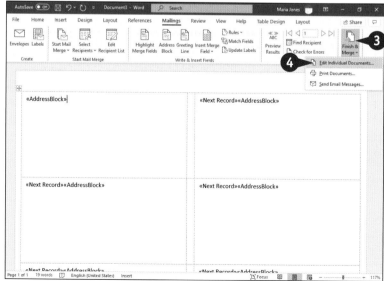

The Merge to New Document dialog box opens.

5 Click **All** (◯ changes to ◉); or click **Current record** (◯ changes to ◉); or click **From** (◯ changes to ◉), and then enter the appropriate numbers in the From box and the To box.

6 Click **OK**.

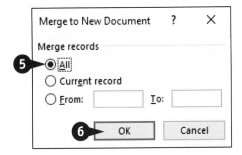

The Merge to New Document dialog box closes.

G Word creates the labels in a new Word document named Labels1.

The new document contains individual labels for each mailing list recipient.

You can now save and print the labels using standard techniques. For example, press Ctrl+S to save the Labels document, and then press Ctrl+P to open the Print screen in Backstage.

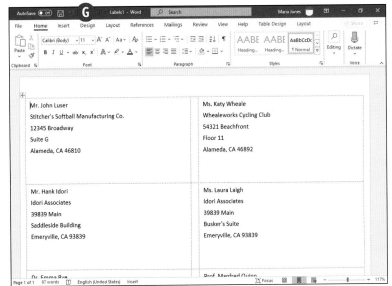

TIP

What does the Check for Errors button on the Ribbon do?

Click **Check for Errors** to display the Checking and Reporting Errors dialog box, and then choose one of the following three options. Click **Simulate the merge and report errors in a new document** (◯ changes to ◉) to test the merge and create a report containing errors; this is often the best choice. Click **Complete the merge, pausing to report each error as it occurs** (◯ changes to ◉) to run the merge and examine each error as it occurs. Click **Complete the merge without pausing. Report errors in a new document** (◯ changes to ◉) to run the merge and create a report containing all errors. Click **OK** to proceed.

Index

A

Actions list, 15
Actions tab, 90
Additional Actions, 90–91
aligning text, 126
    cells (tables), 240
    tabs, 24
    vertical, 164
All Apps screen, 18
Android, Word, 19
antonyms, 104
app window controls, 8
apps
    All Apps screen, 18
    Office Online, 6
area charts, 248
Arrange All windows, 57
Artistic Effects tool, 269
attachments to email, 314–315
AutoComplete, 25
AutoCorrect, 90, 98–99
AutoFit, tables, 233
AutoSave
    collaboration and, 205
    OneDrive documents, 53
AutoText, 101

B

background, 12–13
    images, 269
Backspace key, deleting text, 67
Backstage view, 10
    Actions tab, 90
    AutoCorrect, 90
    document creation, 36
    opening/saving files, 47
    Options, 90
    Options link, 11
    Proofing, 90

bar charts, 248
Bar tab, 136
blank lines, inserting, 68
bold text, 108, 112
bookmarks, 72–73
Border Styles, 242–243
borders
    cells (tables), 242–243
    page borders, 188–189
    paragraphs, 140–141
    pictures, 269
    removing, 141
box and whisker charts, 248
Building Blocks, 100–101
Building Blocks Organizer, 172–173
bulleted lists, 130–131

C

cells (tables), 225
    borders, 242–243
    margins, 234
    merging, 236
    shading, 241
    spacing, 235
    splitting, 237
    text, aligning, 240
Center tab, 136
Change Case panel, 114
Character Map, 63
characters, special characters, 62–63
Chart Design tab, 247
charts
    area, 248
    bar, 248
    box and whisker, 248
    column, 248
    combo, 248

Index